# reviveDAILY

## Year Two

# Other Books in This Series

*revive*DAILY: *A Devotional Journey from Genesis to Revelation, Year One*

Available from Kyle Lance Martin, Time to Revive, and reviveSCHOOL

The Complete Portrait of the Messiah: An Interactive Bible Study from Genesis to Revelation

# *revive*DAILY

**A Devotional Journey
from Genesis to Revelation**

## Year Two

## Laura Kim Martin

*Revive me, O LORD, according to Your word.*
—Psalm 119:107 NASB

time to • **revive**

Richardson, Texas

Time to Revive
Publishing in conjunction with Iron Stream Media
100 Missionary Ridge
Birmingham, AL 35242
IronStreamMedia.com

ISBN: 978-1-63204-092-3 (paperback)
ISBN: 978-1-63204-093-0 (ebook)

1 2 3 4 5—25 24 23 22 21
Printed in the United States of America

Dedicated to each follower of Christ who desires to draw near to the Lord while continuing this journey through the Word.

reviveDAILY: Year Two is for YOU as you press on running the race set before you in the grace, in the power, and in the truth of the Gospel.

———————

*God, You are my God; I eagerly seek You.*
*I thirst for You;*
*my body faints for You*
*in a land that is dry, desolate, and without water.*
*So I gaze on You in the sanctuary*
*to see Your strength and Your glory.*

*My lips will glorify You*
*because Your faithful love is better than life.*
*So I will praise You as long as I live;*
*at Your name, I will lift up my hands.*
*You satisfy me as with rich food;*
*my mouth will praise You with joyful lips.*

*When I think of You as I lie on my bed,*
*I meditate on You during the night watches*
*because You are my helper;*
*I will rejoice in the shadow of Your wings.*
*I follow close to You;*
*Your right hand holds on to me.*
—Psalm 63:1–8

# About the Cover

I sought the Lord for His will regarding the cover for *revive*DAILY. One day, I found myself standing in our guest room, looking at a framed painting by prophetic artist Mindi Oaten. In that moment, something in me leaped! This guest room had hosted many of the reviveSCHOOL teachers over the course of the two years we taught, studied, and wrote through the Bible. In addition, this room, with this one painting on all the walls, served as a source of refuge for me when I needed to rest or dig into the Word and write. And in that reflective moment, I knew this painting was to be the cover for *revive*DAILY!

Mindi painted this particular piece, *Tree of Life*, on Day 185 of reviveINDIANA, while in Fort Wayne. Mindi wrote this description of the piece:

Positioned along the glistening Living Waters, life is found in the tree that is planted and rooted in the Lord. This tree is unlike any other tree. Its fruit is so uncontainable and of every variety. Its leaves glimmer and sparkle in the light of the Lord's love and righteousness. This tree of life when rooted and established in favorable soil will bring healing to every corner of the earth. For God covers and longs to heal the nations.

*And he showed me a river of the water of life, clear as crystal,*
*coming from the throne of God and of the Lamb, in the middle*
*of its street. On either side of the river was the tree of life, bearing*
*twelve kinds of fruit, yielding its fruit every month; and the leaves*
*of the tree were for the healing of the nations.*
—Revelation 22:1–2 NASB

I am grateful for this artwork as the cover of *revive*DAILY: *Year One* and *Year Two* because the message portrays my hope and prayer for each reader of this devotional. This one painting is divided in half between the *Year One* and *Year Two* book covers to portray the image of life transformation and growth in Christ as you spend time in His Word and in His presence. As you press on through the journey of studying the Bible day by day and journey from Genesis through Revelation, I pray you will become like this tree of life: *planted and rooted in the Lord, bearing uncontainable fruit and sparkling in the light of the Lord's love and righteousness!*

---

*Instead, his delight is in the LORD's instruction,*
*and he meditates on it day and night.*
*He is like a tree planted beside streams of water*
*that bears its fruit in season*
*and whose leaf does not wither.*
*Whatever he does prospers.*
—Psalm 1:2–3

---

As you press on reading through the Bible and spending time with Jesus in *revive*DAILY: *Year Two*, a growth, a strengthening, and a transformation is happening in you that you may not even recognize in yourself. In the art image for Year Two, you will notice the image of even more healing, fruit-bearing leaves, but you will also notice the large, thick, strong tree trunk. In nature, a large trunk occurs when time has passed bringing growth, strength, and stability. Trees require sunlight and water, among other elements, to grow in this way. They may endure hardship along the way, but as water and sunlight fuel their growth, they develop a strong root system to endure whatever comes their way. Many fruitful leaves signal a tree's good root system. Even though you can't see what is below the ground surface of most trees, if they look healthy and bear fruit, then you can assume they are rooted and grounded in good soil.

In a similar way, as you spend time again this year in God's Word, you are developing a strong, stable 'trunk' as your roots grow deeper and wider in God's love and in His Word as you daily abide in Him. You are satisfying yourself in His Living Water that never dries up. Jesus alone brings satisfaction. You are soaking in the Son of God and allowing His love and His light to shine into your life. His love and light will continue to *revive you* as you study Genesis to Revelation.

*Therefore, as you have received Christ Jesus the Lord, walk in Him, rooted and built up in Him and established in the faith, just as you were taught, overflowing with gratitude.*
—Colossians 2:6–7

## About the Artist

Mindi Oaten has ministered with the Time to Revive team since 2015 as a prophetic artist working in acrylic on canvas. Mindi lives with her family in Alberta, Canada. As part of the curriculum for revive-SCHOOL, Mindi painted a prophetic painting for each book of the Bible. You can view her biblical artwork at www.reviveSCHOOL.org. You can view and order prints of all her prophetic artwork at www.mindioaten.com.

On the front cover and throughout each devotional page, you will see the shape of a double diamond. A diamond can symbolize light, commitment, faithfulness, promise, victory, and treasures and riches. As you read through the Bible and this devotional, I pray your life becomes transformed by the light of Christ found in the rich treasures of His Word.

# Contents

*A Devotional Journey from Genesis to Revelation*
This is the second year of a devotional journey walking you through the
Word of God from Genesis to Revelation. You will read all 66 books of
the Bible in two years, alternating between sections of the Old and New
Testaments, while recognizing the Messiah in each book. Imagine Paul
discussing the Scriptures with disciples in the Hall of Tyrannus daily for
two years, so that all of Asia heard the message of the Lord (Acts 19). The
purpose for *revive*DAILY is for life transformation through the power of
reading God's Word!

## The Daily Reading Plan: Year Two

### The Wisdom Books

### Paul's Letters

## The Major Prophets

## Other Letters in the New Testament

## The Minor Prophets

## Well Done

You completed the second year of this two-year journey! You read through all ten segments of the Bible, including those in *revive*DAILY: *Year One*:

Pentateuch
Gospels
The Historical Books
Acts

## Now What?

I invite you to do what I did after I wrote *revive*DAILY: *Year One* and *Two*. I invite you to continue to read the Word and spend time with Jesus. Begin another two-year journey through the Word of God. Ask friends to join you as you press on reading, continuing to draw near to Jesus. He will not stop revealing His great love to you as you spend this time with Him and with others.

# Acknowledgments

*And not only that, but we also rejoice in our afflictions, because we know that affliction produces endurance, endurance produces proven character, and proven character produces hope. This hope will not disappoint us, because God's love has been poured out in our hearts through the Holy Spirit who was given to us.*
—Romans 5:3–5

In *revive*DAILY*: Year One*, I acknowledged the people in my life who lifted my arms up while writing through the Bible for two years. I acknowledged how I could not have walked through this revive-SCHOOL and *revive*DAILY writing season without them. That continues to remain true through *revive*DAILY*: Year Two*. Those same people in my life lifted my arms up not only *through writing* this devotional journey for two years but also *through enduring the valleys and mountains life brought my way during that season of my life.*

In *revive*DAILY*: Year Two*, I want to acknowledge the trials, the suffering, the pain, and the joy the Lord allowed me to endure while writing. The Lord promises all of us *joy in the midst of trials, comfort in the midst of affliction, nearness to the brokenhearted,* and *production of endurance, character, and hope* when we walk through pain. The more hardship I walked through these two years, the more closely I knew the heart of my Savior because I depended deeply on Him and His truths as I studied His Word. My time studying His Word became even more intimate and led me to hearing His voice more clearly.

I acknowledge these moments not to glorify the trials but to bring *glory to the Lord for His victory. He brought us through it all!* I know I am not alone in my trials or afflictions. The enemy works vigorously to steal, kill, and destroy our desire to live a life in the Lord. As a reader on this journey, you may be *enduring* suffering, discipline, hardship, or brokenness. You are not alone in your struggle. I want to acknowledge the hardship—*but not dwell in the pain.* I long to walk with the Lord daily and gaze upon His face. Let's give God the glory as we walk in thankfulness, rejoicing at all times and keeping our eyes on Jesus, the author and perfecter of our faith.

---

*My flesh and my heart may fail,*
*but God is the strength of my heart,*
*my portion forever*

. . . . . . . . . . . .

*But as for me, God's presence is my good.*
*I have made the Lord GOD my refuge,*
*so I can tell about all You do.*
—Psalm 73:26, 28

---

I acknowledge that my flesh is weak and weary, but in the power of Christ and by His Holy Spirit, I am made strong.

I acknowledge that fear and worry come and go, but through the Holy Spirit there is life, freedom, and love.

I acknowledge that I have lived in bondage to the lies of rejection, inadequacy, shame, and guilt. Yet, I have sought and received freedom in Jesus and the Holy Spirit to set me free and give me life.

I acknowledge that I have felt alone. I have felt like a strange person, an alien in this world, until I released the desire to please people. I have found my identity and freedom in Christ. I am no longer a slave to man or ashamed of the Gospel.

I acknowledge feeling lonely and sad. I sought the Lord. He faithfully stood by my side and restored the joy of my salvation.

---

*Therefore, no condemnation now exists for those in Christ Jesus, because the Spirit's law of life in Christ Jesus has set you free from the law of sin and of death.*
—Romans 8:1–2

---

I acknowledge that I have made idols in my life, putting other things on this earth in place of my hope and love in the Lord. Even so, the Lord has done the refining work of revealing them to me, so I can tear them down and replace them with the Lord God Almighty as my one and only God.

I acknowledge the hurt caused by the painful words of others and rejection in relationships. In that place of hurt, the Lord walked with me to forgive others and to love anyway.

I acknowledge the lack of control I felt when my husband laid in a hospital bed undergoing tests 1,000 miles away from where I sat. I trusted the Lord for the unknowns and for saving his life.

I acknowledge a season of visiting doctors and of more tests on my husband, wondering the what-if of all the scenarios that went through my head. I trusted that his physical health was in the Lord's hands as we pressed on studying the Word. The Lord sustained us physically, sustained us emotionally, and sustained us in supernatural ways through His power.

I acknowledge the feelings of being overwhelmed with four kids and a busy, traveling husband. Those overwhelmed days led me to lean on the Lord moment by moment for strength and wisdom from His Spirit.

I acknowledge the nights I went to bed wondering, *Will tomorrow be the day the Lord will not be faithful to provide; will tomorrow be the day to close the doors for our ministry; will tomorrow be the day we have to sell our home?* Praying for provision led me to a place of laying everything (my pride, my security, my plans, my life) down in surrender. In that place of laying it down, I woke up to the God who provides in miraculous and faithfully incredible ways.

I acknowledge feelings of grief as Kyle and I both lost our grandmas during these two years of *revive*DAILY and reviveSCHOOL. And yet, the Lord reminded me of the legacy of these two incredible women who went before us and whose strength lives on. The Lord comforts those who mourn.

---

*Dear friends, don't be surprised when the fiery ordeal comes among you to test you as if something unusual were happening to you. Instead, rejoice as you share in the sufferings of the Messiah, so that you may also rejoice with great joy at the revelation of his glory. If you are ridiculed for the name of*

*Christ, you are blessed, because the Spirit of glory and of God rests on you. None of you, however, should suffer as a murderer, a thief, an evildoer, or a meddler. But if anyone suffers as a "Christian," he should not be ashamed but should glorify God in having that name.*
—1 Peter 4:12–16

I acknowledge my heartbreak and agony as I closely walked alongside friends enduring marriage separation. While some ended in divorce, others ended in restoration. I hold on to faith that the Lord works all things together for His good and for His glory to those who put their trust in His name. He is a redeeming Savior at all times and in all ways.

I acknowledge the prayerful nights in tears as I walked alongside close friends enduring the pain from adultery, abuse, addictions, and murder. I hold on with faith believing anything is possible and witnessing the Lord bringing beauty from ashes.

I acknowledge the sorrow felt from tragic events, accidents, sickness, and loss. I know and bear witness that the Lord walks with us through the shadow of death and He restores the joy of our salvation. He is our Great Shepherd.

I acknowledge the sadness from disunity and disfunction the enemy causes in the Body of Christ. I have fought to find love and seek the Holy Spirit for unity in these places.

I acknowledge the feeling of failure after the Lord closed doors that Kyle and I felt led by the Lord to pursue. I have wondered if we missed a sign from the Lord somewhere along the way or if we did something wrong. The Lord pointed us to truth: *"No, child of God—I allow nos so that you can hear the yeses even clearer."* All in His time.

I acknowledge my daily dependence on the Lord as I raise four strong-willed children. Parenting challenges me daily. Yet, I know I am called to it, and the Lord provides and equips me in my calling. Therefore, I fight to live in the Spirit as a mom and not in my flesh. My flesh brings anger, impatience, unkindness, and leads to regret. The Spirit brings love, peace, kindness, gentleness, self-control, faithfulness, and patience. It's so much more fun to walk in the Spirit as a mom!

I acknowledge the temptation to perform and to be self-sufficient. I remember standing firm in truth and intentionally resisting that temptation as it came upon me, leaning in toward the Spirit saying, "Not in my own strength, Lord, but in Your power, in Your grace, in Your trust. Please flow through me."

*And if the Spirit of Him who raised Jesus from the dead lives in you, then He who raised Christ from the dead will also bring your mortal bodies to life through His Spirit who lives in you.*
—Romans 8:11

I acknowledge persecution and enduring mocking for my faith in my community. Yet, I believe it is worth it for Christ's name to be lifted up.

I acknowledge the difficult moments in marriage—communicating, intimacy, lifting one another up more than myself, and living in unity. I have learned the more I can lay myself down, the more beauty comes when two people live as one. The Lord is so good and so faithful. Marriage rooted and grounded in the Lord is a fun adventure!

I acknowledge—I can't do life alone. I am in need of a Savior in my life. I am broken and weak, and I need help from the Lord. I have found that in this place, the Lord's love and grace carries me day by day.

*Taste and see that the* LORD *is good.*
*How happy is the man who takes refuge in Him!*
*You who are His holy ones, fear Yahweh,*
*for those who fear Him lack nothing.*
—Psalm 34:8–9

It's through these moments, *I taste and see that the Lord is good.*
In the presence of the Lord, *the fullness of joy is found.*
In our weakness, *His strength and His power abound even more.*

As I have remained in His Word, rooted and grounded, when the storms come, the Lord's truth leads me in the direction to go. I can hear His voice leading me through.

Through it all, with my eyes on the Lord, I pray others will *acknowl-edge* His strength, His power, and His love on full display—even more. All for His glory. I *acknowledge* this and continue to praise the name of the Lord who is worthy to be praised!

---

*Now the God of all grace, who called you to His eternal glory in Christ Jesus, will personally restore, establish, strengthen, and support you after you have suffered a little.*
—1 Peter 5:10

---

# Introduction

Dear friend,

*Lord, hear my voice when I call;*
*be gracious to me and answer me.*
*My heart says this about You,*
*"You are to seek My face."*
*Lord, I will seek Your face.*
—Psalm 27:7–8

As you hold this devotional book in your hands, you may be picking it up for the first time or you may be reading it as part of your journey through the Bible from Genesis to Revelation. You may have just finished *revive*DAILY: *Year One* and are now pressing on through *Year Two*. Either way, I'm glad you are here. I'm thankful for your hunger to grow in the Lord and read His Word. The Lord promises you will be satisfied in Him.

*For He has satisfied the thirsty*
*and filled the hungry with good things.*
—Psalm 107:9

I want you to first understand how important you are to Jesus. He loves you. He has called you by name, and you are His. He has a beautiful plan for your life. He longs for you to draw near to Him, and He promises as you draw near to Him day by day, He will draw near to you. As you draw near to Him, He will satisfy you. He will be your joy. He will be your peace.

*Draw near to God, and He will draw near to you.*
—James 4:8

As you begin *revive*DAILY*: Year Two*, you may be thinking, *Wow, I don't know if I can do this another whole new year.* I remember taking a deep breath and pressing into writing the second year. I said yes to the Lord walking by my side each day. He had grown as my friend, my shepherd, and my Savior. After the first year writing *revive*DAILY, His voice felt nearer and clearer as I continued reading His Word. I didn't know how reading through God's Word and sitting in His presence would take me to a different, deeper level. I didn't know the new challenges and experiences coming my way that year, and yet, in the midst of it all, I experienced a strength from the Lord like no other. As I spent time in His presence and in His Word, applying it to my own life, His strength became my own and His power worked within me in unimaginable ways.

Therefore, I pray for you as you press on through reading and studying God's Word. May you experience a deeper level in your relationship with Jesus as He calls you to walk by faith, beyond where you have ever walked before. Not just in a way to know the Word, but to know Jesus, receiving and embracing His love for you.

---

*Deep calls to deep in the roar of Your waterfalls;*
all Your breakers and Your billows have swept over me.
—Psalm 42:7

---

Also, I want you to know that as *revive*DAILY*: Year Two* leads you through even more of the Word, it just keeps getting better! It may sound weird to say, but as you grow, the words you read will grow and "taste" even better. It's like drinking milk, but then beginning to eat meat that satisfies a whole new part of you! I'm excited you have said yes to the Lord for year two. The Lord will continue to grow you deeper in Him. I believe He has even more for you, just as He did for me!

---

*Taste and see that the Lord is good.*
How happy is the man who takes refuge in Him!
—Psalm 34:8

---

The book you hold is the year-two collection of daily messages the Lord spoke to my heart as I read through the Bible over the span of two years.

Every day, I read a section of Scripture and asked the Lord to reveal what He wanted for me to understand. I asked how I could apply the truth of His love and grace to my life. I asked the Lord to make it real to me. I asked Him to help me understand the storyline of the Messiah throughout Scripture. I asked the Lord to help me see His heart as I journeyed through the Word, just like you are continuing to do.

## How This Came About

Ever since I was a young child, I trusted the Lord with my life. As a teenager, I began to really read His Word and followed where He led me by faith. When I became a young wife and mom to four, I fully surrendered my life to Him, enduring trials, testing, and discipline. I watched the Lord work miraculously in my marriage, in the lives of my kids, and through the ministry, Time to Revive (TTR), which the Lord led my husband, Kyle, and me to begin. With a heart for reviving the Church, TTR carries out its calling to equip the saints through evangelism and discipleship to be ready for the return of Christ.

Starting in 2010, TTR began traveling to cities and counties across America as the Spirit led, gathering believers to go out and share the Gospel with a focus to love, listen, discern, and respond to others. We would pour into these communities for a short period of time and leave an equipped remnant to go out, to disciple, and to grow in the Lord.

---

*For we walk by faith, not by sight.*
—2 Corinthians 5:7

---

One of these communities was Elkhart County, Indiana. After a season of equipping in 2015, TTR moved on to new communities, but the Lord had a different plan. In 2017, the team felt led to go back to Elkhart County and reengage, similar to Paul when he traveled for the Gospel. In October of 2017, Kyle sensed the Spirit lead him to pause his travel from city to city and spend two years studying the Scriptures with a group of believers, focusing on where the Messiah is found from Genesis to Revelation. And so, a new journey began and reviveSCHOOL was born.

*He withdrew from them and met separately with the disciples, conducting discussions every day in the lecture hall of Tyrannus. And this went on for two years, so that all the inhabitants of Asia, both Jews and Greeks, heard the message about the Lord.*
—Acts 19:9–10

A group of students gathered in Indiana, and then others began to join online and in groups around the world. Kyle began recording daily teachings in a studio in Texas; artist Mindi Oaten painted prophetically through each book; a team created study questions; and another team wrote study notes.

Shortly after a unique time of prayer together as a couple, Kyle said to me, "Laura, I think you should write every day through the Bible." As Kyle said this, the Lord spoke to my heart the words from 1 Peter 5:6–7:

*Humble yourselves, therefore, under the mighty hand of God, so that He may exalt you at the proper time, casting all your care on Him, because He cares about you.*

The Lord has the best plans for us and wants to grant our hearts' desires as we delight ourselves in Him. When His plans unfold, we must be ready and willing to say yes to Him! The best part is you never know where your yes will lead you, but God does and has a plan. At that time, all I knew was to walk in obedience to His voice. Therefore, from that place of obedience, I said, "Yes, I will write every day as You, Lord, lead me."

*Then I heard the voice of the Lord saying:*

*Who should I send?*
*Who will go for Us?*
*I said:*

*Here I am. Send me.*
—Isaiah 6:8

And so, my journey through the Word of God began. As I began, I prayed and asked the Lord for *His power to work within me*, so that the words I wrote would not be in strife or in performance but rather from His heart.

*Now we have this treasure in clay jars, so that this extraordinary power may be from God and not from us.*
—2 Corinthians 4:7

I asked the Lord to *anchor my heart in Him*, that I would not be tossed around or lose focus on my assignment from Him to write. So many things in this world can demand our attention, even great things, but I knew my eyes, heart, and mind had to be fixed on Jesus, anchored in His hope alone.

*We have this hope as an anchor for our lives, safe and secure.*
—Hebrews 6:19

I began every day by reading His word.

*How happy is the man
who does not follow the advice of the wicked
or take the path of sinners
or join a group of mockers!
Instead, his delight is in the LORD's instruction,
and he meditates on it day and night.
He is like a tree planted beside streams of water
that bears its fruit in season
and whose leaf does not wither.
Whatever he does prospers.*
—Psalm 1:1–3

After two years studying the Word of God, this psalm became true in my marriage, in my parenting, and in the entirety of my life. When you read His Word day after day, night after night, delighting in the Lord's love for you, He strengthens you. You become like a tree planted beside the water. Jesus is the living water your soul craves. *NOTHING else satisfies but Jesus.*

*Those who seek the LORD*
*will not lack any good thing.*
—Psalm 34:10

I desire for this devotional to continue to guide you through reading the Bible for yourself. So often we think reading through the Bible is daunting and hard to understand. Perhaps you feel like you don't have the time it takes to read the Word. Or maybe you are dissatisfied with self-help guides and lighthearted devotionals. I believe one of the enemy's greatest schemes is to keep God's children distracted, disinterested, and disillusioned by the Bible. But in Christ we have victory to overcome these schemes when we stand firm in Him. I pray for you to rise up each day and have victory reading the Word.

*Arise, shine, for your light has come,*
*and the glory of the LORD shines over you.*
—Isaiah 60:1

**Here's the Deal**

Jesus wants you to get to know Him and to receive His great love for you. He desires a personal relationship with you. Reading the Word forces you to sit still and be in His presence. Pause the distractions of your life and find a special place to sit each day. Take a deep breath and let go of the worries of the world. Breathe in the promises and the love the Lord has for you.

*Revive*DAILY: *Year One* and *Year Two* comprise a single devotional journey designed to walk with you through the Bible in a span of two years, focusing on seeing the Messiah in each book of the Bible. Following the reviveSCHOOL plan, you will read a section in the Old

Testament and then a section in the New Testament, breaking the Bible into 10 different segments:

1. *Year One:*
   - Pentateuch
   - The Gospels
   - Historical Books
   - Acts

2. *Year Two:*
   - Wisdom Books
   - Paul's Letters
   - Major Prophets
   - Other Letters in the New Testament
   - Minor Prophets
   - Revelation

Each day read the daily Scripture (or listen to the audio version). You will find the daily reading at the top of each page. Then read the devotional for a simplified explanation of the Scripture and a personal word of encouragement for your day. But don't stop there! I encourage you to dig a little deeper into the additional three Bible verses included. Take the time to open your Bible and find these Scriptures. This will help you get to know your Bible and draw closer to the Lord.

When you are done reading each day, write in your journal. An important part of my journey with the Lord is taking time to listen to God's voice. Sit still, ask the Lord questions, and wait to hear His voice: *How does this Scripture apply to my life today? What do You want me to receive from You today? How can I show Your love to others today?*

---

*I am the good shepherd. I know My own sheep, and they know Me.*
—John 10:14

---

If you want to go even deeper, I recommend the added study and teaching tools at www.reviveSCHOOL.org. Sign up to receive daily chapter-by-chapter teachings from the Word. Even if you didn't begin reviveSCHOOL.org in year one, I would encourage you to begin now in year two.

I am excited to *continue with you* on this two-year devotional journey through the Word of God. Perhaps you need to create a new place to read and spend time with Jesus each morning. I pray the Lord will *revive you*. I bless you as you press on, not in your own strength but in the strength of the Lord.

---

*Now to Him who is able to do above and beyond all that we ask or think according to the power that works in us.*
—Ephesians 3:20

---

The Lord is with you. The Lord loves you. The Lord longs for you to love Him with all your heart, soul, mind, and strength. Pressing on reading the Bible, His love letter to you, develops this great love inside you. Enjoy the journey with the Lord one day at a time.

In Christ alone and with love,
Laura Kim Martin

### Week 1, Day 1: Job 1
Job and His Family

Job lived in the country of Uz and was known as the greatest man among all the people of the East. He feared God, turned from evil, and lived with perfect integrity. As Satan roamed the earth, he asked God for permission to attack Job. The Lord granted his request but restricted Satan from laying a hand on Job himself. So Satan brought four specific disasters that resulted in the destruction of Job's animals, his servants, and even his children. In the midst of this great suffering, Job fell to the ground and worshipped God: "The LORD gives, and the Lord takes away. Praise the name of Yahweh." Through this testing, Job continued to walk in integrity, without sin, and did not blame the Lord for anything.

As believers, you will endure suffering. Even today, the enemy prowls, seeking to steal, kill, and destroy. When you lay with your face to the ground, crying out to the Lord in pain and agony, the Lord promises He is with you. God gives you a reason to hope in the midst of disaster. Keep your eyes on *the promised redeemer, Jesus Christ.* The Lord gives and takes away. Even so, will you continue to say, "Praise the name of the Lord"? Choose to praise the Lord even in the midst of suffering. Yes, it's painful, but choose hope moment by moment. The Lord promises He will personally restore, establish, strengthen, and support you after your season of suffering. Hold on to His promises.

---

*Naked I came from my mother's womb,*
*and naked I will leave this life.*
*The LORD gives, and the LORD takes away.*
*Praise the name of Yahweh.*
*Throughout all this Job did not sin or blame God for anything.*
—Job 1:21–22

---

Further Scripture: 1 Samuel 2:6–7; 1 Peter 1:6–7; 5:10; 1 Peter 5:10

### *Week 1, Day 2: Job 2—3*

### Satan's Second Test

Again, the Lord gave Satan permission to attack Job. This time Satan could strike Job physically as long as he spared Job's life. Satan thought Job would surely curse God when his body was attacked with boils from top to bottom. However, Job proved Satan wrong. Through this attack, Job pressed on, living with integrity. He said to his wife, who wanted him to curse God, "Should we accept only good from God and not adversity?" In contrast, Job's three friends traveled to spend time with Job. Upon seeing their good friend in great agony, the friends wept together and sat with Job in silence for seven days.

When you see someone suffering, it can be awkward when you don't know exactly what to do or say. You can be the voice of an accuser, saying: "Go ahead and quit, you have every right to give up." Or you can be a sympathetic voice—a friend who sits with someone else in their pain. You may not know what to do for your friend going through cancer, a job loss, or depression. Sometimes you get stuck and just don't do anything. Today, *ask the Lord for wisdom.* He may just lead you to sit in silence in your car outside their home and pray for them. Or perhaps you give them a hug and sit in the hospital waiting room in silence. Any act of kindness is an expression of God's love. Today, go and show kindness to someone the Lord places on your heart.

---

*Then they sat on the ground with him seven days and nights, but no one spoke a word to him because they saw that his suffering was very intense.*
—Job 2:13

---

Further Scripture: Job 2:11; Proverbs 17:17; Colossians 3:12

## *Week 1, Day 3: Job 4*
## Eliphaz Speaks

After seven days of sitting with Job in his misery, the first of Job's three friends spoke up. Eliphaz brought accusations and arguments against Job because of what had happened to him. As the first to speak, Eliphaz had an agenda. Instead of conveying brotherly love, Eliphaz spoke out of his own wisdom.

You may see things from a different perspective as you observe a friend going through a time of suffering. However, as a friend, truly seek the heart of the Lord for wisdom before blurting out what you think about the situation. *Be slow to speak.* Then, when you do say something, speak from a pure heart, not with ulterior motives. Ask the Lord to help you communicate truth in love at the proper time. Your friend may not be ready to hear the insight you feel you have from the Lord, so pray. Pray for your suffering friend. Ask the Lord to cover your words of truth in His love. Ask the Lord to confirm your words to your friend with a supporting Scripture. Above all, walk it out in obedience, and trust the Holy Spirit to move in ways beyond human words.

---

*In my experience, those who plow injustice*
*and those who sow trouble reap the same.* —Job 4:8

---

Further Scripture: Ephesians 4:15, 29; 1 Peter 1:22

### *Week 1, Day 4: Job 5—6*

## Job Responded

Job responded honestly to his friend Eliphaz. He shared that he was indeed suffering. Because Job was suffering, he was weighed down and heavy-laden. He admitted the boils on his body caused him pain. And yet, despite feeling the bitterness of suffering, despite not agreeing with his friend's response, *Job turned to the Lord in prayer.*

Sometimes it's hard to admit you carry heavy burdens. It's difficult to be vulnerable with family and friends and admit, "I am weary and worried." This admission requires honesty and humility. However, as a believer, you walk with a Savior, a King, and a Friend named Jesus who reaches out His hand and says, "Come to Me, all of you who are weary and burdened, and I will give you rest." Jesus says, "I am your rest." Friend, rest in Jesus. First, admit your burden. Take a deep breath in and breathe out. As you breathe out, say, "God, take this burden from me. I'm worn out from carrying it. I trust You to carry it for me." Now, lift your hands in the air with your palms up as a sign of releasing the burden. He's got it. He is able to carry it, and He is able to equip you with grace and power to walk through this season. *Rest in Him.*

---

*If only my grief could be weighed*
*and my devastation placed with it in the scales.*
*For then it would outweigh the sand of the seas!*
*That is why my words are rash.* —Job 6:2–3

---

Further Scripture: Psalm 62:5–8; 91:1–2; Matthew 11:28–30

***Week 1, Day 5: Job 7—8***
The Threat of Traditions

Bildad examined Job's season through the lens of tradition. Without really knowing what caused Job's pain and suffering, Bildad responded with the traditional thought: *If you earnestly seek God, then ask Him for mercy. If you are pure and upright, then God will respond.* Bildad implied that because God wasn't releasing Job from the pain, then something must be wrong with Job. Job responded to Bildad's reasoning by proclaiming God as a sovereign God. Sometimes both the blameless and the wicked endure pain and disaster. Even so, all things point back to God. He alone is God, and He alone is sovereign.

Allow Bildad's response to serve as a reminder to not get stuck in tradition looking at every situation the same. Each painful situation will not always make sense. It may not always fit in a specific category. *And yet God remains in control.* He sees the heart. He sees the motives. He carries all understanding. In the New Testament, God sent the Holy Spirit to guide, counsel, and grant you understanding. Therefore, as you walk through life upholding Scripture to be true, also seek the Holy Spirit for help in each situation. As the Holy Spirit moves in your life, He will grant you patience and wisdom for His glory and for lives to enter His kingdom. In each new situation, ask the Lord for help and guidance, and trust Him to lead you in all your ways.

*For ask the previous generation,*
*and pay attention to what their fathers discovered,*
*since we were born only yesterday and know nothing.*
*Our days on earth are but a shadow. —Job 8:8–9*

Further Scripture: Mark 7:5; John 16:13; Colossians 2:8

## *Week 1, Day 6: Job 9—10*
### Needing a Mediator

Job replied to Bildad as he persevered through suffering. Job asked the question: "How can a person be justified before God?" And then, even in the midst of his pain, Job proceeded to recognize God's attributes— God is wise and all-powerful. He removes mountains without their knowledge. He alone stretches out the heavens and treads on the waves of the sea. He does great and unsearchable things—wonders without number. Even in the midst of suffering, Job spoke forth the greatness of God.

If God is such a magnificent God, *then how are you justified before Him?* How do you get to God? *The answer is Jesus, our Promised Redeemer.* Jesus is your mediator. He came to earth so that you don't have to defend yourself before God. Jesus came to set you free from sin. He came as a gift from God for you to receive. As you receive Jesus into your life, walk with Him, fix your eyes on Him, and He will transform your life. If you haven't received Jesus as your Savior and Lord but believe you have sinned and want to be justified freely by Christ, receive Him today. Say to the Lord, "I believe in You, Jesus, the resurrected Messiah, and I give You my life. I receive You as my Savior and Mediator." When you ask Jesus to take control of your life, even in the midst of suffering, you will be able to stand with His hope in you and praise the Lord for His mighty attributes.

---

*Yes, I know what you've said is true,*
*but how can a person be justified before God?* —Job 9:2

---

Further Scripture: Romans 3:23–24; 1 Timothy 2:5–6; Hebrews 9:15

*Week 1, Day 7: Job 11—12*

Practical Encouragement

Job's third friend, Zophar, responded to Job's pain and suffering with wise, biblical truth. However, Zophar did not know that Job didn't need to repent. Zophar didn't know Job's heart. Only the Lord knew Job's heart and what caused his suffering.

Only the Lord knows your heart. He sees the pain and knows your thoughts. Even so, if you find yourself in a season of suffering, Zophar gave some practical encouragement to consider. *Ask the Lord if these practical steps are for you.* Redirect your heart to God. Literally lift your hands up in the air as an outward expression of surrender and submission to the Lord. Remove any sin in your life and put it far away. Don't allow any temptation to sin in your home. Today, take time to process through these and act on them as the Lord leads you. As you do this, the Lord will walk with you. Although you may still endure suffering, even through the hard days, you will find hope, joy, confidence, and freedom as you seek the Lord with a pure heart.

*As for you, if you redirect your heart*
*and lift up your hands to Him in prayer—*
*if there is iniquity in your hand, remove it,*
*and don't allow injustice to dwell in your tents—*
*then you will hold your head high, free from fault.*
*You will be firmly established and unafraid. —Job 11:13–15*

Further Scripture: Psalm 28:2; 2 Timothy 2:21; 4:5

### Week 2, Day 8: Job 13
#### Job's Initial Response to Zophar

Job was covered with boils from head to toe when he responded to his three friends. He had listened to their logic and truth. He understood them and yet believed he was not inferior to them. As Job saw into their hearts and motives, he believed they were missing something in their counsel to him. At one point, Job told Zophar: "If only you would shut up and let that be your wisdom!"

Many families or schools have rules against saying the phrase "Shut up." In most cultures, this phrase comes across as impolite and crass in its direct approach of telling someone to stop talking. However, Job directed the phrase at his three friends, equating shutting up with wisdom. Yes, sometimes keeping your mouth closed and not offering advice is indeed the best wisdom. Today, be intentional and don't say everything you think, even on your social media comments, posts, or text messages. Before you say something, pause, close your mouth, and listen longer than you normally would. Rest in the fact you don't have to get your point across. God is sovereign. God is in control. When you exercise self-control with your words, you allow the Lord to move in the situation. So do as Job said, "Shut up and let that be your wisdom."

---

*If only you would shut up*
*and let that be your wisdom!* —Job 13:5

---

Further Scripture: Proverbs 17:28; 18:2; James 1:19

## Week 2, Day 9: Job 14
### Losing Hope

Job continued to respond to his friends' advice. In his response, his hopelessness is palpable. He was weary in the suffering. Eventually he began asking God all kinds of questions. As Job's pain intensified, he even questioned life after death.

What do you do when you are at the end of your rope? Do you think about death more than you think about life? You may ask yourself: *Is there really anything to hope for? What is my purpose here on earth?* Here's the answer. Hope remains. Hope lives on. You have *the Promised Redeemer*, the hope of this world, Jesus Christ. He is the anchor for your soul. He is safe and secure. Allow the Holy Spirit to fill you up with this hope found in Christ. He fills you with joy and peace as you believe in Christ Jesus. Then, through believing in Jesus, you will have eternal life. If you are questioning life right now, listen to these words for you: You have purpose. You are worthy of Jesus coming to earth just for *you*. You are loved. You are not alone. You have hope. Hold on to the *hope* found in Jesus, and ask the Holy Spirit to fill you up. Today, you may need to pray this moment by moment, trusting that the Lord hears you and will answer you.

*When a man dies, will he come back to life?*
*If so, I would wait all the days of my struggle*
*until my relief comes.*
*You would call, and I would answer You.*
*You would long for the work of Your hands.* —Job 14:14–15

Further Scripture: Romans 15:13; 2 Timothy 1:10; Hebrews 6:19

## *Week 2, Day 10: Job 15*
### Suffering Through Trials

Job's friends began a second round of responses. Eliphaz went first, and this time he intensified his comments, almost rebuking Job. He responded to Job's suffering with a works-based perspective, believing Job surely did something wicked to earn the suffering he was experiencing.

Here's the deal. *You cannot earn your way to God.* God's love and mercy are a free gift. He is kind and patient. It's not based on what you do or don't do. Yes, there are times you may have consequences to your choices or sin. However, as you go through trials, understand that God's ways are not your ways. The Lord is a God of grace and mercy. Yes, as believers, the Lord promises you will endure suffering. Everyone. However, hope remains by understanding even if you suffer from various trials, as you keep your eyes on Jesus, you will come out refined by the fire. You will be purified as gold, resulting in praise, glory, and honor to Jesus. *Ask the Lord for endurance and strength.* May the Lord cover you with His love and allow His kindness to wash over you today.

---

*Listen to me and I will inform you.*
*I will describe what I have seen.* —Job 15:17

---

Further Scripture: Romans 2:4; 1 Peter 1:6–7; 2 Peter 3:9

## Week 2, Day 11: Job 16
### Miserable Comforters

Job replied to Eliphaz's second, more blunt comments directed toward his suffering. Job responded honestly and shared how Eliphaz didn't encourage him. He called Eliphaz's words empty, just a string of words together. Job even said if Eliphaz was the one suffering, Job would offer him more encouragement and more encouraging words resulting in relief to the soul rather than discouragement.

Your words are important. They matter and have impact. Are you an encouraging friend? Or are you the one who quickly points out the problems and criticizes the situation? The Lord says to treat others the way you want to be treated. As you receive love from your heavenly Father, pour His love out to others. Forgive as you want to be forgiven. Help as you want to be helped. *Encourage as you want to be encouraged.* Be the friend you would like to have. When in doubt, remember love is patient, kind, not envious, not boastful, not conceited, doesn't act improperly, is not selfish, and not provoked to do something wrong. Instead, love rejoices in truth and never ends. Today, ask the Lord for an encouraging, loving word to share with a friend. Then deliver the message with love and watch God show up!

---

*If you were in my place I could also talk like you.*
*I could string words together against you*
*and shake my head at you.*
*Instead, I would encourage you with my mouth,*
*and the consolation from my lips would bring relief.* —Job 16:4–5

---

Further Scripture: 1 Corinthians 13:4–6; Colossians 3:13–14; Hebrews 3:13

*Week 2, Day 12: Job 17—18*

## Death Is Not the End

As Job spoke in frustration and helplessness for his situation, his friend Bildad responded for the second time. This time he responded with such criticism toward Job it was almost to the point of death and destruction. Bildad warned Job about what happened to the wicked, the one who does not know God. But here's the truth: *Job knew God.*

Can you imagine getting these harsh words from a friend as you walked through the most intense suffering and pain of your life? It may seem rare to have a friend like this. However, the enemy prowls around daily, seeking to bring about a similar destruction and death to your life. He comes to steal your joy and break up your relationships. He even speaks lies to you, leaving you feeling depressed, helpless, and hopeless. But here's the deal. You have the power within you to stop the lies. Jesus has won the battle. Remember, through the power of the Holy Spirit, you have everything you need to fight back. Take every thought captive by gaining control over what you think about yourself and believe God's truth. Lift up your shield of faith. Don't allow yourself to fall into the traps the enemy places in your life. Walk with victory because the battle belongs to the Lord! So press on in great faith, believing God's promises.

---

*Indeed, such is the dwelling of the unjust man,*
*and this is the place of the one who does not know God.* —Job 18:21

---

Further Scripture: Deuteronomy 20:4; 2 Corinthians 10:4–5; 1 John 5:4

*Week 2, Day 13: Job 19*
A Living Redeemer

Job responded to Bildad with exhaustion, saying:

> How long will you torment me
> and crush me with words? . . .
> He has removed my brothers from me;
> my acquaintances have abandoned me. . . .
> My breath is offensive to my wife,
> and my own family finds me repulsive.

Nevertheless, even in the midst of despair and exhaustion, Job found hope, saying: "But I know my living Redeemer, and He will stand on the dust at last." Yes, Job knew the living Redeemer, the one who was still to come, the promised Redeemer, Jesus. Job found hope.

Each day, you will walk through situations that may bring discouragement: spilled coffee on your computer, a lost phone, infertility, a friend who won't speak to you, being confined to bed or your house . . . there are so many situations on any given day that can lead to discouragement. As you walk through these difficult moments, remember there is always a *but*. There is always the truth. *You have a living Redeemer, Jesus Christ.* He gave His life in order to set you free from sin and death. And now, your Redeemer lives. Even at the end of a difficult day, choose to say: "*But* I know my Redeemer lives." Now you can face tomorrow, because your Redeemer lives. God's got you, friend. Hang on to the hope in Christ.

*But I know my living Redeemer, and He will stand on the dust at last.*
*Even after my skin has been destroyed, yet I will see God in my flesh.*
—Job 19:25–26

Further Scripture: Isaiah 43:1; Romans 8:1–2; Ephesians 1:7–8

## Week 2, Day 14: Job 20
### Complete Satisfaction

Zophar responded to Job a second time. This time Zophar's unsettled thoughts forced him to angrily answer Job. Zophar strongly explained how the joy of the wicked would be brief and how happiness for the godless would only last a minute. He went on to say that the wicked person's appetite would never be satisfied.

Those without Jesus, who are without the presence of the living God inside them, will search and search for meaning and fulfillment in their lives, but they will never find satisfaction. They will chase after everything they desire but never truly find peace. However, in Christ's presence, there is fullness of joy. Even when life is dry and parched, He will be your living water. He will be your strength. He will forgive your sins and heal your diseases. He will redeem your life from the pit and satisfy you with goodness. As you delight in the Lord, He will give you the desires of your heart and will give you the strength you need for every situation. Christ is enough. When you hunger and thirst for life with Christ, you will be filled. Stop chasing after the things of the world. *Only Christ can give complete satisfaction.*

---

*Because his appetite is never satisfied,*
*he does not let anything he desires escape.* —Job 20:20

---

Further Scripture: Psalm 103:2–5; Isaiah 58:11; Matthew 5:6

*Week 3, Day 15: Job 21*

Waiting on the Lord

Job responded to his friends' reasoning about why he was experiencing this time of suffering, living day and night with painful boils. Job's thoughts and emotions had been up and down, and yet he continued to wait upon the Lord for the day when he would be free from the suffering.

*Waiting.* When you walk in the Spirit, the Lord will fill you with patience. In contrast, when you walk in your flesh, you will naturally grow impatient, experience worry and fear, get irritated, and lose perspective. Whether you are waiting for coffee to brew, the line at the grocery store to move, or traffic to clear, everyday situations may cause you to grow impatient. Waiting for a health test result over the weekend or for a loved one to get out of surgery can really cause unrest in your heart. However, the Lord says those who wait upon the Lord will renew their strength. No matter what you are waiting for, you can release your prayers to the Lord and wait expectantly, trusting that He hears you! As you wait for something in your life today, believe one thing—*the Lord knows.* He hears you. So trust His timing even through traffic. Wait with thanksgiving. Rest in His promises. Resist the urge to fear and fret. *The Lord your God is with you through the waiting.*

---

*As for me, is my complaint against a man?*
*Then why shouldn't I be impatient?*
*Look at me and shudder;*
*put your hand over your mouth.* —Job 21:4–5

---

Further Scripture: Psalm 5:3; Isaiah 40:31; Micah 7:7

## *Week 3, Day 16: Job 22—23*
## The Bottom Line

Once again Job heard from his friend Eliphaz, who questioned the reasons for Job's suffering. Eliphaz offered answers to Job, essentially saying: If only Job would work on X-Y-Z, then his suffering would stop. However, Job understood that life doesn't happen like a formula. Job admitted he couldn't find God anywhere from the north, south, east, or west, and *yet* Job kept his faith saying, "*Yet* He knows the way I have taken; when He has tested me, I will emerge as pure gold." Job acknowledged he was terrified and afraid of God, and *yet* Job held onto hope saying: "*Yet* I am not destroyed by the darkness, by the thick darkness that covers my face."

Today, you may be in the middle of a trial like Job. You can't see God's hand in your life anywhere, and *yet* you know He is with you. You may be terrified, and *yet* you trust and are not destroyed. You have faith and hope carrying you through the difficult, painful days. Remember, through the affliction, the Lord is producing endurance, character, and hope in you. Today, as you walk through the darkness, God knows the way you have taken. You are not destroyed. You will emerge like pure gold. Press on in faith, and hold on to the hope within you.

---

*When He is at work to the north, I cannot see Him;*
*when He turns south, I cannot find Him.*
*Yet He knows the way I have taken;*
*when He has tested me, I will emerge as pure gold.* —Job 23:9–10

---

Further Scripture: Isaiah 48:10; Romans 5:3–5; Hebrews 11:6

*Week 3, Day 17: Job 24*
Look Around You

As Job responded to his friends, he brought attention to others suffering around him: the injustices happening, the crimes in the city, and the curses on the wicked. Rather than just focusing on his own suffering, Job noticed how the orphans, the widows, and other misfortunate, helpless people needed help, hope, and love.

In the midst of your own suffering, *take your eyes off yourself and look at others around you.* You may be in the hospital for treatment or at an insurance office making a claim for an accident, but for a moment, open your eyes to see those around you. As a believer in Jesus, you are called to love God and love others—and not just when things in your life are going smoothly. Who knows, maybe in the midst of sickness or loss, the Lord wants to use you to bring hope to another person. You never know how the Lord will move when you take your eyes off yourself and show someone compassion and love. Even when you feel weary and have nothing left to give, God's grace is sufficient and will give you strength. Love others even through the pain. It may be just what you need to get through your own painful situation.

---

*They prey on the childless woman who is unable to conceive,*
*and do not deal kindly with the widow.*
*Yet God drags away the mighty by His power;*
*when He rises up, they have no assurance of life.*
*He gives them a sense of security, so they can rely on it,*
*but His eyes watch over their ways.* —Job 24:21–23

---

Further Scripture: Ephesians 5:2; Philippians 2:3–4; 1 John 4:19–21

### *Week 3, Day 18: Job 25—26*

Focus on Giving Thanks

Bildad spoke to Job again, this time calling Job a maggot and a worm. Bildad's advice and comments were not likely what Job needed to hear. Job responded strongly to Bildad with a series of direct questions. Job put his foot down and said to Bildad, "I have heard enough from you." And then, in the midst of his own personal misery and suffering, Job focused on Who he knew was certain—the God who created the universe and all creation. "He stretches the northern skies over empty space; He hangs the earth on nothing. . . . He laid out the horizon on the surface of the waters."

Today, as you press on through the Lord's plan for your day—whether it's a day filled with joy and delight or a day filled with heartache and unknowns—*give thanks to God, the creator of heaven and earth*. Praise the Lord for His power that stirs the sea. Praise the Lord for His breath that gives the heavens their beauty. Open a window, walk outside, breathe in the fresh air, let the sun soak your face or the raindrops drench your hair, and give thanks to the Lord for His mighty, powerful creation. The same God who created the universe longs for a relationship with you. The God of miracles and wonders loves you. Stop and pause at His wonders today.

---

*He stretches the northern skies over empty space;*
*He hangs the earth on nothing.*
*He wraps up the waters in His clouds,*
*yet the clouds do not burst beneath their weight.* —Job 26:7–8

---

Further Scripture: Psalm 104:24–25; John 1:3; Romans 1:20

*Week 3, Day 19: Job 27*

Hold Fast

Job's friends didn't offer Job much hope as he pressed on through suffering. Even so, Job affirmed his commitment to the Lord, to his integrity, and to holding on, clinging to hope. He stated to his friends, "I will never affirm that you are right." Then Job expressed he would "cling to [his] righteousness and never let it go."

To *cling* means to hold fast, to persevere, to not quit, to hold on to what God has asked you to do. Imagine plastic wrap—they kind you use for leftovers. The purpose of it is to keep two pieces connected as they cling to each other, oftentimes covering a dish of food. Plastic wrap's purpose fails when it stops clinging to the side of a container of food. The spaghetti sauce may slip out, causing a mess. In the same way, you must hold fast and cling to the Lord so His purposes and plans for you are carried out to completion. The Lord will give you strength as you hold fast to His love and grace in your life by faith. Don't lose hope, even when bumps in the road come. Instead, *cling to the hope you have in Christ.* The Lord is faithful to fulfill His promises as you hold fast to Him.

---

*I will never affirm that you are right.*
*I will maintain my integrity until I die.*
*I will cling to my righteousness and never let it go.*
*My conscience will not accuse me as long as I live!* —Job 27:5–6

---

Further Scripture: Philippians 1:6; Hebrews 10:23; Revelation 2:10

## *Week 3, Day 20: Job 28—29*
### The Mystery of Wisdom

Job asked the question, "Where can wisdom be found, and where is understanding located?" It's not found in the ocean depths. It's not exchanged for gold, silver, precious pearls, sapphire, coral, or quartz. Wisdom is beyond all the riches the world offers. Job knew that the source of wisdom was found in the all-seeing, all-knowing God.

Like Job, you may ask yourself, *What is wisdom and where does it come from?* The Word of God says that the fear of the Lord is wisdom and to turn from evil is understanding. You can search through books and online resources or seek your mentor's advice, but ultimate wisdom comes from fearing God. To fear God means to have a reverent respect for all He is capable of, believing He holds all the mysteries of the world together. As you walk in God's ways, resisting evil and temptations, you display understanding. You must believe God is bigger than all of the things of the world. Wisdom is worth more than any precious stone. Wisdom is greater but not unattainable. Today, ask the Lord for wisdom, and He promises it will be given to you!

---

*But where can wisdom be found,*
*and where is understanding located?*
. . . . . . . . . . . . . .
*He considered wisdom and evaluated it;*
*He established it and examined it.*
*He said to mankind,*
*"The fear of the Lord is this: wisdom.*
*And to turn from evil is understanding."* —Job 28:12, 27—28

---

Further Scripture: Ephesians 1:7–9; Colossians 2:2–3; James 1:5

*Week 3, Day 21: Job 30*

Enduring Never-Ending Pain in the Hope

Job persevered in his suffering, but he still expressed his misery, his aching, and the mockery he received from the community. His physical pain never ended—day and night the pain gnawed at him. And yet Job knew the Lord was with him; even if it meant to his deathbed, the Lord would lead him. He found hope in a living Redeemer.

Today, you may need to hear you are not alone in your pain, how someone else has also endured great pain day and night. You may be sick and in such physical pain that words can't even begin to describe it. You may see no end in sight except through death. The days are hard, and the nights are no different. Just as Job knew this pain, your Savior, Jesus Christ, experienced this intense pain as well. People rejected and despised Jesus. People turned away from and devalued Him. The apostle Paul, in the midst of his own suffering, responded with the hope that no matter what he went through, nothing would separate him from the love of God. So today, in the mist of your pain, understand in your heart that you are not alone, even if it feels like it. Others have endured this pain too. Hold on to the hope that nothing will ever separate you from Christ. Dear friend, *the Lord will see you through.*

---

*Night pierces my bones,*
*but my gnawing pains never rest.*
*My clothing is distorted with great force;*
*He chokes me by the neck of my garment.* —Job 30:17–18

---

Further Scripture: Job 19:25–26; Isaiah 53:3; Romans 8:38–39

### *Week 4, Day 22: Job 31*
### Lay It All Out

Job believed he had walked in integrity and righteousness toward others. However, in the event he had done anything wrong in the Lord's eyes, he laid it all on the line. If he had lived an impure life and acted in lustful ways, if he had not given to the poor or not given to a person in need of clothing, if he had placed his confidence in gold and rejoiced in wealth, if his heart had been enticed in any other way, then Job was willing to receive the consequences. He was ready for his indictment. Job understood God saw his ways and numbered his steps. God would surely know if Job walked in falsehood.

Are you able to open all the pages of your life before God? Is there a page or two you'd want to keep secret and covered up? Here's the deal—God sees everything. He knows all. There is nothing you can hide from God, so it's really not worth the effort. Even though God knows everything about your life, you need to understand in your head and believe in your heart that He loves you no matter what. Not only does He love you, but His grace covers your sin, your guilt, and your shame. Christ died for you to be *set free*. You don't have to carry the weight of your sin. It is done. Child of God, the Lord longs for you to walk in freedom. *Receive God's grace and mercy and open all the pages of your life to Him.*

---

*Does He not see my ways*
*and number all my steps?* —Job 31:4

---

Further Scripture: Proverbs 5:21; Romans 6:22; Hebrews 4:13

## *Week 4, Day 23: Job 32–33*
### Elihu's Response

After Job responded to his three friends, a new friend emerged with a message for Job. Elihu witnessed the previous interactions among Job, Bildad, Eliphaz, and Zophar, and a word from the Lord rose within him to the point he could not stay quiet anymore.

If the Lord has given you a message, a verse, or an edifying word for another person, speak those words out. If you wake up every day with the same person and message on your heart or if you think about it several times throughout the day, then that's when you know you have to communicate it! Ask the Lord for the opportunity to talk with that person, trust the Lord will grant clarity for your words, and then, go for it! Yes, it will take courage. Yes, it will take boldness. Yes, it will take faith. But friend, God will be with you. Speak it out. The Lord says you are *His mouthpiece, His vessel, and His ambassador* to proclaim the good news in boldness and in power through the Holy Spirit. Today, rise up and say the message on your heart delivered with love.

---

*My heart is like unvented wine;*
*it is about to burst like new wineskins.*
*I must speak so that I can find relief;*
*I must open my lips and respond.* —Job 32:19–20

---

Further Scripture: Exodus 4:11–12; 2 Corinthians 5:20;
2 Timothy 1:7–8

*Week 4, Day 24: Job 34—35*

Crying Out

Elihu continued speaking to Job about the message so heavy on his heart. Elihu spoke from his perspective and gave possible reasons for God's silence through Job's suffering. Elihu confronted the pride he witnessed creep into Job's heart. Because of Job's pride, God did not answer when he cried out.

You may think to yourself, *I need help, but asking for help from the Lord or others—no way.* You may believe asking for help or crying out reveals weakness, or you fear you may have to release control to someone else. You'd rather pretend you have it together than let go of your pride. However, the Lord desires for you to ask Him for help. He already knows you need it. He wants you to ask Him because it's in the asking for help that you finally surrender. In asking, you reveal your humility, your helplessness, your faith in God's power and God's resources, and your trust in God for victory. It is *okay* to cry out. Christ came to earth for you. He sent the Holy Spirit to *help* you. You have the body of Christ to *help* you. The Lord promises to hear your cry for help. He will save you and deliver you from your troubles. Open your heart and cry out for help today. The Lord is with you and will answer your humble cry for help.

---

*There they cry out, but He does not answer,*
*because of the pride of evil men.* —Job 35:12

---

Further Scripture: Psalm 34:17; 145:19; John 15:5

*Week 4, Day 25: Job 36*
Turn to the Lord

Elihu continued speaking into Job's life and even asked Job to be patient with him a little longer. In many ways, Elihu answered Job's plea for a mediator. As one who received knowledge from a distant place, Elihu spoke different truths into Job's life in the midst of his suffering. Elihu warned Job to be careful not to turn to sin in the midst of his affliction.

When you are stuck in a pit of despair, this is not the time in your life to turn to sin. Lord willing, through your affliction, you will be refined and will grow in perseverance, character, and hope. Don't give up on hope and choose sin. When life gets tough, don't turn to alcohol and begin drinking your sorrows away. When life gets tough, don't just go out shopping and accumulate debt. When life gets tough with your marriage, don't turn to other relationships to fill the void. Instead, *turn to the Lord.* Press on in hope through the affliction. *Nothing else but Christ will satisfy your heart.* Nothing. No woman. No man. No drink. No purchase. Nothing but the love of Christ. Keep your eyes fixed on Jesus until He shows up. And He will show up because He is faithful. Don't lose hope.

---

*Be careful that you do not turn to iniquity,*
*for that is why you have been tested by affliction.* —Job 36:21

---

Further Scripture: Psalm 37:24; Romans 5:3–5; 2 Corinthians 4:1–2

## *Week 4, Day 26: Job 37*
### Fear Before God

In Elihu's final words to Job, he passionately described the Lord's great and mighty works through the weather and creation. He clearly presented his case for how the Lord can handle control of our lives, and he wanted Job to stop and just listen. In doing so, the final point Elihu spoke into Job's life was to fear God with a pure heart. As Elihu stated, God frowns upon those who carry themselves with superior wisdom. The God of all creation holds all wisdom, so why be prideful about it and think you know better than God?

In just moments, pride can easily creep into your heart. You may think you already know the outcome of a situation or believe you know the reasons why something happened or assume you have it all together. Remember, God is the God of all creation and all wonders—yes, He created you, and He knows your heart. He longs for you to fear Him with all your heart and without any pride. As you walk through any trial or suffering, *focus on God's creation, and read through His Word to know Him more.* As you do these two things, it will help you turn from self-centeredness to *fearing God* with a pure heart. The same God who set the boundary of the sea and gives the rain controls your life. He is more than able. Allow Him to teach you His way.

---

*Therefore, men fear Him.*
*He does not look favorably on any who are wise in heart.* —Job 37:24

---

Further Scripture: Psalm 19:9; 86:11; Jeremiah 5:22–24

## *Week 4, Day 27: Job 38*
### Creator of the Universe

After Elihu addressed Job's prideful heart and the importance of fearing God, the Lord answered Job from a whirlwind. The Lord gave Job His opinion in the form of several questions about creation, essentially asking Job, *Can you make and control My creation?* Yes, Job may have walked in integrity, but did he fully recognize the full magnitude of God's hand in all of creation? Clearly Job never had a reason to challenge God, even during his suffering.

Although you may have great character and success in life, *God is still God.* There is no one besides the Lord. He is your rock and a refuge, who makes your way perfect. He counts the number of stars and gives names to them all. He is great, vast in power, and His understanding is infinite. Today, realize how much you do not know and how amazing God is. This truth will keep you humble and at a place of dependency before the Lord. Even when you walk through difficulty, remember God, the creator of the universe, also holds your life in His hands. You may know God, but do you really *know* God?

---

*Who is this who obscures My counsel*
*with ignorant words?*
*Get ready to answer Me like a man;*
*when I question you, you will inform Me.*
*Where were you when I established the earth?*
*Tell Me, if you have understanding.* —Job 38:2–4

---

Further Scripture: 2 Samuel 22:32–33; Job 38:34–35; Psalm 147:4–5

### *Week 4, Day 28: Job 39—40*
## God Captured the Behemoth

God gave Job a chance to answer. Job admitted he had no words and covered his hands over his mouth. Then the Lord resumed questioning Job about how he had challenged God's justice. Because the Lord saw his heart, God knew Job had developed an attitude problem that needed to be smoothed out so that his relationship with God could be restored. God went on to describe a Behemoth, possibly a dinosaur-type creation, and questioned if anyone could capture such a super beast apart from Himself. If Job couldn't capture this beast, then how could Job justify himself before God?

God is capable of being in charge. So let go of control in your life and let God's will be done. How do you do that? Pause. Pray. Don't force things to happen. Find security in God. If God puts a burden on your heart and opens the door to something new, even if it doesn't make sense, walk through that door in obedience to God. If you know God is in it, then let Him be God. God owns the cattle on a thousand hills. If you are praying for a loved one to come back to Christ, wait upon the Lord. If God can turn the heart of a king, then He is also able to turn the heart of a wayward child. Again, *God is capable of being in charge.* Rest in the Lord. Seek the Lord. Then go and follow Him. He is in control!

---

*Would you really challenge My justice?*
*Would you declare Me guilty to justify yourself?*
*Do you have an arm like God's?*
*Can you thunder with a voice like His?* —Job 40:8–9

---

Further Scripture: Psalm 50:10; Proverbs 21:1; Revelation 1:17

## *Week 5, Day 29: Job 41—42*
Knowing God Better

After the Lord spoke to Job about His strength and majesty over creation, He gave Job a chance to respond. At last, Job completely humbled himself, acknowledged God's greatness, and replied to the Lord, "I know that You can do anything and no plan of Yours can be thwarted." Job *repented* of his prideful words when he realized he had spoken about things he did not understand. The Lord accepted Job's prayer of repentance for himself and later on behalf of his three friends as well. After Job prayed, the Lord *restored* his prosperity and *restored* his relationships with his brothers, sisters, and former acquaintances. The Lord blessed the subsequent part of Job's life even more than the first.

*Repent and restore.* It may take a lifetime for a father to repent of wrongdoing toward a son, but when repentance occurs, the Lord promises restoration. A husband and wife may endure an entire weekend without speaking to each other because of a misunderstanding. But the moment they repent before the Lord and one another, restoration begins. Repentance reveals a humbled heart. Humble yourself, repent to God and to others, and you will be restored. The Lord promises this over and over and over. What are you waiting for? Ask the Lord to reveal any areas in your life that need repentance. If He *reveals* an area, *repent* with a broken and contrite heart, ask the Lord for forgiveness, and you will be *restored!* Today, take a minute to seek the Lord and repent. His mercies are new each morning, and He promises healing and restoration.

---

*Therefore I take back my words and repent in dust and ashes.*

. . . . . . . . . . . . . . .

*After Job had prayed for his friends, the* Lord *restored his prosperity and doubled his previous possessions.* —Job 42:6, 10

---

Further Scripture: 2 Chronicles 7:14; Hosea 6:1; 1 Peter 5:10

### *Week 5, Day 30: Psalms 1—3*
### Make the Choice

The Book of Psalms opens with a choice: follow the advice of the wicked, take the path of sinners, and join a group of mockers *or* delight in the Lord's instruction and meditate on it day and night. The Word of God says if you choose the second option you will be happy! Happiness expresses feelings of joy and satisfaction. All those who take refuge in the Lord are happy. Even so, happiness is not based on circumstances or trials. You are to find joy in the Lord in every circumstance, even through trials. You do so by keeping your eyes fixed on Jesus and not on yourself as you go through your day.

So today, try something. Make the choice to open the Word of God and ask the Lord for one verse to focus on all day long. Intentionally listen to music with edifying lyrics. Spend time with people who also delight themselves in Jesus. Then, at the end of your day, ask the Lord to show you how considering His Word and truth all day long had an effect on your day. Try this for a several days in a row as a discipline *to stay connected with the Lord,* and it may just turn your life around!

---

*How happy is the man*
*who does not follow the advice of the wicked*
*or take the path of sinners*
*or join a group of mockers!*
*Instead, his delight is in the* LORD's *instruction,*
*and he meditates on it day and night.* —Psalm 1:1–2

---

Further Scripture: Psalm 2:12; Ecclesiastes 2:26; James 1:2

## *Week 5, Day 31: Psalms 4—6*

### Praying in the Morning

What do you do first when you wake up in the morning? Check your phone? Go make coffee? Care for young kids who need your attention? Today, begin with prayer. While the coffee brews, before you click on the Facebook app, open Instagram, check your email, or even in the midst of watching morning cartoons with your little ones, *pause and pray.* Call upon the name of the Lord. Allow Him to hear your voice as you begin your day. Think of a few of His attributes you are grateful for and give Him praise. Share with Him what's on your heart for the day and ask Him to help you.

He hears your prayers, and He promises to answer when you call upon His name. And because you know He hears you, expect Him to answer. He may answer with a no, a yes, or a not right now, but He will answer, making your paths straight and giving you understanding along the way. Remember, *wake up* and pray with expectation!

---

*At daybreak, LORD, You hear my voice;*
*at daybreak I plead my case to You and watch expectantly.* —Psalm 5:3

---

Further Scripture: Psalm 6:9; Jeremiah 29:12; 1 John 5:14

### *Week 5, Day 32: Psalms 7—9*
### Reason to Celebrate

These days, people host all kinds of celebrations and get special treats for everything—like scoring a goal at soccer, getting promoted at work, losing a tooth, or any calendar holiday. Today, celebrate the work of God's hands! Not only did God make you, but He made the heavens, moon, and stars. He made the sheep, oxen, birds in the sky, and fish in the ocean. All of it was made by His hands. And He made man to rule over it all. He put everything under your feet, all His wonderful works. God describes you as a clay vessel holding all His power to do the work He called you to do.

So when you feel defeated, when you feel knocked down, when you feel you've messed up and don't measure up, it is time to stand up. You are a child of God. You are the work of His hands—and He cares for you. You are able to press on because the creator of the universe, God Almighty's power is at work in your life. *Give thanks to the Lord throughout the earth. Celebrate and have a special treat today* because the Lord has done great things and has given you so many reasons to rejoice, boast, and sing about His name!

---

*What is man that You remember him,*
*the son of man that You look after him?*
*You made him little less than God*
*and crowned him with glory and honor.*
*You made him lord over the works of Your hands;*
*You put everything under his feet. —Psalm 8:4–6*

---

Further Scripture: Psalm 8:9; 9:1–2; 2 Corinthians 4:7–9

*Week 5, Day 33: Psalms 10—12*

The Lord Your Guard

The Lord will guard you and protect you, even in a world full of wicked people wandering everywhere: people boasting in themselves, living with greed, despising the Lord, and believing God doesn't exist. God allows hard things to happen in this fallen world, and you may not understand why. Sometimes His protection comes in the form of peace and strength in the middle of a trial. Sometimes God's protection doesn't look like you thought it would. You endure a car accident or a house fire, a bad word spoken to you, or a sickness. You don't feel protected. Trust that God is in your midst. He sees something you may not see, and He's working on the bigger picture. He is with you.

With faith in Jesus, trust and believe His promises. When you find yourself in a fearful situation, *pray and believe God* is your shield, your horn of salvation, your stronghold, your refuge, and your Savior. When you call to Him, you will be saved. Rest in knowing whatever trial you face today the Lord will protect and guard you.

---

*You, LORD, will guard us;*
*You will protect us from this generation forever.*
*The wicked wander everywhere,*
*and what is worthless is exalted by the human race.* —Psalm 12:7–8

---

Further Scripture: 2 Samuel 22:3–4; Psalm 10:3–4; 2 Thessalonians 3:3

## *Week 5, Day 34: Psalms 13—15*
### Living Righteously Intentionally

Where do you intentionally seek the presence of the Lord? Is it in a chair every morning before the sun rises? Is it on the bathroom floor before you hop in the shower? Is it on the commute to work with the radio off? Seeking God's presence may look differently for everyone, *but the key is to be intentional.*

The Lord's strength flows through your life from your time in His presence. In His presence, your will, wants, and desires are emptied. Your walk becomes godly and righteous as you depend on His power and strength. You will live honestly, practice righteousness, and acknowledge God's truth in your heart through your time in His presence. These behaviors happen not because they are forced through your effort but because your love for the Lord increases through His ongoing presence and power within you. Security in Jesus as your rock and your firm foundation are found in His presence. Ultimately, as a follower of Jesus, you will live in the presence of God forever. Until that time comes, *intentionally seek His ongoing presence*, and His love and grace will overflow from your life.

---

*LORD, who can dwell in Your tent?*
*Who can live on Your Holy Mountain?*
. . . . . . . . . . . . . .
*the one who does these things will never be moved.* —Psalm 15:1, 5

---

Further Scripture: Micah 6:8; Matthew 7:24–25; 1 Corinthians 3:16

## *Week 5, Day 35: Psalms 16—17*
Keep the Lord in Mind Always

As a follower of Christ, keep the Lord on your mind always. *Always.* When you wake up, make breakfast for your family, walk into that board meeting, play that sports game, walk up the steps to preach that sermon, wait on the doctor's report, tuck your kids to bed at night, or burn the midnight oil writing papers for school . . . keep the Lord on your mind *always!* Why? Because when you do, you won't be shaken or feel defeated in life. You won't be shaken when you lose the game or your kids won't listen to you. You won't feel defeated when you don't have approval from your peers, your coworkers, or your teachers, or when the health test reveals unwanted results.

Keep your mind focused and your eyes fixed on Jesus, the author of your life. He has plans for you, not to harm you but to prosper you for good. He holds your future and will reveal the path of life to you even through the trials. As you keep the Lord in mind and rest in His presence, He promises you will experience *joy.* Try it today. Keep the Lord on your mind *at all times.* Read His Word. Give thanks to Him for His promises. Sit in the quiet and let His Spirit speak to your heart. Rest in Him. Not in yourself. Not in your things or your agenda. Not in strife or in fret. *Rest in Him.* In Him, you won't be shaken.

*I keep the LORD in mind always.*
*Because He is at my right hand,*
*I will not be shaken.*
*Therefore my heart is glad*
*and my spirit rejoices;*
*my body also rests securely.*
. . . . . . . . . . . . . .
*You reveal the path of life to me; in Your presence is abundant joy;*
*in Your right hand are eternal pleasures.* —Psalm 16:8—9, 11

Further Scripture: Psalm 16:5—6; Jeremiah 29:11; Hebrews 12:2

### *Week 6, Day 36: Psalm 18*
## Worship the Lord

Think of a time when you cried out to the Lord with an emotional, heartfelt prayer. Perhaps you needed healing, an impossible provision, supernatural wisdom, or protection from harm's way. And then God moved—He answered in an "only God" type of way. Did you stop and worship, giving praise and thanksgiving to the Lord? Maybe you didn't have the words to praise the Lord? Maybe you want to enter His gates with thanksgiving and His courts with praise, but you just feel stuck when you try to articulate it. Take a minute and read David's words in Psalm 18 aloud. Seriously, do it. David praised the Lord with such a depth of worship and praise. You can learn from this man who cried out to the Lord through every circumstance and witnessed the Lord move in impossible, "only God" ways to deliver and heal him.

Today, begin praising the Lord with the phrase: "I love You, Lord, my strength." It may seem simple, but repeat the words out loud, over and over, until it comes from a place of real adoration to the Lord. *God is glorified when you worship Him.* Call to the Lord who is worthy of praise, and you will be saved.

---

*I love You, Lord, my strength.* —Psalm 18:1

---

Further Scripture: Psalm 18:2–3; Mark 12:30; Revelation 14:7

## *Week 6, Day 37: Psalms 19—20*
### Lift Your Banner High

You face a spiritual battle every day as you seek first the kingdom of God and His righteousness. The enemy sets out to destroy your heart, your life, and your mind to keep you from fulfilling your whole purpose from the Lord. Nevertheless, you have the Lord on your side as you pray to answer you, protect you, help you, sustain you, and remember you. *Do not fear.*

God asks you to delight in Him with a pure heart. As you do so, your desires will line up with His desires for you. His strength, timing, wisdom, and protection allows you to fulfill your purpose from the Lord. Some people may take pride in chariots and horses, but as a believer, take pride in the Lord your God. As things on this earth collapse and fall apart, guess who stands firm forever? The King of Glory! *The Lord who is strong and mighty will give you the victory.* Raise your banner high in the name of the Lord. He is worthy to be praised.

---

*May He give you what your heart desires*
*and fulfill your whole purpose.*
*Let us shout for joy at your victory*
*and lift the banner in the name of our God.*
*May Yahweh fulfill all your requests.* —Psalm 20:4–5

---

Further Scripture: Psalm 20:7–9; 37:4; Ephesians 6:12

## *Week 6, Day 38: Psalms 21—22*
### The Fifth Gospel

Have you ever thought, *No one understands my pain, my misery, my distress. I just feel all alone. Where is God in this?* David prophesied about the Messiah's pain and distress generations before God sent Jesus to the earth. When it came to pass, Jesus cried out to God, His father, just as David had written: "My God, My God, why have You forsaken me?" David first prophesied it, and then, you read the story of Jesus—He indeed suffered pain, but God delivered Jesus from His suffering. Jesus was resurrected, going from death to life. In fact, Psalm 22 is quoted, referenced, or alluded to fifteen times in the New Testament. Some in the early church even refer to it as the "fifth gospel."

And just as Scripture prophesied of Jesus, the same is true for you. God will resurrect your life from the pit and what feels like death. *He will redeem your pain as you trust Him through any circumstance.* One day He will lift you up, and you will praise His name. You will testify to others about His great name. So press on. Just as Jesus held on to the hope in His father, hang on to hope found in Christ's love.

---

*My God, my God, why have You forsaken me?*
*Why are You so far from my deliverance*
*and from my words of groaning?*
*My God, I cry by day, but You do not answer,*
*by night, yet I have no rest.*
*But You are holy,*
*enthroned on the praises of Israel.*
*Our fathers trusted in You;*
*they trusted, and You rescued them.*
*They cried to You and were set free;*
*they trusted in You and were not disgraced.* —Psalm 22:1–5

---

Further Scripture: Psalm 22:27–31; Matthew 27:46; Acts 2:29–30

## *Week 6, Day 39: Psalms 23–25*
## The King of Glory

Have you ever stopped and wondered what the phrase "King of glory" means? The word *glory* is defined as weight. When used to describe a person, it denotes that the person carries power and solemnity, deserving honor. Describing the Lord as the *King of glory* prompts you to give the Lord the appropriate respect and honor that He deserves as the awesome, almighty, one and only King of your life. "Lift up your heads" and "rise up" direct you to get ready for the coming King.

The psalmist says to have clean hands and a pure heart, not setting your mind on anything false. The Lord doesn't ask you to be perfect but rather to live with actions and an inner attitude honoring God. Rise up and make Jesus the King of your life, serve Him with all your heart, and *expect the King of glory to appear.* Seek the Lord's face and trust Him. He is worthy of it all.

---

*Lift up your heads, you gates!*
*Rise up, ancient doors!*
*Then the King of glory will come in.*
*Who is this King of glory?*
*The LORD, strong and mighty,*
*the LORD, mighty in battle.* —Psalm 24:7–8

---

Further Scripture: Psalm 24:3–4; Matthew 17:5; Revelation 19:1

### *Week 6, Day 40: Psalms 26–28*
This One Thing

If you could ask the Lord for one thing, what would it be? David prayed for fellowship with the Lord all the days of His life. Today, focus your attention on this one thing—to dwell with the Lord. *Dwell means to remain for a time.* Yes, you still have to go through your day, but as you do, rest in Jesus. Abide in the Lord like a branch on a vine. Read His Word. Take the time to know God day after day after day. The more you know God, the more strength you will have to press on.

When you are nervous about an upcoming test, ask the Lord for wisdom and peace. When you carry a heavy burden, admit you can't do it on your own, and ask the Lord for help. When you have a temptation in front of you, pause and ask the Holy Spirit for power to resist the enemy and flee. Focus on Christ, and don't be distracted by the things of the world. The world may entice you, but the Lord is enough. Dwell with Him.

---

*I have asked one thing from the LORD;*
*it is what I desire:*
*to dwell in the house of the LORD*
*all the days of my life,*
*gazing on the beauty of the LORD*
*and seeking Him in His temple.* —Psalm 27:4

---

Further Scripture: Luke 10:39, 41–42; John 15:4; 1 John 3:6

## *Week 6, Day 41: Psalms 29—30*
### Lamenting into Dancing

God never lets you go. He loves you. No matter how far in the pit you have fallen, He loves you. Even at rock bottom, the Lord will pick you up. If you cry out to Him for help, He will heal you. He never stops loving you. You may have sinned. You may feel trapped and caught, not able to see a way out. Your whole life may feel like a blur.

Remember, *with God there is always a way out.* He promises to restore, to reconcile, and to redeem every situation. Begin by crying out for help, let go of any pride or selfishness, and allow the Lord's light to shine into the cracks of your brokenness. You may have cried all night in your sorrow. You may have lost your marriage, your job, your children, or a loved one. The Lord hears every cry. He promises to turn your lament into dancing. He'll remove your sackcloth and clothe you with gladness. As you open your eyes to begin each new day, His mercies never ever end. They are new every morning. Great is His faithfulness each and every day. Give thanks to God for His great faithfulness.

*For His anger lasts only a moment,*
*but His favor, a lifetime.*
*Weeping may spend the night,*
*but there is joy in the morning.*
. . . . . . . . . . . . . . .
*You turned my lament into dancing;*
*You removed my sackcloth*
*and clothed me with gladness,*
*so that I can sing to You and not be silent.*
Lord *my God, I will praise You forever.* —Psalm 30:5, 11–12

Further Scripture: Lamentations 3:22–23; Romans 8:28; Ephesians 1:7

### *Week 6, Day 42: Psalms 31–32*
## Acknowledge Sin

Have you felt tired of keeping the secret of unconfessed sin? Have you told lies to keep others from knowing the truth? Did hiding sin wear your body down? Friend, life with Christ isn't meant to be like that. Jesus came to forgive you of your sin so you can walk with freedom, joy, and peace. If you acknowledge your sin to Him, no matter how difficult it may feel or what a mess you will find yourself in, *He has promised to forgive you and redeem your life.* He will cleanse you from all unrighteousness and restore the joy of your salvation. The Lord will take away your guilt and groaning.

Stop running away from the Lord and begin to take steps toward Him. Humble yourself, acknowledge your sin, release it to the Lord, and trust Him for what will happen next. Pray to the Lord: "But I trust in You, God, You are my God. The course of my life is in Your power, deliver me from the power of my enemies." The Lord will restore your life one step at a time as you *trust* in *Him.* Why don't you begin today? Take that first step. The Lord will be with you.

---

*When I kept silent, my bones became brittle*
*from my groaning all day long.*
*For day and night Your hand was heavy on me;*
*my strength was drained*
*as in the summer's heat.*
*Then I acknowledged my sin to You*
*and did not conceal my iniquity.*
*I said,*
*"I will confess my transgressions to the LORD,"*
*and You took away the guilt of my sin.* —Psalm 32:3–5

---

Further Scripture: Psalm 31:14–15; Acts 3:19; 1 John 1:9

## *Week 7, Day 43: Psalms 33–34*
## Praising God for His Provision

Do you wake up in the morning thinking about a certain situation? Do you continue to wait for the Lord to move in a specific way? Is there something that pains your heart? You can't see the future. You don't know the outcome. All you can do is live one day at a time. You know the truth—to not worry, to cast all your anxieties on the Lord, and to believe He is able to do the impossible. And yet all you can do is wait, hope, trust, and rejoice in the Lord. It doesn't feel like enough, but the situation remains out of your control.

Today, remember God's promise that He is *your help and your shield*. Rejoice in the Lord for strengthening you in weakness and for providing you with wisdom and protection. Even during times of suffering, even during the waiting, even during this trial—*rejoice in His holy name*. As you rejoice through your affliction, the Lord promises to produce endurance and character. Your hope will grow stronger day by day as God pours out His everlasting and consistent love. As you wait, picture God's love covering you like a warm blanket wrapping around you. You must sit and rest long enough to feel His love pouring out over you. Yes, circumstances may remain difficult, but God's love for you is even greater. Hang on to hope, and don't let go.

---

*We wait for Yahweh;*
*He is our help and shield.*
*For our hearts rejoice in Him*
*because we trust in His holy name.*
*May Your faithful love rest on us, Yahweh,*
*for we put our hope in You.* —Psalm 33:20–22

---

Further Scripture: Psalm 34:1; Romans 5:3–5; 1 Thessalonians 5:16–18

## *Week 7, Day 44: Psalms 35—36*
### Pray for Deliverance

As a believer in the Lord, Scripture says you will face enemies: the world, the flesh, and the devil. You must stay alert, walk in the Spirit, and put on the full armor of God. Remember, the enemy prowls around seeking to destroy you. Even so, trust the Lord will deliver and protect you from these enemies. God will fight for you. The Lord will be your help and your deliverer. He will calm the storm.

No matter what harm goes on around you, no matter how difficult circumstances appear, remember to trust in God's great love. You can't love both the things of this world and the Lord. Choose to love the Lord your God with all your heart, soul, and mind. His faithful love reaches the heavens. His faithfulness reaches the clouds. His righteousness is like the highest mountains and His judgments like the deepest sea. From this great love, *the Lord powerfully fights for you, friend. He desires victory over your life.* He takes pleasure in your well-being. In Christ, you are an overcomer. So do not fear. Instead, delight in the Lord's deliverance as you yield to Him.

---

*Oppose my opponents, LORD;*
*fight those who fight me.*
*Take Your shields—large and small—*
*and come to my aid.*
*Draw the spear and javelin against my pursuers*
*and assure me: "I am your deliverance."* —Psalm 35:1–3

---

Further Scripture: Psalm 36:5–6; 1 Peter 5:8; 1 John 2:15–16

## *Week 7, Day 45: Psalm 37*
Commit Your Way

Committing your way to the Lord means to *dedicate, give, or devote* your plans, your time, your heart, and your thoughts to the Lord. *Everything.* It's not a neutral, halfway, only-when-you-feel-like-it sort of thing. It's dedication, and it may mean giving up other things to keep your commitment to the Lord. Commitment isn't negotiable. It's saying, "I'm all in." In this world, commitment seems like a fading character quality. If you don't feel like doing something, the world accepts your lack of commitment. However, that's not how the Lord designed your walk with Him.

Committing to the Lord is how you journey with Him; it's how you have a relationship with Jesus. If you just show up when you feel like it or when you are desperate, you miss out on the beauty and peacefulness of walking with Jesus. He longs for you to commit to walking with Him. God says, "Trust Me with all your heart." As you commit to Him and trust Him . . . the Lord *promises to act.* So today, what is your role? Commit your way to Him and trust Him. Get out of the way. Stop taking control and forcing the action. God is in control. He's got it, and He will act!

---

*Commit your way to the LORD;*
*trust in Him, and He will act.* —Psalm 37:5

---

Further Scripture: Psalm 37:23–24; Proverbs 3:5–6; Isaiah 40:28–29

### Week 7, Day 46: Psalms 38–39
## Hope in Christ

The guilt of sin can rest on your shoulders like a heavy weight. After a season of living in sin, making choices you know are against God's will, even your body can be affected physically. This lifestyle of sin becomes a burden too heavy to bear, leaving you with no physical strength. You feel stuck and hopeless.

Hear this today: *you have hope in Christ*. It begins with repenting before the Lord. He has not left you. He stands near you with wide-open arms like a father welcoming a child home. But you—*you*—need to walk toward the Father's arms and receive His loving embrace. If the steps ahead seem too difficult and healing from all that has been destroyed feels impossible . . . *hang on to the hope in Jesus*. Nothing is impossible with Jesus. He died so you may live. He died so you may be free. Therefore, humble yourself and turn from your sinful ways to receive His love. He will answer you when you walk into His loving arms, wash away your guilt, and cleanse you from your sin. He will help you with the steps ahead as your Savior and your Redeemer. Run into His open arms of love. He is there waiting for you. What are you waiting for?

---

*For I am about to fall,*
*and my pain is constantly with me.*
*So I confess my guilt;*
*I am anxious because of my sin.*

. . . . . . . . . . . . . .

*Lord, do not abandon me;*
*my God, do not be far from me.*
*Hurry to help me,*
*Lord, my Savior.* —Psalm 38:17–18, 21–22

---

Further Scripture: Psalm 38:15; 51:1–3; 1 John 1:9

## *Week 7, Day 47: Psalms 40—42*
## Thanksgiving and a Cry for Help

Life is full of highs and lows. One moment you find yourself in a pit of despair, and the next moment you feel on top of a mountain. Everyone goes through these emotions and feelings as life continues with unexpected joys and trials. One thing remains certain—Christ came to put a new song in your mouth. Christ came to hear your cry for help and fill you up with His great love. Christ came to lift you out of the pit of muddy clay, set your feet on the firm rock of salvation, and make your steps secure. In Christ, you are a new creation.

So, when you are in the middle of a mess, *cry out to Him and He will hear you.* No matter how many troubles surround you, if your sins have overtaken you or if you are unable to see clearly, the Lord will rescue you. He will deliver you and help you. Friend, the Lord delights in you. You don't need to walk in a place of darkness. Put your hope in God. Praise Him—your Savior and your God. Praise Him through the storm, the fog, the heaviness. Praise the name of the Lord!

> *I waited patiently for the LORD,*
> *and He turned to me and heard my cry for help.*
> *He brought me up from a desolate pit,*
> *out of the muddy clay,*
> *and set my feet on a rock,*
> *making my steps secure.*
> *He put a new song in my mouth,*
> *a hymn of praise to our God.*
> *Many will see and fear*
> *and put their trust in the LORD. —Psalm 40:1–3*

Further Scripture: Psalm 40:17; 42:11; 2 Corinthians 5:17

## *Week 7, Day 48: Psalms 43–45*
## A Royal Wedding Song

Just as a bride prepares to marry her groom, the Church must prepare to reunite with Jesus when He returns. A groom prepares and leaves his father and mother, and a bride leaves her home in order to unite together as one, as husband and wife. The Church, the bride of Christ, must prepare herself to see Christ again—by being washed clean of sin and walking in righteousness, blameless before the Lord. *Are you ready for Christ to return?*

Are you hanging on to your past? Are you clinging to the comfort of this world, not fully committed to the Lord? To prepare for the return of Christ as a believer, you must leave behind your old ways and hold fast to the hope in Christ. Allow His Spirit to transform you into a new creation. Allow the Lord to come in and create His beauty in you. Trust that He is able. As a believer, the Lord molds you to resemble Christ. Therefore, when Christ returns, you can stand ready and prepared to meet the King of glory. You can be ready for His glory to come. Get ready because Jesus is coming back!

---

*Listen, daughter, pay attention and consider:*
*forget your people and your father's house,*
*and the king will desire your beauty.*
*Bow down to him, for he is your lord.* —Psalm 45:10–11

---

Further Scripture: Ephesians 5:25–27; Revelation 19:7–8; 21:1–2

## *Week 7, Day 49: Psalms 46—48*
Be at Rest

Are you in a situation that feels like it's just too much for you to figure out how to get through it? The battle seems hard and hopeless. You just don't know what to do, what to say, whom to turn to. You feel alone. Isolated. Frozen. Stuck.

Here's the good news: *God promises to fight your battles for you.* He goes before you. He goes behind you. He says not to worry. He even says to be still. Stop trying. Stop researching. Stop thinking through "what if" scenarios. Stop trying to be right or make excuses. Stop it. Be at rest. Surrender to the Lord. The same God who is exalted over the nations promises to care, love, and be with you wherever you go. God is able to fight your battle. He is able to make the enemies cease. He is able to cut through chains of iron and break any strongholds and years of bondage. Moment by moment, day by day, trust the Lord. When He gives you direction and guidance, then make the move, say the word, and read the Scripture. But until then, rest in *Him.* He's got you in His loving hands!

*"Stop your fighting—and know that I am God,*
*exalted among the nations, exalted on the earth."*
*Yahweh of Hosts is with us;*
*the God of Jacob is our stronghold.* —Psalm 46:10–11

Further Scripture: 2 Chronicles 32:7–8a; Psalm 46:1–3; Isaiah 45:2

### *Week 8, Day 50: Psalms 49—50*
Misplaced Trust in Wealth

Do you ever find yourself looking at your neighbors and comparing your life to theirs? Perhaps they seem more successful or wealthier from the world's perspective. Whether you have much or little on this earth, *the key is to focus your heart and mind on the Lord,* not on the things of this world. Jesus said it is easier for a camel to enter through the eye of a needle than for a rich man to enter the kingdom of God. So keep your eyes on Jesus and not on others or on accumulating more wealth.

Today, give thanks for the gifts God has given you—both material and spiritual, remembering every good and perfect gift comes from the Lord. Resist the temptation to compare yourself to others or even to judge others and their success. Trust the Lord with a pure heart and live obediently to the things the Lord is calling *you* to do. Whether rich or poor, the Lord desires all people to give up their lives for the sake of the Gospel. The more you give up, the richer you become in the Lord. You can never outgive God!

> *They trust in their wealth*
> *and boast of their abundant riches.*
> *Yet these cannot redeem a person*
> *or pay his ransom to God.* —Psalm 49:6–7

Further Scripture: Matthew 16:25–26; Mark 10:24–25; Luke 16:14–15

## *Week 8, Day 51: Psalms 51—53*
### David's Confession of Sin

Psalm 51 recounts David's prayer of confession after committing his sins of adultery, murder, and cover-up regarding his relationship with Bathsheba. If you have concealed sin in your life, you will not prosper in your relationship with the Lord. Eventually, others will discover your hidden sin. And the Lord sees all. He knows your heart, and, yes, He sees your sin as well. Nevertheless, the Lord loves you. If you confess your sin to Him, He will show you mercy. He longs for you to turn away from sin and back to Him.

Today, ask the Lord, "*Is there anything I need to confess?*" Pause, close your eyes, and just listen to the Holy Spirit. If He brings anything to mind, release it to Him and ask for forgiveness with a genuine heart. You can't fake repentance. The Lord knows your heart. Then, turn away from your sin and commit your life to the Lord. Ask Him to create in you a clean heart and renew a steadfast spirit within you. Ask Him to restore to you the joy of your salvation and renew a right spirit within you. Remember, Jesus died to prove His love for you, saving you from your sin. He forgives you and loves you so much. Turn to Him today.

*Wash away my guilt*
*and cleanse me from my sin.*
*For I am conscious of my rebellion,*
*and my sin is always before me.*
*Against You—You alone—I have sinned*
*and done this evil in Your sight.* —Psalm 51:2–4

Further Scripture: Psalm 51:10–13; Proverbs 28:13; Romans 5:8

### *Week 8, Day 52: Psalms 54—56*

God Is for You

*God is for you.* The God of the universe, the Almighty Maker of heaven and earth, *He is for you.* The Father God who sent His Son Jesus to earth to die for the sins of the world . . . yes, *He is for you.* He loves you. He holds your life in His hands.

You have nothing to fear. Nothing. Run to Jesus when you are afraid and trust Him. *He is for you.* God is your friend, your protector, and your deliver. He is always with you and will never leave you. *He is for you.* Today, hang on with hope to this one thing: *God is for you.* Repeat this until you believe it deep in your soul: God is for you. *God is for you. God is for you.* Now walk in this promise today—at school, at work, at home, or in your car. Even as you lay under the covers not wanting to get up, do the hard thing, get up, and remember—*God is for you.* Amen and amen.

---

*This I know: God is for me.* —Psalm 56:9

---

Further Scripture: Psalm 56:3–4, 13; Romans 8:31

## *Week 8, Day 53: Psalms 57—59*
## Make a Choice

Today, *choose to find your confidence in the Lord.* Choose to sing praises to the Lord. Choose to proclaim His promises about His far-reaching, faithful love. No one is too far away for His love to reach. His love is as high as the heavens, and His faithfulness reaches the clouds.

You may feel as though you are in a pit today. Still, lift up your head and begin to muster praises to the Lord. Your praises will bring Him glory and exalt Him. What the enemy may have wanted for evil, you can turn to praise. Therefore remain steadfast and immovable, keeping your eyes on the Lord. Remain faithful to proclaim His praises in the midst of heartache, and He will give you eyes to see what He sees. It's a choice. Ask yourself: *Am I going to complain and dwell on negative thoughts or am I going to rise up and praise God for His faithful love?* Today, choose to rise up, friend! Rise up and find your confidence in the Lord one day at a time!

---

*My heart is confident, God, my heart is confident.*
*I will sing; I will sing praises.*
. . . . . . . . . . . . . .
*For Your faithful love is as high as the heavens;*
*Your faithfulness reaches the clouds.*
*God, be exalted above the heavens;*
*let Your glory be over the whole earth.* —Psalm 57:7, 10–11

---

Further Scripture: Genesis 50:19–20; 1 Corinthians 15:58;
2 Timothy 4:6–7

## *Week 8, Day 54: Psalms 60—62*
Trust in God Alone

You will face moments in life, such as sickness, failure, consequences of sin, and fear. There may be times you simply want to run away and hide. However, God has more for you than avoiding the hard times in life. You have to wake up and face reality. You have to face the diagnosis. You have to face the consequence. You have to face your fear. *With God by your side, you can do this.*

To *rest in God alone* means to have a silent confidence in the Lord. Believe in your heart and live with confidence knowing that no matter what happens, the Lord is with you and has control. And that is enough. Consider Jesus through everything. He is more than enough, and He is more than able to help you. Trust in the Lord *at all times.* And just talk to Him—pray, pray, pray, and then pray some more. The Lord never grows weary of hearing the heart of His people. You won't be shaken as you set your mind on God, your rock, your salvation, your stronghold, and your refuge. It will be okay. Rest in the Lord.

---

*Rest in God alone, my soul,*
*for my hope comes from Him.*
*He alone is my rock my salvation,*
*my stronghold; I will not be shaken.*
*My salvation and glory depend on God, my strong rock.*
*My refuge is in God.*
*Trust in Him at all times, you people;*
*pour out your hearts before Him.*
*God is our refuge.* —Psalm 62:5–8

---

Further Scripture: Psalm 118:6–8; Isaiah 43:1–2; John 14:1

## *Week 8, Day 55: Psalms 63—65*
### Knowing God

Walking with Jesus is a two-way street. It takes discipline and devotion. If you are thirsty, the Lord will satisfy you. When you gaze upon the Lord in His presence, you will see His strength and His glory. As you think of your need for the Lord, He will be your helper. When He hides you in the shadow of His wings in protection, rejoice in Him. Follow closely to the Lord, and He will hold your hand.

As you spend intentional time with Him, your life will be transformed. Remain in Him, and He will remain with you. Seek the Lord, and you will find Him when you search with all your heart. Don't just know the Word, *know the God of the Word.* Today, seek to know the God of your salvation.

*I will follow close to You;*
*Your right hand holds on to me.* —Psalm 63:8

Further Scripture: Psalm 63:1–2; Jeremiah 29:13; James 4:8

## *Week 8, Day 56: Psalms 66—67*
Praise the Lord

Have you seen the Lord at work in your life today? *Praise the Lord!* Are you having a difficult day and struggling? *Praise the Lord!* Let His praise always be on your lips. *Praise the Lord* as a weapon in the battle! *Praise the Lord* in expectation for fulfillment of His promises.

Today, spend time praising the Lord through different ways of expression: raise your hands, kneel, dance, shout aloud, or sing a new song! Let praise arise from your heart! Fear God and testify of His love in your life. Let all the people and all the nations praise the name of the Lord so the whole world will know the great and mighty Lord of your salvation!

---

*Come and listen, all who fear God,*
*and I will tell what He has done for me.*
*I cried out to Him with my mouth,*
*and praise was on my tongue.* —Psalm 66:16–17

---

Further Scripture: 2 Samuel 6:14–15; Psalm 67:3–4; Daniel 2:19–20

## *Week 9, Day 57: Psalm 68*
### God's Majestic Power

Do you feel surrounded by the enemy? Are you hearing lies from the enemy, tempting you to fall into his traps or luring you to seek comfort in anything but the Lord? Perhaps you feel heaviness all around you, almost as though you are paralyzed and unable to do anything.

Rise up, friend, rise up. Allow God's majestic power to arise within you. Abide in Him. Hold every thought captive and remind yourself of God's truth. The Lord promises He will always be with you. His presence goes where you go just as the Ark of the Covenant went with David when he traveled. And David's enemies were scattered by the presence of God. Remember, submit to God, resist the devil, and he will flee from you by the power of Jesus Christ's presence in you. *Rise up.* You are not defeated. Victory belongs to the Lord. May the Lord arise within you. Rise up!

---

*God arises. His enemies scatter,*
*and those who hate Him flee from His presence.* —Psalm 68:1

---

Further Scripture: Numbers 10:35; Matthew 28:20; James 4:7

### *Week 9, Day 58: Psalm 69*
David's Request to Be Saved

David endured persecution. Christ endured persecution. They both endured lies, insults, and even felt like strangers around their brothers and sisters—all because of their zeal and devotion to God Almighty. As you follow Christ, He promises that you, too, will endure hardship and persecution. When you cry out for help, you may receive silence in return. When you cry out for help, you may receive sour-tasting advice that doesn't satisfy, just as Christ received vinegar and gall. Even so, endurance will come as you find hope in Christ and through His Scriptures. He gives power and strength to His people.

If you are enduring hardship or persecution today, remember you are not alone. The world, your enemies, and the devil do not like the sovereign, mighty, majestic God of your salvation. However, when you draw near to the Lord, He will redeem your life. He will rescue you. Do not fear. The Lord is near to those who love His name. Allow praise and worship to rise up within you and praise His name—Yahweh, Elohim, Adonai, Lord God, God of our Salvation. Praise His holy name!

*You know the insults I endure—*
*my shame and disgrace.*
*You are aware of all my adversaries.*
*Insults have broken my heart,*
*and I am in despair.*
*I waited for sympathy,*
*but there was none;*
*for comforters, but found no one.*
*Instead, they gave me gall for my food,*
*and for my thirst*
*they gave me vinegar to drink.* —Psalm 69:19–21

Further Scripture: Psalm 69:9; Matthew 27:33–34; Romans 15:3–4

## *Week 9, Day 59: Psalms 70—71*
### God's Help in Old Age

Everyone knows someone younger to whom they can proclaim and bear witness of God's power to. Think about it for a minute: each generation can offer something to the next because, in reality, everyone is "older" than someone. You are never too old or too young to begin to pour into the generation behind you. There is no excuse.

As the Lord continues giving you hope, take time to proclaim His power to others. Share about the Lord's mighty acts of faithfulness as you stand upon Him, your firm foundation, rock, and refuge. As you received forgiveness and redemption from the Lord, share the story of God's amazing grace. There's no retirement from walking with Jesus. So even when you think no one cares, *remember the Lord gave you the responsibility to proclaim His name to another generation.* Today, open your eyes and ears to someone you can share God's love with. Impact another generation even if it means putting on your glasses or turning up your hearing aids! As you walk in obedience, watch God move in your life!

---

*God, You have taught me from my youth,*
*and I still proclaim Your wonderful works.*
*Even when I am old and gray,*
*God, do not abandon me.*
*Then I will proclaim Your power*
*to another generation,*
*Your strength to all who are to come.* —Psalm 71:17–18

---

Further Scripture: Psalm 71:6–8; 119:90; 2 Timothy 2:2

## *Week 9, Day 60: Psalms 72–73*
### All the Nations Will Bow

Jesus is the name above every other name. He sends you out with joy and guides you with peace. He rescues the poor and helps the afflicted. He acknowledges the helpless. He redeems the oppressed and ceases the violent. He sees each person as perfectly and wonderfully made. You, child of God, are precious in His sight. No other god on earth offers the unconditional love of the Lord God Almighty, who was, who is, and who is coming. He is the author and the perfecter of your faith, and He is worthy to be praised. His glory will fill the entire earth.

Today, intentionally pray for the day every knee *will* bow and every tongue *will* confess Jesus Christ is Lord. Pray all nations *will* bow down and serve the one true living God! Come, Lord Jesus, come. May you believe in faith it will come to pass. As you pray, ask Jesus to make a way for all people over all the earth to know the name of the Lord our God and bow down to Him. Amen and amen!

*Let all kings bow down to him,*
*all nations serve him.* —Psalm 72:11

Further Scripture: Psalm 72:18–19; Isaiah 55:12; Philippians 2:9–11

*Week 9, Day 61: Psalm 74*
Feeling Abandoned by God

Do you ever wonder why God doesn't just stretch out His hand and cure the sick, destroy the evil in the world, or make the pain go away? By faith, you believe He can. By faith, you trust He will. By faith, you believe He has a plan. You have seen the work of His hands in the past, you have witnessed miracles, and you know the power of the Lord God Almighty. But in this moment, in this circumstance, He doesn't seem to be moving like you know He can, and you begin to feel abandoned by God.

And yet you wait. You wait and you remember the works of His hands and give thanks for the times in your life you witnessed Him perform saving acts on the earth. And you surrender your will to the Lord. You say: *"Not my will, but Your will be done."* Because even when you don't see Him moving, the Lord God is in your midst, working in ways you cannot see. Today, hold on to the hope, be on watch, and expect the Lord's power to reign in your life for His glory.

---

*Why do You hold back Your hand?*
*Stretch out Your right hand and destroy them!*
*God my King is from ancient times,*
*performing saving acts on the earth.* —Psalm 74:11–12

---

Further Scripture: Isaiah 65:24; Luke 22:42; John 5:17

## *Week 9, Day 62: Psalms 75—76*
## Know God

Allow God's name to be known: His identity, His reputation, and His character. As a believer, the Lord entrusts you to make His name known and to love others with the same love you receive through Jesus. But first, ask yourself, *Do I really know God? Do I know God in a way that I trust Him, fear Him, and obey Him?*

Press on to *know* God, not in a scholarly way, but in an intimate-relationship way. God has given you the Holy Spirit. God deliverers you from battles, fighting off the enemy as a mighty warrior. He shatters the schemes of the enemy. His strength surpasses your knowledge. God offers grace and mercy each day through His unconditional love. Love people as Christ loves you and share His truth with others. They will even be jealous of the love you receive from the Lord as you walk through life in joy, peace, and love. The day will come when all will praise the name of the Lord, and He will be feared by the kings of the earth. Until then, press on to know God and make His name known.

---

*God is known in Judah;*
*His name is great in Israel.*
*His tent is in Salem,*
*His dwelling place in Zion.*
*There He shatters the bow's flaming arrows,*
*the shield, the sword, and the weapons of war.* —Psalm 76:1–3

---

Further Scripture: John 13:34; Acts 1:8; Romans 10:16b–19

Remembering the Past, Present, and Future

The Israelites shared stories of God's faithfulness from one generation to the next. They shared how the Lord split the sea, led the Israelites with a cloud by day and a fiery light by night, and how He provided streams of water out of stone. These were spiritual markers in their lives, and they signified God's faithfulness. They also shared stories of their own unfaithfulness and sin toward God. And yet, the Lord was compassionate and forgiving and did not destroy them.

Each generation must remember and learn from the past in order to protect the future and appreciate the present. Like the Israelites, you have spiritual markers in your life. Today, *what story would you share with this generation to convey God's faithfulness?* Don't waste another day—share with your kids around the dinner table tonight, send an email to your grandchildren, or share a video with your extended family about God's faithfulness in your life. It may feel raw and vulnerable, but it's in those intimate, weak, tender moments of life that you receive the Lord clearly and powerfully. Do not be ashamed of your need for Him to move. God is a God who provides and redeems. The next generation will need to stand on these promises just as much as you did! Go and share your story so it won't be forgotten!

---

*I will declare wise sayings; I will speak mysteries from the past—*
*things we have heard and known*
*and that our fathers have passed down to us.*
*We must not hide them from their children,*
*but must tell a future generation*
*the praises of the LORD, His might, and the wonderful works*
*He has performed. —Psalm 78:2–4*

---

Further Scripture: Deuteronomy 6:5–7; Psalm 78:6–7;
1 Corinthians 10:11–12

## *Week 10, Day 64: Psalms 79—80*
Revival with the God of Israel

Have you chosen to turn away from the Lord? Have you given in to temptation? Do you try and live life in your flesh by your own strength? Do you believe in God but don't really include Him in your everyday life? Have you slipped further and further away from God? Do you realize you are in desperate need for the Lord to save you and restore you?

*You are never too far gone.* God is able to restore. He is able to save. God is all-powerful and loves you unconditionally. However, you must be willing to repent and turn back to Him. You are the only one who can make this decision. If you are ready, say, *"Yes, Lord, I'm willing to turn to You."* Then, in faith, turn away from your sin and turn toward God. Receive His grace and mercy. Find refreshment and revival for your soul in His presence. Take steps by faith and believe He will bring you restoration and strength. Make that choice today as you trust God's great love.

---

*Rally your power and come to save us.*
*Restore us, God;*
*look on us with favor,*
*and we will be saved.* —Psalm 80:2–3

---

Further Scripture: Numbers 6:24–26; Amos 9:14; Acts 3:19

## *Week 10, Day 65: Psalms 81—82*
Remember What God Has Overcome!

The Lord promises His people He will provide. He says, "I am Yahweh." He is the Lord God. The Lord God delivered you from wherever you were before accepting Jesus. The Israelites were in slavery in Egypt, and the Lord brought them back to Israel. He said, "Remember I am your God, and I delivered you and will provide for you. You need to *open your mouth*, and then I will fill it." God promises the same deliverance and provision for you.

To fix your eyes on Jesus, you must face Him. As you do, naturally, your mouth will face Him. Open your mouth. Surrender. Acknowledge your weakness and expect Him to give you strength. The Lord promises to *fill you up*. He promises to *provide for you*. He provides because He cares, He knows, and He has the power to do so. Today, turn to the Lord your God, seeking Him first. In humility, open your mouth. And as you do, you will walk in His promises for your life beyond anything you can imagine.

---

*I am Yahweh your God,*
*who brought you up from the land of Egypt.*
*Open your mouth wide, and I will fill it.* —Psalm 81:10

---

Further Scripture: Psalm 81:11–13; Matthew 6:31–33; 2 Peter 1:3

*Week 10, Day 66: Psalm 83*
Need to Hear God's Voice

As a follower of Christ, the Holy Spirit dwells in you and speaks to you. As a believer, you hear God's voice in various ways—through prayer, Scripture, dreams, visions, other believers, and creation. But here's the deal . . . you must be intentional to hear God's voice. The concept is similar to your inability to steer a car while it's sitting idle. The car won't steer until you have the key turned on, the car in gear, and begin to move forward. *To hear the Lord's voice in your life, you need to walk with Him.* Trust in Him with all your heart and intentionally acknowledge the Lord in your life. Then He will answer you and direct your steps.

But remember the enemy has a voice as well. It can be loud—telling you lies and luring you into disbelief. Be on guard and intentionally ask the Lord to not be silent. When you call upon Him, He promises He will answer you. God has victory over the voice of the enemy, and you have the power to tell the voice of the enemy to stop in Jesus' name. Today, may you hear the voice of the Lord guiding you in truth.

*God, do not keep silent.*
*Do not be deaf, God; do not be idle.*
*See how Your enemies make an uproar;*
*those who hate You have acted arrogantly.* —Psalm 83:1–2

Further Scripture: Proverbs 3:5–6; Isaiah 30:21; John 14:16–17

## *Week 10, Day 67: Psalm 84*

## Happiness on the Journey

Happiness. How do you find it? The world seems to have all the answers to finding happiness. But in reality, happiness by the world's standards will fade away. Those who spend time in the Lord's presence, praising Him continually, are truly happy. *You find happiness when you find your strength in the Lord along your journey.* You are happy when you trust in God alone. Relationships on earth will wither, disappoint, and fade away. Things on this earth will rust and get destroyed. The Lord provides many good gifts for you to enjoy, but they are not meant to fulfill your happiness. Therefore, set your mind on the Lord, set your mind on His kingdom, and spend time in His presence.

If you make decisions based on what makes you the happiest, stop. Happiness will not be found in that one thing for very long. Make your decision with the Lord's guidance, His Word, and His truth. Call to Him, and He will answer you. He is your helper. Today, do not search out for happiness. Instead, seek the Lord's will for your life.

*How happy are those who reside in Your house,*
*who praise You continually.*
*Happy are the people whose strength is in You,*
*whose hearts are set on pilgrimage.* —Psalm 84:4–5

Further Scripture: Psalm 32:8; 84:11–12; 1 Peter 1:24–25a

### *Week 10, Day 68: Psalm 85*

## Prayer for Revival

"Will You not revive us *again*, Lord?" Do you ever wonder if the Lord thinks to Himself: *Seriously, how many times do I need to revive you? I'm tired of you continuing to turn away from Me to other gods and the things of this world. And then you turn back to Me and I revive you again. And the cycle continues.*

The crazy thing is, the Lord doesn't think like that. That's our human perspective—not feeling worthy to receive His redemptive love. Your Heavenly Father stands with open arms and a heart full of love and compassion saying, "Welcome back, child of Mine. I love you. Welcome back, child."

The Lord will revive you again. He forgives you. No matter where you are today, turn back to the Lord. Thank Him for His amazing grace and faithful love. Ask Him to forgive you, and then listen to His message for you and follow His ways. It's time to wake up to the truth. Stop living for yourself. Turn back to the Lord and allow Him to renew your mind and revive your life. Today, pray for the church to wake up.

---

*Will You not revive us again*
*so that Your people may rejoice in You?* —Psalm 85:6

---

Further Scripture: 2 Chronicles 7:14; James 4:8; 1 John 3:1

## *Week 10, Day 69: Psalms 86—87*
### God Is in the Highs and Lows

Ask yourself: *Is my whole source of joy in the Lord?* Rather than living dry and weary, let the living water of the Lord be your whole source for joy. He alone can satisfy your heart.

May all things in life funnel and filter their way through the Lord. May He deliver you from the pit and pull you out with His compassion and graciousness. The Lord will be slow to anger, rich in truth, and faithful to love. That's who God is. Let the river of His great love and the streams of His grace and mercy flow together as the one true source of joy. Stop looking elsewhere. Stop looking for some joy from the things of this world, some joy from temporary pleasures, some joy from earthly relationships, and then some joy from Jesus. Instead, let the Lord be the source of joy through everything. And once you discover the Lord as your whole source for joy, it will make you want to dance!

---

*Singers and dancers alike will say,*
*"My whole source of joy is in you."* —Psalm 87:7

---

Further Scripture: Psalm 86:13; Isaiah 58:11; 2 Corinthians 3:5

### *Week 10, Day 70: Psalm 88*
### A Cry of Desperation

No matter how difficult, dark, sad, painful, overwhelming, or depressing your life may be, can you still muster the words: *You are the God of my salvation?* If you have walked through a season of desperation, you know salvation in God may be the only thing you have to hang on to, the one, single glimmer of light. This hope in Christ, trusting that He is the author and perfecter of your faith, allows you to press on and cry out in desperation during the long nights and the never-ending days.

No matter how far down in the pit you are, no matter how weary you feel, you are not alone. The Lord is with you. He hears you. He is your salvation. Cry out to Him in desperation. He will set your feet on a rock and make your steps secure. He will raise up your life. Cry out to Him, and He will lift you up.

*Lord, God of my salvation,*
*I cry out before You day and night.*
*May my prayer reach Your presence;*
*listen to my cry.* —Psalm 88:1–2

Further Scripture: Psalm 30:1; 40:2; Jonah 2:6

*Week 11, Day 71: Psalm 89*

God's Promises

Has there ever been a time in your life when you knew the Lord was calling you to something or was raising you up for something specific? Perhaps, years ago, someone gave you a prophetic word, but you have yet to see the Lord fulfill it in your life. God anointed David and made a covenant to establish generations forever. And yet David questioned God's call on his life. He believed in the Lord's faithfulness. He praised Yahweh and knew God's hand would strengthen him always. Even so, David walked through difficult times when his faith was tested.

You may question, doubt, or wonder: *Did I really hear from the Lord? Is He really a faithful God?* Remember to seek first His kingdom. Delight yourself in the Lord. Cultivate and pour into the place the Lord has you in today. Don't look too far ahead, only living for that one golden moment you think is coming. Keep your hands to the plow. Press on, fixing your eyes on the author and perfecter of your faith, Jesus Christ. The Lord will lead you and guide you in His timing. He hasn't left you. Hold on and keep your eyes on Jesus.

---

*But You have spurned and rejected him;*
*You have become enraged with Your anointed.*
*You have repudiated the covenant with Your servant;*
*You have completely dishonored his crown.* —Psalm 89:38–39

---

Further Scripture: Psalm 37:3–4; 89:20–21; Proverbs 4:25

## *Week 11, Day 72: Psalm 90*
### Established in Christ

Life can be difficult and trying, but as you press on with hope, even through the pain, begin to seek the Lord in the morning. He alone satisfies you and fills you up with His faithful love. You may even bring your questions to the Lord: what you should do, where you should go, how to spend your time in this quickly fleeting life. Remember, the Lord will teach you and give you wisdom on how to number your days when you seek Him.

Today, you don't need to wander aimlessly or without hope. Pray and ask for the favor of the Lord to be upon you. Ask the Lord to establish the work of your hands. *God's timing is not always your timing,* but that doesn't mean it's a closed door. Sometimes He simply wants you to wait. Your Heavenly Father may be saying to you: *"I'm preparing you for something. Just wait, My child!"* May the Lord confirm and establish the work of your hands today. He has a plan for you. Above all, remember you are established *in Christ*. You are rooted and grounded in Him. You are His, and He will establish the work He has for you.

---

*Let the favor of the Lord our God be on us;*
*establish for us the work of our hands—*
*establish the work of our hands!* —Psalm 90:17

---

Further Scripture: Psalm 90:12; Colossians 2:6–7; 1 Peter 5:10

### *Week 11, Day 73: Psalm 91*
## Protection Through Intimacy

Trusting in God's protection doesn't mean you will have a perfect, trial-free, healthy, never-get-hurt kind of life. Yes, God watches over you. Yes, He is your refuge. Yes, He is your deliverer. Yes, you can trust Him. His faithfulness will be your protective shield, and He will cover you under His wings. *But what does that look like as you walk it out in faith?*

Keep in mind you live in a fallen world with fallen people, and God works in mysterious ways. His ways are higher than our ways. God says you may be pressured in every way, but He promises you will not be crushed. You may be perplexed, but you will not despair. You may be persecuted, but you are never abandoned. You may even be struck down, but you won't be destroyed. You may be weak, but you are strong in Christ. You may have nothing, but you will have peace that passes all understanding. You may be in the midst of trials and tribulation, but even so, consider it joyful because God promises He will never leave you nor forsake you. He will protect you and provide. He will be your refuge. *The key is to never stop trusting Him.* Say out loud: *"You are my refuge and my fortress, my God, in Whom I trust."* Make that your battle cry and open your eyes to see the Lord's protection in your life as you trust Him.

---

*The one who lives under the protection of the Most High*
*dwells in the shadow of the Almighty.*
*I will say to the LORD, "My refuge and my fortress,*
*my God, in whom I trust." —Psalm 91:1–2*

---

Further Scripture: Psalm 91:3–4; 2 Corinthians 4:8–9;
2 Thessalonians 3:3

## *Week 11, Day 74: Psalms 92—93*
God's Love and Faithfulness

As you wake up today, declare the Lord's faithful love over your life. Declare the praises of God. Before you head to bed tonight, declare the Lord's faithfulness in your life. No matter what you may be facing, the burdens you carry, or the battle you are in, declare God's faithfulness. He is faithful yesterday, today, and tomorrow. God is faithful in your life—something powerful happens as you proclaim this truth out loud!

Give a voice to the truth resounding in your head. Shout the word *"Joy"* out loud. Look at someone near you and say, *"Joy!"* Perhaps you aren't feeling joyful, so just begin by whispering, *"Joy."* Then say it in a louder whisper, *"Joy."* Then say it with a regular voice, *"Joy."* Now a little bit louder, *"Joy."* Now shout, *"Joy!"* Are you smiling yet? Smiling itself doesn't mean you have joy. However, smiling sure does make your situation feel less burdensome for the moment as you remember God's great love and faithfulness for you! Release this joyful sound to the Lord in praise! The Lord loves you, and He is working for you! *Joy!*

*It is good to praise Yahweh,*
*to sing praise to Your name, Most High,*
*to declare Your faithful love in the morning*
*and Your faithfulness at night. —Psalm 92:1–2*

Further Scripture: Psalm 92:4; 100:4; James 1:12

## *Week 11, Day 75: Psalms 94—95*
## Hear His Voice

Jesus described Himself as the Good Shepherd. As a believer in Christ, you are His sheep. Like any good shepherd who learns the bleats of his flock, the sheep learn to hear and follow the shepherd's voice. And because they follow the voice, the sheep avoid trouble and live a fuller life. In the same way, you are to listen and follow the voice of God. As a believer, you have the Holy Spirit guiding you and counseling you in the way you should go. But sometimes, even though you know the truth and the Scripture, you still don't follow the Lord's voice.

*What if you just followed God's voice in faith without any hesitation—* without a hardened heart, rebellious spirit, or hanging on to hurts of the past, without being distracted with the busyness of life? What if you truly listened and *followed God's voice with a pure, uninhibited heart?* Ask the Lord to create in you a heart willing to listen, willing to follow, and willing to walk in truth. Walk as you hear His voice. Take that step you don't want to but feel nudged to take. Do that thing you are questioning. You don't know what is on the other side of obedience. Chose to listen, be obedient, and walk out God's caring faithfulness in your life. There's an indescribable grace on the other side of obedience.

---

*Today, if you hear His voice:*
*Do not harden your hearts as at Meribah,*
*as on that day at Massah in the wilderness.* —Psalm 95:7–8

---

Further Scripture: Psalm 95:6–7a; 139:23–24; John 10:4

## *Week 11, Day 76: Psalms 96—97*
King over the Earth

The world is firmly established because *the Lord reigns as King over the earth*. Let that sink in for a minute. All the nations proclaim: "The Lord reigns." Not only is the Lord the creator of the heavens and earth, but He is also the King. And because the Lord God Almighty reigns as King, the world will not be shaken. Put your hope in the One who reigns over all . . . the King of glory.

Today, sing a new song. Declare God's glory, proclaim His salvation, and praise Him for His wondrous works to all people in every nation. Find a moment while you are at home alone, or in your car, or out for a run, and begin to sing a song of praise and proclamation to the Lord. Ready? Open your mouth and let the words flow out as a melody! God is so worthy to be praised!

---

*Say among the nations: "The LORD reigns.*
*The world is firmly established; it cannot be shaken.*
*He judges the peoples fairly."* —Psalm 96:10

---

Further Scripture: Nehemiah 9:6; Psalm 47:8; 96:1–3

## Week 11, Day 77: Psalms 98—99
### All Will Be Judged

All the nations will gather with shouts of joy and singing from the tops of the mountains to the depths of the sea. During this time, the Word of God declares a time of judgment for all people. The Bible calls the Lord a judge for a reason. It's not a warm, cozy message, and sometimes it's difficult to hear as truth. But yes, *all people will be judged.* The all-knowing and all-seeing God knows if a person believes in Jesus as the way, the truth, and the life or not. Those who believe will have eternal life with Jesus, and those who do not will be thrown into the lake of fire.

If you haven't surrendered your life to Christ, *what are you waiting for?* You don't know the day or the time, but Jesus is coming back. That means the time of judgment is coming. Give your life to the Lord, and you will have security of eternal salvation on the Day of Judgment. No fear. No wonder. No questioning. Just peace. If you surrender your life to the Lord, you will be with Him for eternity. To God be the glory great things He has done.

*Let the rivers clap their hands;*
*let the mountains shout together for joy*
*before the LORD,*
*for He is coming to judge the earth.*
*He will judge the world righteously*
*and the peoples fairly.* —Psalm 98:8–9

Further Scripture: Isaiah 44:23; John 3:16; Revelation 20:11–12, 15

## *Week 12, Day 78: Psalms 100–102*
## Following with Integrity

Integrity is a big deal to the Lord. It includes being honest—allowing your actions to match your words and your heart. It means no hidden secrets but instead being real, authentic, and pure. The Lord says, *"Let your word 'yes' be 'yes,' and your 'no' be 'no.'"* The enemy gains ground when you live your life deceitfully. The enemy lures you into building upon your lies, making you believe it'd be easier to keep being dishonest. But in truth, you are quenching the Holy Spirit as you continue to sin.

The Holy Spirit came to give you a clean heart, to remove your heart of stone, and to replace it with a heart of flesh. Therefore, if you are stuck in a lie or a place of deceitfulness, surrender your heart to the Lord. Jesus told His disciples, "Blessed are the pure in heart, for they will see God." Today, walk away from the lies through the power of the Holy Spirit. Be honest with the Lord, with yourself, and with others. *Honesty brings freedom*, allowing you to serve the Lord more fully.

*My eyes favor the faithful of the land*
*so that they may sit down with me.*
*The one who follows the way of integrity*
*may serve me.*
*No one who acts deceitfully*
*will live in my palace;*
*no one who tells lies*
*will remain in my presence.* —Psalm 101:6–7

Further Scripture: Proverbs 6:16–19; Ezekiel 36:26–27; Matthew 5:8, 37

## Week 12, Day 79: Psalms 103—104
God's Benefits to Us

Can you recall all the Lord's benefits in your life? You are called to give thanks to the Lord and praise His name. But perhaps there are days when you wonder, *What do I praise the Lord for? I am in a pit. I am feeling blah. Does He even know what's going on with me?* Open your Bible right now and turn to Psalm 103. The psalmist recounted more than thirty *benefits* of the Lord. You can read verse after verse of God's great blessings for you.

So even if you don't feel like praising the Lord right now, *your soul can praise and bless the holy name of the Lord.* As you proclaim and release these words of thanks from your mouth, the enemy's grasp and lies will be undone in the face of truth! Give thanks for His great love that satisfies you with goodness and renews your youth. For as high as the heavens are above the earth, so great is His faithful love toward those who fear Him. Be reminded of this great love and the Lord's many benefits just for you today.

---

*My soul, praise Yahweh,*
*and all that is within me, praise His holy name.*
*My soul, praise the* Lord,
*and do not forget all His benefits.* —Psalm 103:1–2

---

Further Scripture: Psalm 103:8; 2 Corinthians 4:6–7; Galatians 2:20

## *Week 12, Day 80: Psalms 105—106*
### God's Faithfulness

Think about a moment when you experienced God's undeniable faithfulness—a moment you want to remember and never forget throughout generations to come, such as a healing from a serious health issue, a timely provision, a moment of conviction followed by redemption, or a time the Lord miraculously showed up! Take time today to give thanks to the Lord and proclaim His deeds to the people around you.

As you remember the wonderful works of the Lord, perhaps you want to organize a celebration for His faithfulness. Why not have a piece of cake to celebrate the memory of God's faithfulness in your life? Maybe you'd like to give a special gift to someone as a way to celebrate the time in your life God provided for you. However the Lord may lead you as you look back and remember, the key is to press on walking with Jesus while you *remember His faithfulness* and sing hallelujah!

---

*Give thanks to Yahweh, call on His name;*
*proclaim His deeds among the peoples.*
*Sing to Him, sing praise to Him;*
*tell about all His wonderful works!* —Psalm 105:1–2

---

Further Scripture: Deuteronomy 8:2; Psalm 105:3–5;
1 Corinthians 11:26

## *Week 12, Day 81: Psalms 107–109*
### Godly Character Through Opposition

Even in the moment of accusation, let the words of your mouth praise the Lord. Thank the Lord even as opposition arises. You may be tired, you may doubt your strength, and even then, praise the Lord.

The psalmist described thanking the Lord "fervently," which means, "passionately or enthusiastically." Imagine passionately cheering for a sports team or enthusiastically singing during a concert. Now imagine turning your passion and enthusiasm to the Lord. In *all of it—even in the midst of opposition*, give thanks and praise. Even if you don't feel it from the depth of your soul, begin to praise and give thanks to the Lord. Eventually, you will begin to unleash that passion and enthusiasm from within. The Lord sees your need. He is your provider. He sees your hopelessness. He is your hope. He sees your weakness. He is your strength. He sees your brokenness. He is your healer. He covers you with His love. Praise the Lord and give thanks for His great name.

---

*I will fervently thank the LORD with my mouth;*
*I will praise Him in the presence of many.*
*For He stands at the right hand of the needy*
*to save him from those who would condemn him.* —Psalm 109:30–31

---

Further Scripture: John 16:33; 1 Peter 2:9, 12

## *Week 12, Day 82: Psalms 110—112*
## The Priestly King

God reigns as the King and the Priest of glory. God will defeat His enemies. God will extend His kingdom. A great army is coming with Jesus' return. But until then, Jesus sits at the right hand of God. The time will come when God will defeat all enemies and crush kings, bringing forth His anger.

*Are you ready?* What does it mean to be ready? Acknowledge God's power. Acknowledge who He is. *You have no need to live in fear of the world.* So stop fearing the things in this world. Rather, live in fear of the Lord for that is the beginning of wisdom. Fear the Lord for His mightiness and power. Praise His name because *great* is the name of the Lord. Call upon the name of the Lord to subdue your enemies and proclaim His victory so others will know Jesus Christ is the King and Priest of glory. Yes, proclaim victory in Jesus so others will know Jesus Christ. Amen.

---

*The Lord is at Your right hand;*
*He will crush kings on the day of His anger.*
*He will judge the nations, heaping up corpses;*
*He will crush leaders over the entire world.* —Psalm 110:5–6

---

Further Scripture: Psalm 47:3; Acts 7:55–56; 15:17–18

### *Week 12, Day 83: Psalms 113—115*

## God Reaches the Poor, Needy, and Barren

The Spirit of the Lord is upon you. In order to demonstrate His love for you, God the Father sent His Son Jesus to earth to endure the Cross so you could be saved. Now you have the love of God within you. His love flows through you. And it is your responsibility to *love* others out of God's great love within you. *How do you demonstrate love to others?* Love those in need of a hand to lift them up and out of the ashes. Help them to set their feet on the one true solid ground.

Who do you know that needs to fill the void in their life with Jesus? They may be empty and unsatisfied with the things of this world and are ready for the Lord to quench their thirst and fill their emptiness. *Will you be love to them? Will you fill them up with the Father's love?* The Lord will equip you as you walk in His ways, listening to His voice, and loving even the least of these. Not for your own glory but for His glory alone. Today, ask the Lord to lead you to someone to love in Jesus' name.

---

*He raises the poor from the dust*
*and lifts the needy from the garbage pile*
*in order to seat them with nobles—*
*with the nobles of His people.*
*He gives the childless woman a household,*
*making her the joyful mother of children.*
*Hallelujah!* —Psalm 113:7—9

---

Further Scripture: Psalm 115:1; Romans 5:8; 1 John 4:7–8

### *Week 12, Day 84: Psalms 116—118*
### Rejoice and Be Glad

Today is the day the Lord has made; *choose to rejoice and be glad in it.* You have a choice today. Give the Lord praise and honor for the day. Recognize the day is His and walk into it with Him. Rejoice, praise, honor, and give thanks to the Lord. You have breath, you have life, you have salvation in Him. Choose to be glad. Be positive. *What do you have to lose?*

Some people may wake up on the "wrong side of the bed." Others may see the cup half-empty rather than half-full. But either way, child of God, today is a gift. Look up! Fix your eyes on Jesus and give thanks! Let the first words out of your mouth be pleasing to the Lord and edifying to someone else. Look at someone you care about or someone sitting next to you right now and say: "This is the day the Lord has made, *let us rejoice and be glad in it!*" Just do it! It may turn your whole day around because *you* have chosen to focus on the Lord and not on yourself! He's right there with you no matter what the day may hold. Now, get after it! Cheers to a new day!

*This is the day the* LORD *has made;*
*let us rejoice and be glad in it!* —Psalm 118:24

Further Scripture: Deuteronomy 28:13; Psalm 19:14; Isaiah 50:4

## *Week 13, Day 85: Psalm 119*
Delight in God's Word

Take a minute to picture yourself on a journey walking along an unknown path. You don't know when or where you will turn left or right or when you will stop for a bit. It's dark outside, but thankfully, you have a lamp to light the path in front of you and guide your feet. However, it only illuminates far enough for the next step, *requiring you to take one step at a time.*

That lamp represents the Word of God. The Word of God brings light into the darkness. The Word reveals your path of life. It may not reveal a five-year plan or even a detailed step-by-step outline, but it will reveal your next step. The Word will instruct you, help you, and shield you. The Word is sweeter than honey on your mouth and brings you hope and understanding. So what do you do with the Word of God? Do you just read it on a Sunday morning and think that time alone will guide your steps for the week? That's not how the Lord intended it. Open the Word every day. Yes, every day. It will light your path daily on your journey. Today, open your Bible and read the Word.

*Your word is a lamp for my feet*
*and a light on my path.* —Psalm 119:105

Further Scripture: Psalm 16:11; 119:103–104; John 1:1, 14

### *Week 13, Day 86: Psalms 120—121*
Delight in the Journey

Think of a time when you were on a journey: a road trip, a hike up a mountain, or a mission trip overseas. Perhaps you've been on a journey through a specific season of life: a sickness, junior high years, unemployment, healing from a difficult relationship, or grieving the loss of a loved one. Whatever comes to mind when you hear the word *journey*, picture the Lord with you just as He was with the Israelites on their journey up to Jerusalem.

The Lord is your helper. The Lord is your protector. The Lord is your shelter. The Maker of heaven and earth knows you. He walks with you. No matter what journey you face today, lift your eyes up to Jesus. You are not alone. Day and night the Lord is with you because the Lord God, your protector, doesn't sleep! He will protect your coming and going forever. Lift your eyes up, dear child of God. The Lord is with you on your journey today!

---

*I lift my eyes toward the mountains.*
*Where will my help come from?*
*My help comes from the LORD,*
*the Maker of heaven and earth.* —Psalm 121:1–2

---

Further Scripture: Psalm 121:3–4; Isaiah 41:10; Jeremiah 29:11

*Week 13, Day 87: Psalms 122—123*

A Prayer for Jerusalem

Peace is the opposite of anxiety and turmoil. During days of war, people will say, "Peace not war." The same remains true for your life. You'd rather have peace, not anxiety. Your heart longs to feel settled, secure, and serene. The world doesn't bring or offer lasting peace. David and Isaiah prophesied and prayed for peace in Jerusalem. And then Jesus came as the Prince of Peace. The peace of Jesus controls your heart and guards your mind.

As you let go of control, trouble, fear, and unknowns, receiving the peace of Christ into your life, *you will have peace that passes all understanding*. Release to the Lord your anxious thoughts about a relationship, a tryout, a surgery, or a bill. Say it out loud: *"I release this to You, Lord."* As you let it go, receive and replace that anxiety with peace from the Lord, trusting the Lord to go before you. Christ Jesus is your peace as you allow Him to control your heart and your mind. Rest in Him and not in your own strength or control. And as you prepare for Jesus to return one day, pray for His peace in Jerusalem.

---

*Pray for the peace of Jerusalem:*
*"May those who love you prosper;*
*may there be peace within your walls,*
*prosperity within your fortresses."*
*Because of my brothers and friends,*
*I will say, "Peace be with you."* —Psalm 122:6–8

---

Further Scripture: Isaiah 9:6; Philippians 4:7; Colossians 3:15

## *Week 13, Day 88: Psalms 124—125*
## The Lord Is on Your Side

The Lord is with you all the time. He is on your side. Yes, the Maker of heaven and earth promises to be your helper. He is for you. He is with you in battle. He is with you through the storm and through the fire. He is with you today. Have you paused and acknowledged Him in your day? Recognize the Lord is mighty to save and able to offer counsel and guidance.

From the moment you wake up, the Lord is with you. Talk to Him. Invite Him into the day. *Pause and say: "Yes, the Lord is with me."* The Lord fights the battle for you. Cease striving and trying to figure things out on your own. Ask the Lord for His wisdom, power, and strength to flow through you. He can move the enemy. He can heal the sick. He can cause the spirit of doubt and fear to flee. Today, humble yourself and invite the Lord into your day.

---

*If the Lord had not been on our side*
*when men attacked us,*
*then they would have swallowed us alive*
*in their burning anger against us.* —Psalm 124:2–3

---

Further Scripture: 2 Samuel 5:19; 1 Chronicles 10:13–14; Romans 8:31

## *Week 13, Day 89: Psalms 126–127*
## Zion's Restoration

The Lord restored Zion (the nation of Israel) after years of captivity, and He desires to bring restoration to your life. You need to decide "Yes, I am willing to seek freedom, to seek life, to seek the fullness of *joy* the Lord has for me through Him!"

Just as a garden takes time—pulling weeds, plowing soil, planting seeds, waiting for seeds to grow—the same is true in your life with Christ. You can decide to just walk by the garden and do nothing—not enjoy the beauty or taste the fruit. Or you can choose to embrace the work, cultivate beauty, and seek the Lord for healing through repentance and humility. *What's your choice today?* The Lord is willing to do great things in your life and is waiting to bring you full healing! He desires to fill your mouth with laughter and shouts of joy and bring restoration. It may take time, *but it's worth it for freedom.*

---

*When the LORD restored the fortunes of Zion,*
*we were like those who dream.*
*Our mouths were filled with laughter then,*
*and our tongues with shouts of joy.*
*Then they said among the nations,*
*"The LORD has done great things for them." —*Psalm 126:1–2

---

Further Scripture: Isaiah 61:7; Amos 9:14; Galatians 6:9

## *Week 13, Day 90: Psalms 128—129*
### Protection of the Oppressed

The Lord has faithfully protected Israel over the years, and He promises to protect you from the enemy just the same. Remember, in Christ, there is life. In Christ, there is victory. In Christ, there is freedom. No weapon formed against you will succeed. You may be attacked over and over, but *as you stay rooted and grounded in Christ Jesus, you will find victory.* The enemy's plans will not prevail.

What does it look like to keep fighting even in the midst of attacks? Stand in confidence from the Lord. Keep walking by faith, trusting that God is victorious, and therefore you have victory in Him alone. Victory comes from fixing your eyes on Jesus and His wisdom. Seek Him. Spend time in His Word. Allow His voice to lead you and guide you. But know, even when you are still, He is fighting for you. The enemy will not prevail. Remain in Christ. He is your stronghold.

---

*Since my youth they have often attacked me—*
*let Israel say—*
*Since my youth they have often attacked me,*
*but they have not prevailed against me.* —Psalm 129:1–2

---

Further Scripture: Isaiah 54:17; Jeremiah 1:19; 1 John 4:4

## *Week 13, Day 91: Psalms 130—131*
### More than Watchmen Wait

As the sun comes up over the horizon, the watchmen breathe a sigh of relief. The light of morning has come. The darkness of night and any potential attack now ends with the dawn. The light from the sun has arrived, and the watchmen feel hopeful for a new day.

As you wait today for a job, a child, joy, peace, healing, finances, or whatever it may be, find your hope in the Lord. The Son of God has come. He is your light. His Word brings forth healing, truth, joy, and salvation. Just as a watchman stands alert and waiting, you too must stand alert and waiting for the Lord to move in your life. Picture yourself waiting for the light to shine forth on the horizon. He is with you. Proclaim His love. Proclaim His light. Yes, it may be difficult to wait through the darkness . . . *but wait with hope in the Son of God, Jesus.* Wait with hope in the Lord.

*I wait for Yahweh; I wait*
*and put my hope in His word.*
*I wait for the Lord*
*more than watchmen for the morning—*
*more than watchmen for the morning.* —Psalm 130:5–6

Further Scripture: Isaiah 52:7–8; Ezekiel 3:17; Micah 7:7

## *Week 14, Day 92: Psalms 132–133*

Unity in Love

When there is unity on a sports team, the game is more likely to end in victory. When there is unity in the body of Christ, it leads to victory in the kingdom. The Lord longs for oneness and unity. The world will believe in Jesus when they witness harmony among brothers and sisters in Christ.

How do you make every effort to live in harmony with one another? Love binds everything together in perfect unity. *So put on love.* Remember love comes from above—from the love of your Heavenly Father. Allow your love to overflow from the love you receive from Him. Love your family. Love your brothers and sisters in the body of Christ. Don't keep records of wrong. Forgive others and seek forgiveness. As you love others, the world will take notice and witness the oneness. Through the power of the Holy Spirit, lay yourself aside and walk in humility. If you feel a lack of unity with a brother or sister, it is time to seek reconciliation. Begin with asking the Lord how to love them today, and walk it out in obedience, trusting He will be with you.

---

*How good and pleasant it is*
*when brothers live together in harmony!* —Psalm 133:1

---

Further Scripture: John 17:20–23; 1 Corinthians 13:4–8a; Colossians 3:14

## Week 14, Day 93: Psalms 134—136
### His Love Is Eternal

The psalmist reflected on God's eternal love from the time of creation to when Israel settled in the land of Canaan. God's eternal love lasted not only through the miraculous moments and times of faithfulness but also through the challenging times and seasons of discipline. Through each high and low of life, the psalmist knew God's love was eternal, His mercy endured forever, His love never quit.

Today, reflect on the word *eternal*—something that lasts forever and ever with no beginning and no end. Because God loves you, He sent His Son Jesus to save you from death so you could live eternally with Him—*a forever love.* Your citizenship now rests in heaven. Even when you walk through the valley of the shadow of death, the Lord's love abides with you. His mercies are new each morning. Through your temptations and weaknesses, God's love remains full of compassion. It is gracious, slow to anger, and rich in faithfulness and truth. His love won't quit on you. Receive it. Accept it. Rest in it. Child of God, God's love for you is eternal.

---

*Give thanks to the Lord of lords.*
*His love is eternal.*
*He alone does great wonders.*
*His love is eternal.* —Psalm 136:3–4

---

Further Scripture: Psalm 86:15; John 3:16; Romans 8:35–37

## *Week 14, Day 94: Psalms 137–139*
## Maturing in Discipline

The God of the universe created you in your mother's womb. He knit you together. He calls you remarkable and wonderfully made. He knows your eyesight, your height, the number of hairs on your head, and even your thoughts. *Nothing is hidden from Him.* All your days were written in His book before a single one of them began for you. Isn't that amazing? From the moment of your conception, He has been at work maturing you and disciplining you into His image.

Not only is the Lord all-knowing, but His presence is also always with you to strengthen and guide you as you mature. There's nowhere you can hide, no distance you can run, no height too high, or depth too low, where He is not with you and able to move on your behalf. His hand is always there to lead you and hold on to you. As you walk through today, *believe these truths from the Lord*: You are known. God has plans for you. You, child of God, are beautifully and perfectly created. God designed you and has a specific plan for you! Hold on to these powerful promises for your life today!

---

*For it was You who created my inward parts;*
*You knit me together in my mother's womb.*
*I will praise You*
*because I have been remarkably and wonderfully made.*
*Your works are wonderful,*
*and I know this very well.* —Psalm 139:13–14

---

Further Scripture: Psalm 139:1–5; Ephesians 2:10; 1 Peter 2:9

## *Week 14, Day 95: Psalms 140–142*

### An Honest Prayer

Day after day, David turned to the Lord in prayer. His prayer life is a model for you. Are there ever times when you turn to the Lord to seek Him but don't know what to say? Today, use Psalm 141 as an outline for your prayer as you seek the Lord. David's honest words will resonate within your heart.

As you begin to pray, call upon the Lord and ask Him to hear you. Then lift up your hands in worship as a symbol of surrender, vulnerability, and honesty to the Lord. Next ask the Lord to guard your mouth and keep watch over the door of your lips. How many times in the middle of hardship is your first inclination of the flesh to spew words of hatred, jealousy, or anger? *The Lord knows the power of your tongue.* Therefore, ask Him to put a guard over your mouth. When you welcome the Lord into your situation, He will answer. He will protect you, discipline you, and expose evil. Turn to the Lord in prayer. He is faithful, and His promises are true day after day after day.

*LORD, I call on You; hurry to help me.*
*Listen to my voice when I call on You.*
*May my prayer be set before You as incense,*
*the raising of my hands as the evening offering.*
*LORD, set up a guard for my mouth;*
*keep watch at the door of my lips.* —Psalm 141:1–3

Further Scripture: Ezra 9:5; Ephesians 4:29; James 3:5–6

## *Week 14, Day 96: Psalms 143–145*

## A Cry for Help

Friends often greet each other with, "How are you doing?" Many will smile and say, "I'm good." But what if one day you aren't good? What if that day, when someone asked how you were doing, you said, "My spirit is weak within me; my heart is overcome with dismay." David told the Lord this honest truth and even said, "Answer me quickly!" David's spirit was failing, and he didn't want to go further into the pit.

Can you relate to this place of despair, loneliness, and depression? Release your feelings to the Lord and let go of any shame or guilt. Then reach out and tell someone as you seek their wisdom. Remember, you are not alone. You don't have to stay in this place of despair. Others will relate to you. Receive and believe these promises from the Lord today: *The Lord loves you and cares for you. He is your rock, stronghold, deliverer, and shield. Take refuge in Him because the Lord is gracious and compassionate, slow to anger and great in faithful love.* Today, if your spirit is weak and your heart is overcome with dismay, *the Lord will listen* to your prayer for help.

---

*LORD, hear my prayer.*
*In Your faithfulness listen to my plea,*
*and in Your righteousness answer me.*
. . . . . . . . . . . . . .
*My spirit is weak within me;*
*my heart is overcome with dismay.* —Psalm 143:1, 4

---

Further Scripture: Psalm 143:7–8; 144:2; 1 Peter 5:6–7

## *Week 14, Day 97: Psalms 146–147*
Hallelujah!

What do you place your hope in? Is it in the things of this world? Your financial investments? A powerful boat or fast car? Perhaps a remodeled home or an amazing vacation? Maybe even the success of your children? Keep in mind, the things of this world will come and go. Yes, the Lord gives you good gifts to enjoy, but when these good things from the Lord begin to identify who you are, God is not pleased. You will never be truly satisfied or strengthened in the things of this world. Eventually they will collapse and fade away.

Instead, *put your hope in the Lord*. He remains faithful forever. Fear the Lord more than you place value on the things of this world. These earthly things will fall and vanish. You don't even know what tomorrow will hold, so why trust in something that may not be here tomorrow? But—Hallelujah!—*with the Lord you can stand firm. With the Lord you can have freedom and victory.* You can place your confidence in the Lord because He will be with you forever. Seek the Lord for help daily. Fear the Lord, then you will be blessed. Hallelujah!

---

*He is not impressed by the strength of a horse;*
*He does not value the power of a man.*
*The Lord values those who fear Him,*
*those who put their hope in His faithful love.* —Psalm 147:10–11

---

Further Scripture: Psalm 20:7–8; 146:5–6; James 4:13–14

### Week 14, Day 98: Psalms 148–150
## Adoration Through Praise

Jesus said the greatest command is to love God with all your heart, all your soul, and all your mind. Love God with everything. Praising God with everything you have shows your love to God. Just as you would encourage or praise a son or daughter to demonstrate your love for them, praise the Lord for the good things He has done.

Don't let an off-tune singing voice, lack of musical gifting, or uncoordinated dance moves slow you down. You can *praise the Lord* with everything *you* are and with all *you* have. Anything that has the breath of life can praise the name of the Lord. So that includes you! Today, pause for a moment and praise the Lord. Simply say out loud, "Blessing and honor and glory and dominion to the One seated on the throne, *and to the Lamb, forever and ever!* Amen!" Life is full of highs and lows, but one thing that remains the same yesterday, today, and tomorrow is the Lord God Almighty. Hallelujah!

---

*Let everything that breathes praise the* Lord.
*Hallelujah!* —Psalm 150:6

---

Further Scripture: Psalm 148:7–11; Matthew 22:36–38; Revelation 5:13

## *Week 15, Day 99: Proverbs 1–2*
Wisdom and Discipline

Have you ever wondered: *What is the fear of the Lord?* Solomon described fear of the Lord as "the beginning of knowledge." He also wrote, "To fear the LORD is to hate evil." Solomon wisely instructed his son to search for wisdom and understanding as though it were a treasure, and by doing so, "then you will understand the fear of the LORD." Later, in the New Testament, the author of Hebrews told believers, "Hold on to grace. By it, we may serve God acceptably, with reverence and awe, for our God is a consuming fire."

As you wrestle with comprehending the fear of the Lord, *press in and seek the Lord for wisdom and understanding.* Make the choice to seek Him in all your ways like searching for a treasure. In your decision to seek the Lord for answers, for help, and for grace, you will demonstrate your reverence toward Him and your faith in trusting Him. Additionally, you will display your confidence in God as a consuming fire. The more you discover the Lord, the more you will hate evil. You will know your God is able, and this will compel you to stand in awe and reverence at His ways. *You will find yourself walking in the fear of the Lord.* Nothing else will ever compare to the treasure discovered in seeking Him.

---

*The fear of the LORD*
*is the beginning of knowledge;*
*fools despise wisdom and discipline.* —Proverbs 1:7

---

Further Scripture: Proverbs 2:3–5; 8:13; Hebrews 12:28–29

### *Week 15, Day 100: Proverbs 3—4*

## Learning to Trust God

When you lean against a tree, you place trust in the tree's ability and strength to hold you up. You believe the tree won't fall down, which allows you to keep standing. Now, imagine the tree as God. You believe that He is strong enough to hold you up. Just like the tree, you will keep standing as long as you *lean on God*, relying on His strength to keep you from falling over.

*Are you leaning on God to hold you up, or are you leaning on something else?* God has given you promise after promise, encouraging you to rely on Him in all your ways for understanding. He is with you. He is your God. He will strengthen you. He will help you. He will hold on to you. Therefore, *trust the Lord with everything*, believing in His ability, strength, and reliability to hold you up and guide you on the right paths. Lean on that tree—the Tree of Life—the Lord God Almighty. Can you picture yourself leaning on God? Rest in Him alone. He will hold you up and guide you!

---

*Trust in the LORD with all your heart,*
*and do not rely on your own understanding;*
*think about Him in all your ways,*
*and He will guide you on the right paths.* —Proverbs 3:5–6

---

Further Scripture: Psalm 62:1; Proverbs 3:7–8; Isaiah 41:10

*Week 15, Day 101: Proverbs 5*

Avoid Seduction

Seduction from the wrong source will kill a marriage, but it can be avoided. Pay attention! Often a seductive person lures another person away from a husband or wife, seeking to destroy a marriage with the help of the devil, who tells you the lie that you will find happiness and satisfaction with someone else.

Heed Solomon's advice: Don't go near the door of seduction! It leads to destruction and into even deeper sin. Listen, it may look enticing and seem like everything you have ever wanted, but it won't really satisfy or last. *Make the choice* to flee, block the person's phone number, avoid places where your paths may cross, walk on the other side of the road, and even drop out of the shared committee or group. Take action and do whatever you need to do to resist the lure of seduction. Admit your weakness to the Lord and ask Him for strength. Fix your eyes on Jesus daily. Ask for help from a trusted friend. The Lord will give you strength. *He is a God of transformation and power!* But you must also make the decision to stay away and flee from seduction.

*So now, my sons, listen to me,*
*and don't turn away from the words of my mouth.*
*Keep your way far from her.*
*Don't go near the door of her house.* —Proverbs 5:7–8

Further Scripture: Proverbs 5:22–23; 1 Corinthians 6:18; 2 Timothy 2:22

### *Week 15, Day 102: Proverbs 6—7*
### Seven Deadly Sins

An earthly father shows his love for his children by giving instructions and setting boundaries. In the same way, your Heavenly Father has given you commands and teachings to follow. Yes, He loves you unconditionally. Yes, He forgives your sins. Yes, His grace and mercy will follow you all the days of your life. *But that doesn't mean you intentionally stray from His commands, His teaching, and His Word.* His Word should guide you away from doing evil and away from the things the enemy wants you to believe are okay. The seven things the Lord hates are a good example of things to flee from: eyes that are arrogant, a tongue that lies, hands that murder the innocent, a heart that hatches evil plots, feet that race down a wicked track, a mouth that lies under oath, and a troublemaker in the family.

The Lord hates how the devil tempts you. He detests the destruction sin brings to your life, and *He wants to protect you from evil.* Therefore, it is important to read the Word of God. It will guide you as a lamp to your feet and a light for your path. The Lord will provide the strength to follow His commands as you walk, lie down, and wake up. Just take one step at a time towards following Him.

---

*My son, keep your father's command,*
*and don't reject your mother's teaching.*
*Always bind them to your heart;*
*tie them around your neck.*
*When you walk here and there, they will guide you;*
*when you lie down, they will watch over you;*
*when you wake up, they will talk to you.* —Proverbs 6:20–22

---

Further Scripture: Psalm 119:105; Proverbs 6:16–19; 6:23–24

## *Week 15, Day 103: Proverbs 8—9*

Wisdom vs. Foolishness

An invitation to walk on the path of wisdom is available to anyone—no experience needed. You don't have to have it all together. You don't have to have tons of knowledge. You don't have to do good works and earn your way to walk along the path of wisdom.

Jesus shed His blood and died to save the entire world from death so anyone who believes in Him may receive His grace and eternal life. But the choice to get off the path of folly, to instead walk along the narrow path of wisdom and pursue understanding, rests on you. *The Lord offers the invitation to everyone—yes, even the inexperienced.* You are welcomed and invited to come and receive Jesus, the bread of life. The choice is yours. What path will you choose to walk?

---

*"Whoever is inexperienced, enter here!"*
*To the one who lacks sense, she says,*
*"Come, eat my bread,*
*and drink the wine I have mixed.*
*Leave inexperience behind, and you will live;*
*pursue the way of understanding."* —Proverbs 9:4–6

---

Further Scripture: Matthew 7:13–14; John 3:16; Ephesians 2:8–9

## *Week 15, Day 104: Proverbs 10–11*
Generous Obedience

The Lord loves a cheerful giver. As the Lord counsels you in all your ways, He will direct your path as you steward the resources He has given you. The truth is you can't take anything with you to eternity. Wealth is not profitable on the day of judgment. The hope you place in your finances will vanish when you die. So while you are on earth, do not put your hope in earthly possessions.

Ask the Lord how to steward the different gifts He has given you: your time, your talents, and your resources. *The Lord says a generous person will be enriched and a person who sows generously will also reap generously.* Seek the Lord, and He will direct your path. It may require you to be stretched, it may require you to walk by faith, and it may seem crazy. But the Lord is faithful when you walk in obedience. Take that step and watch the Lord honor your faithful, generous, obedience! May you be flooded with His living water poured over you!

---

*One person gives freely,
yet gains more;
another withholds what is right,
only to become poor.
A generous person will be enriched,
and the one who gives a drink of water
will receive water.* —Proverbs 11:24–25

---

Further Scripture: Proverbs 11:4, 7; 2 Corinthians 9:6–7; Philippians 4:19

*Week 15, Day 105: Proverbs 12—13*

Tame Your Tongue

Make a specific effort to think before you speak. Before you let words out of your mouth, pause long enough to think if your words are worth the time, energy, and impact they may have on others. If it's too hard to take a breath and pause, put your hand over your mouth as a literal guard for five seconds. And then say your words.

Have you ever tried putting toothpaste back into a tube? Probably not. The process is very messy, time-consuming, and nearly impossible. When a person squeezes toothpaste out of the tube, the toothpaste remains out of the tube for good. The same is true for your words. *Once you speak your words, you can't take them back.* When you think before you speak and display self-control through the power of the Holy Spirit, you help prevent offending or hurting someone. Today, may your words speak life and love into others as you practice self-control.

---

*The one who guards his mouth protects his life;*
*the one who opens his lips invites his own ruin.* —Proverbs 13:3

---

Further Scripture: Luke 6:45; James 3:5–6; 1 Peter 2:23

### *Week 16, Day 106: Proverbs 14—15*
## The Gift of Speech

The Lord gave you words as an incredible gift that allows you to communicate. He empowers you to use your words to turn away anger, share knowledge, and encourage others. *And yet* words can also be used for evil. Your words can stir up wrath, blurt out foolishness, and cause hurtful wounds to those around you. The tongue can cause destruction and harm to the world, or it can spread the love of Jesus by declaring the Gospel. *There is power in your words both for good and for evil.*

How can you control your tongue and use it for good and not for harm? Do you know what you want to do but have a hard time controlling what you say? Self-control is a fruit of the Spirit. Therefore, abide in Christ, walk in the power of the Spirit, and then you will demonstrate the fruit of the Spirit. Your words will become more life-giving as you abide in the love of the Lord. The Lord will strengthen you to slow down and think before you speak as you release control to Him. Ask the Lord to transform your heart and mind in Him so that your words bring love and not destruction to those around you.

---

*A gentle answer turns away anger,*
*but a harsh word stirs up wrath.*
*The tongue of the wise makes knowledge attractive,*
*but the mouth of fools blurts out foolishness.* —Proverbs 15:1–2

---

Further Scripture: Proverbs 15:3–4; John 15:4; Galatians 5:16–17

## *Week 16, Day 107: Proverbs 16—17*
God Evaluates Our Motives

Do you have a plan for the day? Perhaps you wrote down some goals you hope to achieve in the years ahead. Now what? Have you thought to pray through those plans or goals and commit your steps to the Lord? God promises He has a plan for your life. Therefore, as you make plans, as you set goals, commit your activities to the Lord and ask Him to determine your steps.

Commit each moment, each activity, and each decision to the Lord with a pure heart and pure motives. Take the next step you know to do and trust the Lord will provide. *If you feel stuck, delight yourself in the Lord, ask Him for wisdom, and keep walking.* The Lord's grace will follow you because He promises to remain faithful and never leave you. Try not to overthink the plans. The end result may look different from or even beyond what you imagined, but if your heart is aligned with the Lord's, it will reflect His love . . . and that's the ultimate goal in everything!

> *All a man's ways seem right to him,*
> *but the LORD evaluates the motives.*
> *Commit your activities to the LORD,*
> *and your plans will be achieved.*
>
> . . . . . . . . . . . . . .
>
> *A man's heart plans his way,*
> *but the LORD determines his steps.* —Proverbs 16:2–3, 9

Further Scripture: Psalm 22:8; 119:133; Jeremiah 29:11–12

## *Week 16, Day 108: Proverbs 18—19*
## Love, Listen, Discern, and Respond

Stay quiet. Stay quiet. Stay quiet. Gossip, harsh words, sarcasm, lies, and foolish and quick-spoken words can lead to strife and devastation. Remember the classic saying, "If you don't have anything good to say, then don't say anything at all." Put this into practice today.

On the flip side, when you aren't talking, you're listening. Listen to understand. Listen because you truly care and seek to love. If you hear something you don't like, be slow to respond. This allows room for the Lord to move in your midst. The Lord promises to fight your battles. You need only to be still. Choose to remain quiet and see what happens today. If you get upset, *stay quiet*. If you get impatient, *stay quiet*. Even if you think you know better, *stay quiet*. Wait for the moment when the Holy Spirit prompts you to speak. *Then say something.* Speak with love. Speak with gentleness. Speak with the peace of Christ. *The key is to take your time and choose your words wisely.* So, stay quiet until the Holy Spirit says, "Go!" Then overflow like a river with God's love!

---

*The one who gives an answer before he listens—*
*this is foolishness and disgrace for him.* —Proverbs 18:13

---

Further Scripture: Proverbs 18:4; Matthew 12:36–37; Colossians 4:6

*Week 16, Day 109: Proverbs 20—21*

## The Lord Directs

Do you ever wish you could just change the course of someone's life? Maybe a cold-hearted spouse, a prodigal child, an estranged parent, or an unwise friend? The Lord sees your hurting heart and promises that He is there. Hang on to this truth: *If the Lord is able to direct the heart of a king, then the Lord is able to turn the heart of your loved one.*

What can you do in the waiting? Take your hands off the wheel, stop trying to control the rudder of their lives, and *pray*. The Lord hears your prayers. Trust He is at work. He is in control, so allow Him to guide your child, your spouse, or your friend back to Him. While you wait, continue to love the Lord your God with all your heart, all your soul, and all your mind. This way, you will remain strong in the Lord and be able to resist the enemy's plans to discourage you. Remember to trust that if the Lord is able to direct the heart of a king, then He is more than able to change and direct the heart of those you love. Hang on to this promise.

*A king's heart is like streams of water in the LORD's hand:*
*He directs it wherever He chooses.* —Proverbs 21:1

Further Scripture: Exodus 15:6; Psalm 27:14; 1 Corinthians 10:13

## *Week 16, Day 110: Proverbs 22—23*
## Dedicate a Child

Parents and other adults have the responsibility to instruct children in the way they should go. The child's path begins with the parent and loving adults in their lives. Are you grounded in the Word of God and walking in love and humility as Christ walked? Do you love the Lord with all your heart, soul, and strength?

As you walk with the Lord, as you talk about the Word of God, the children in your life will learn from your example. Children will bear witness to a person following Christ. Teaching children how he or she should walk with the Lord will not just happen from a Sunday morning visit to church. *No, it comes from discipline, established boundaries, and reflecting Christ's love all week long!* Therefore, share with children how the Lord impacted your day or read a meaningful Bible verse together. Ask a child to pray for you, and then ask how you can pray for them. *Be intentional to train up children in the Lord.* Make it a priority. The Lord is faithful and will bless your efforts and sacrifice.

---

*Teach a youth about the way he should go;*
*even when he is old he will not depart from it.* —Proverbs 22:6

---

Further Scripture: Deuteronomy 6:4–9; Ephesians 6:4; 1 John 2:6

### Week 16, Day 111: Proverbs 24

Honey

In the Bible, honey often symbolizes the Word of God or a desired gift from the Lord. Just as honey can naturally help your body heal wounds and soothe sore throats, the Word of God does the same in your life. Feeling stressed, worried, angry, confused, or lonely? *Turn to the Word of God as your source of relief and help.* Read the Word and allow the Lord to transform your heart moment by moment, seven days a week.

God promises the Word will never fade away. He promises you will find a future and a hope. His Word will be soothing to your soul and healing for your bones. Christ will bring you peace. Watch what happens to your soul as you rest in the Word *every day.* Go ahead and eat a spoonful of honey while you're at it!

---

*Eat honey, my son, for it is good,*
*and the honeycomb is sweet to your palate;*
*realize that wisdom is the same for you.*
*If you find it, you will have a future,*
*and your hope will never fade.* —Proverbs 24:13–14

---

Further Scripture: Exodus 3:7–8; 1 Samuel 14:29; Psalm 119:103

### *Week 16, Day 112: Proverbs 25–26*
### Control the Temper

Raise your hand if there is an area in your life lacking self-control. It's hard to stop yourself, isn't it? You don't want to scream at your kids or your spouse. You don't want to constantly judge people with harsh comments. You don't want to be in debt. You just don't know what to do, and you feel out of control. But before you know it, it's too late and the damage is done. In an effort to maintain control of a difficult situation, you lost control of yourself. *Child of God, you are not alone in this place.*

If you lack self-control right now, take a break. The Word of God says to put to death the things of your flesh. First, you need to die to yourself and surrender this area in your life to the Lord. Read the Word of God, perhaps focusing on Scripture about self-control. Let the Word of God fill you up. As you rest in the Lord, the Spirit of God will lead you. Take time to renew your mind in the Word. Not just one day, *but day after day.* Before you know it, the Spirit will guide and direct your thoughts and your actions, allowing you to bear the fruit of self-control. *God is the God of breakthrough.* Trust Him to fill you up with His fruit of the Spirit as you daily abide in Him.

---

*A man who does not control his temper*
*is like a city whose wall is broken down.* —Proverbs 25:28

---

Further Scripture: Romans 8:13; 12:2; Galatians 5:22–23

## *Week 17, Day 113: Proverbs 27—29*

Iron Sharpens Iron

If you leave a piece of iron alone, it will grow dull, never fulfilling its ultimate purpose to cut things. It needs to hit against another piece of iron to remain sharp. In a similar way, people need people. When people are left alone, they tend to grow dull, unmotivated, and may even make unwise decisions. But when two people are together, they bring out the best in each other, sharing thoughts, laughter, encouragement, and wisdom. God intended for people to be with people. Jesus said the greatest command is to *love God* and *love others. He has a purpose for you to be with others.*

Everyone has an excuse about why they don't pursue friendships: "I'm sure he's busy" or "She won't want to." These excuses leave both people alone. You are meant for each other! Pray and ask the Lord for guidance. Then initiate something with someone. Be a friend. Just show up. And then show up again. Before long, it will feel natural, and you'll begin to sharpen one another through the love you have for the Lord and each other. What are you waiting for? Say a prayer and contact someone today!

*Iron sharpens iron,*
*and one man sharpens another.* —Proverbs 27:17

Further Scripture: Proverbs 27:9; Ecclesiastes 4:9–10; John 15:12

### *Week 17, Day 114: Proverbs 30—31*

### Security in the Lord

God promises His Word is pure. He is a shield to those who take refuge in Him. So today, focus on taking refuge in Him. Be careful not to find security in what you will eat or in successful business deals or awards. Rather, take refuge in the Lord. Hide yourself in Him. Surrender your will to His. Depend on Him in all aspects of life. Sometimes, when you start gaining wealth, success at work, or even an ease in your regular routines, it is easy to become self-sufficient. *You can get to the point where you don't recognize your need for the Lord.*

Wealth, success, and ease here on earth are not bad in and of themselves. It's the tension of *not being consumed by it all and still seeking the Lord* as your security rather than the things on earth. God may have more for you, but perhaps you have gotten to a place of saying, "Who is God?" Continue to give thanks for your circumstances, and seek the Lord for His strength, His wisdom, and His refuge. The Lord will grant peace and guide you as you give Him honor, praise, and glory!

---

*Keep falsehood and deceitful words far from me.*
*Give me neither poverty nor wealth;*
*feed me with the food I need.*
*Otherwise, I might have too much*
*and deny You, saying, "Who is the* LORD*?"*
*or I might have nothing and steal,*
*profaning the name of my God.* —Proverbs 30:8–9

---

Further Scripture: Proverbs 30:5; 1 Thessalonians 5:18; Hebrews 13:20–21

### *Week 17, Day 115: Ecclesiastes 1–2*
## Absolute Futility

Solomon labored to achieve all the pleasures in the world: wealth, possessions, fame, women, servants, achievements, and wisdom. He attained everything under the sun, and yet he called it *absolute futility*—meaning it vanished like a vapor or a breath and had fleeting value. What can you learn from Solomon?

What are you living for? Maybe it's time to shift your focus of what's most important to you. Shift your focus from attaining more and bigger and better toward things that will last for eternity. This world has more and more to offer, but *will it satisfy you and quench your thirst and hunger?* Solomon called it all futile. It's time to stop seeking and searching for contentment from things *under the sun*. Instead, focus on the *Son, Jesus Christ*, the same God yesterday, today, and tomorrow. Jesus, the Son, brings life, love, peace, and joy and will be with you through eternity. In His presence there is fullness of joy, more than anything under the sun could ever bring. Today, focus on the true Son, and His joy will last forever.

*"Absolute futility," says the Teacher.*
*"Absolute futility. Everything is futile."*
*What does a man gain for all his efforts*
*that he labors at under the sun?* —Ecclesiastes 1:2–3

Further Scripture: Psalm 107:9; Ecclesiastes 2:20; 1 John 5:11

### *Week 17, Day 116: Ecclesiastes 3—4*
Short but Meaningful

Do you ever think to yourself: *If I can just get through this season of life, then it will be better?* Or maybe you think: *I can't wait until I am at that level.* The truth is, there will always be another level above and another season you wish you were in. Late nights with crying babies, teenagers and emotions, aging parents: it's all a part of life. *There is a time for everything.* God has appointed the seasons and the moments of your life for you to grow into who you are in Christ and to give Him glory.

The key is to fix your eyes on Jesus through each season. Choose to focus on eternity with your Savior Jesus Christ. When you are changing a diaper in the middle of the night, thank the Lord and imagine eternity. There is a time for everything: *a time to weep and a time to laugh, a time to mourn, and a time to dance.* Embrace the season you are in right now. Today is a gift from the Lord. Today has purpose. The Lord has something for you to learn today. Give thanks even in the middle of the hard or the mundane. Ask the Lord what He has for you today!

*There is an occasion for everything,*
*and a time for every activity under heaven.* —Ecclesiastes 3:1

Further Scripture: Ecclesiastes 3:4; Philippians 4:11; 1 Thessalonians 5:18

## *Week 17, Day 117: Ecclesiastes 5—6*
## Satisfaction in the Lord

Solomon wisely said *money never satisfies.* You may earn more and more money, but it will never truly satisfy. Will you ever think you have enough? In this world, there will always be more to attain. But just when you attain that one thing, your eyes will be set on something new. Even money is futile and fleeting—here today and gone tomorrow. The Lord created your soul for eternity. The only 100-percent secure investment in life is giving yourself fully to the Lord. In Him, you have rest. In Him, you have peace. In His presence, there is joy. He meets your every need.

Money and wealth will never bring the satisfaction you search for. There may be times when you feel it is easier to trust in the security of money more than the ultimate security and promises found in the Lord. Do a heart check today and *seek the Lord* for true satisfaction.

*The one who loves money is never satisfied with money, and whoever loves wealth is never satisfied with income. This too is futile.* —Ecclesiastes 5:10

Further Scripture: 2 Chronicles 9:23; Luke 12:15; 1 Timothy 6:9–10

## *Week 17, Day 118: Ecclesiastes 7—9*

## Pause Before You Respond

You may have times in life when you immediately get angry about something. It's your first reaction. You get irritated, you feel your heart race, and your face gets flushed. In this situation, do not rush to anger. You may want to, you may even have a right to, but *anger abides in the heart of fools.* Take a deep breath, say a prayer, and ask the Lord for wisdom in responding to the situation.

There are two sides to every situation, and often the Lord wants to move in ways beyond what you can see. So, give God time to move before you speak. Give time for understanding. Don't be the fool and rush toward anger. Anger often defends something—perhaps yourself, your territory, or your reputation. Anger rises within you as you defend your rights. *Just pause before you respond.* Allow the Lord to be your defender. Walk out the promise, trusting God to work all things together for His good and His purpose. His work is perfect, His ways are entirely just, and He is a faithful God. Trust Him instead of taking control of the situation and risk acting like a fool.

*Don't let your spirit rush to be angry,*
*for anger abides in the heart of fools.* —Ecclesiastes 7:9

Further Scripture: Deuteronomy 32:4; Romans 8:28;
2 Thessalonians 3:3

### *Week 17, Day 119: Ecclesiastes 10–12*
What Is It All About?

After all his searching, Solomon concluded that fearing God and keeping His commands was the ultimate life goal. And the same is true for us. Fearing God and keeping His commands alone will result in true satisfaction. God will bring judgment. That's not your job. Your job is to fear the Lord. You're responsible to love the Lord your God with all your heart, soul, strength, and mind and to love your neighbor the same way. Keep this as your singular focus. *Be in awe of the Lord to the point it spurs you on to keep His commands.*

Don't get suckered into the things of the world, searching to find happiness and satisfaction. Resist getting angry, impatient, and discontent. The Lord will take care of you because He sees all. As you press on to love Him and love others, and you will find the other things will work out. Stand firm and fear the Lord. God promises you will lack nothing. *This truth is amazing grace.* Today, focus on the narrow path of fearing the Lord and following Him.

---

*When all has been heard, the conclusion of the matter is: fear God and keep His commands, because this is for all humanity. For God will bring every act to judgment, including every hidden thing, whether good or evil.*
—Ecclesiastes 12:13–14

---

Further Scripture: Psalm 34:9; Luke 10:27–28; Revelation 14:7

### *Week 18, Day 120: Song of Songs 1—3*
## The Bridegroom and the Bride

Song of Songs portrays the love between the church and the bridegroom, Jesus Christ, as Solomon communicated and demonstrated his love for his first wife, beginning with attraction to one another and courtship. In a similar way, the Lord sees you. He sees you as beautiful. He sees you as precious in His sight. He understands you. He knows your strengths and your weaknesses. He sought you out and pursued you. He longs to draw you into His great love. He desires for you to come to Him and be His beloved.

Look at the Lord. *Open your eyes to His great love for you.* Allow His love to draw you in. He says He will hide you under the shadow of His wings. He will cover you with His protective feathers. He is your peace, your life, your helper. Today, may you be drawn into the intimate presence and love of Jesus. Believe you are desired and wanted. Believe you are loved with an everlasting love. Believe you are God's beloved. You belong to Him.

---

*How beautiful you are, my darling.*
*How very beautiful!*
*Your eyes are doves.*
*How handsome you are, my love.*
*How delightful!*
*Our bed is lush with foliage.* —Song of Songs 1:15–16

---

Further Scripture: Song of Songs 2:4; Jeremiah 31:3; Ephesians 5:25

## Week 18, Day 121: Song of Songs 4—5

Sex in Marriage

The Lord designed marriage for one man and one woman. He designed sexual intercourse for one man and one woman in a marriage covenant, joining together as one flesh. This covenant is not meant to be broken—not before marriage and not with multiple partners. After great anticipation and waiting, Solomon and his wife enjoyed one another on their wedding night. It was worth the wait as they fully relished and celebrated the love and connection between each other, just as the Lord designed it.

God's original design and intent was for purity and wholeness. Anything apart from His original plan may have spiritual and physical consequences. Walk and rely on strength from the Spirit of God to resist any temptation for sex and other impure actions outside the marriage covenant. *Beauty comes as you wait, resist temptation, and rely on the Lord for strength.* God will be with you in the waiting. And then, when the time arrives for a husband and wife to "enter the garden" together as the Lord designed it, He will bless and honor your decision and commitment to one another. Intimate love is *worth the wait.*

*Awaken, north wind—*
*come, south wind.*
*Blow on my garden,*
*and spread the fragrance of its spices.*
*Let my love come to his garden*
*and eat its choicest fruits.* —Song of Songs 4:16

Further Scripture: Matthew 19:5–6; 1 Corinthians 7:2; Hebrews 13:4

### *Week 18, Day 122: Song of Songs 6—8*
### Restored Marriage

The bond of love in marriage is strong. Solomon and his wife displayed the balance of communication and sexual pleasure in their relationship of love. They went through a time of restoration and came back to enjoy each other like they had on their wedding night. To do so, they had to pause and *get back to their first love.*

God designed marriage for a husband and wife to enjoy pleasure and emotional and physical intimacy together like a "love so strong even a mighty river cannot sweep it away." In your marriage, do you make time to communicate emotionally and physically connect intimately as one flesh as the Lord designed? Be honest. It is easy to let kids, work, and busy schedules get in the way of pursuing love with your spouse. *But it is not an excuse.* Today is the day to pray for restoration in your marriage. Say to each other: "Where has your love gone? Come back, come back, so I may look at you." *The Lord intended for your love to remain as one, united forever.* Today, pray for a restored affection, a restored communication, and a restored intimacy. First, seek the Lord together, and He will rekindle the flame of love. Step out in faith and love one another as Christ first loved you.

---

*Love's flames are fiery flames—*
*the fiercest of all.*
*Mighty waters cannot extinguish love;*
*rivers cannot sweep it away.* —Song of Songs 8:6–7

---

Further Scripture: Song of Songs 6:1,13a; Ephesians 5:25–26; 1 John 4:19

## *Week 18, Day 123: Romans 1*
### The Power of the Gospel

Paul was eager to preach the good news in Rome. He excitedly antici-
pated proclaiming truth to first the Jew and then the Greeks. Why? He
was eager because he wasn't ashamed of the Gospel. Paul knew it was
God's power, not his own strength, that would bring salvation to those
who believed. Therefore, Paul expected God to do great things through
his ministry.

How often do you hear the words "Go share the Gospel" and
immediately get nervous? "Who? Me? Isn't that for the preachers and
missionaries? Surely not me!" Dear child of God, *perhaps you need to
rethink this.* Are you ashamed of the Gospel? Are you relying on your
own strength and power to share the good news? As a believer, *God's
power works through you.* As you walk with Him and He leads you to
share, guess what happens? Fear slips away, and His power shows up.
So, stand up, open your mouth, and share the good news of Jesus Christ
to those the Lord leads you to. He is at work in their lives already, preparing them for the Gospel. You have nothing to lose and everything
to gain in the power of God at work within you!

---

*So I am eager to preach the good news to you also who are in Rome.*
*For I am not ashamed of the gospel, because it is God's power for salvation*
*to everyone who believes, first to the Jew, and also to the Greek.*
—Romans 1:15–16

---

Further Scripture: Acts 4:12; Galatians 6:14; 2 Timothy 1:8

### Week 18, Day 124: Romans 2
## God's Righteous Judgment

God sent His Son Jesus into the world to save the world. God chose to do this knowing sin leads to death. He loves His people and desires to give them eternal life. Therefore, out of the riches of His kindness, restraint, and patience, God allows the opportunity for repentance to all people. Because all people sin, all people need a Savior.

If you are prone to judge others and point out their sin, *stop.* There's a good chance you have a few issues of your own and need God's mercy, love, and forgiveness just the same. Allow the Lord to deal with others. Allow the Lord's kindness to draw a person to repentance. *You are called to love others. You are called to discern when to speak truth in love.* You are not called to judge and criticize. By judging others, it's like taking matters into your own hands, trying to correct someone else's behavior. God is in control. He is working in ways you can't see to draw each person to repentance. Be kind and compassionate, rich in love, and full of mercy, just as Christ is to the church. Trust God loves and cares for each person even more than you do, pray without ceasing, and give it time.

---

*Do you really think—anyone of you who judges those who do such things yet do the same—that you will escape God's judgment? Or do you despise the riches of His kindness, restraint, and patience, not recognizing that God's kindness is intended to lead you to repentance?* —Romans 2:3–4

---

Further Scripture: John 3:17; Romans 2:1–2; James 4:11

### *Week 18, Day 125: Romans 3*
## No Differences Between Jews and Gentiles

Every person, both Jew and Gentile, has sinned. Everyone is unrighteous apart from God's grace in their lives. But thankfully, God has a plan for all His people. Every single person can be justified freely by God's grace through the redemption found in Christ Jesus. This means you can't boast about keeping the law. Also, you can't boast about your good works.

Jesus Christ died on the Cross so you could be saved from death, the penalty for sin. Jesus died in your place. He is your justifier. Because everybody sins, *Jesus is everyone's justifier through faith.* Believe God has a plan for His people. And Jesus, as your justifier, is a part of God's ultimate, loving, gracious plan. In Jesus, you receive freedom, grace, and eternal life.

---

*For all have sinned and fall short of the glory of God. They are justified freely by His grace through the redemption that is in Christ Jesus.*
—Romans 3:23–24

---

Further Scripture: Romans 3:21–22; 2 Corinthians 5:21; James 4:17

## *Week 18, Day 126: Romans 4*
## Justification Through Faith

Abraham was considered righteous and received justification from sin because of His faith in God's promises. *Abraham believed.* Abraham believed God's words were true. He didn't work hard to earn righteousness—he received it through faith. Abraham did not waiver in unbelief at God's promise but was strengthened in his faith and gave glory to God. He did what God asked of him, fully convinced that what God had promised He was also able to perform.

There is no amount of human effort, good works, or keeping of the law that will result in righteousness. *You are saved by grace through faith.* Through believing. God grants you righteousness through faith as you receive Him and His promises. Stop striving. Stop attempting to earn right standing with God by following laws and rules. Just believe in God's promises by faith. Today, believe in what you can't see, and trust God and His promises.

---

*This is why the promise is by faith, so that it may be according to grace, to guarantee it to all the descendants—not only to those who are of the law but also to those who are of Abraham's faith. He is the father of us all in God's sight.* —Romans 4:16–17

---

Further Scripture: Genesis 12:2, 4; Romans 4:20–21; Ephesians 2:8–9

## *Week 19, Day 127: Romans 5*
## Longing for Peace

People long for peace in their lives. They search for peace in every corner of the world. Why? Because God created you to long for something more than this world offers. However, nothing in this world will deliver the peace your soul longs for. You may be going through a crisis, persecution, or affliction, and as you walk through this hardship, you long for peace. *The Lord Jesus Christ is that peace your soul longs for.*

Jesus is your Prince of Peace. You find peace with God through faith in Jesus Christ. Yes, the Jesus who demonstrated His love for you while you were a sinner—that Jesus— is the peace of this world. When you search for peace, turn to Jesus in faith and receive His grace. He will be your peace—even in the midst of despair. As you walk through affliction, Jesus will grant endurance, grow your character, and give you hope. His love has been poured out for you. Give thanks to Him in all circumstances, and His peace that passes all understanding will guard your hearts. Let go of control and walk with Jesus. Remember, He is the peace your soul longs for.

---

*Therefore, since we have been declared righteous by faith, we have peace with God through our Lord Jesus Christ. We have also obtained access through Him by faith into this grace in which we stand, and we rejoice in the hope of the glory of God.* —Romans 5:1–2

---

Further Scripture: Isaiah 9:6; Romans 5:3–5; 2 Thessalonians 3:16

## *Week 19, Day 128: Romans 6*
## Dead to Sin

Everyone has sinned and fallen short of the glory of God. People live in bondage to a variety of sin: false gods and idols, addiction, pride, deception, and more. People live as slaves to sin. Just as a slave would obey a master, a slave to sin obeys whatever sin dictates. However, if you live as a slave to righteousness, then you will obey your master, Jesus Christ.

In Christ, you are set free and are no longer a slave to sin. In Christ, you are dead to sin and alive in Him, which leads to righteousness. Christ came to set you free from the bondage of sin. He has given you eternal life through grace, an unearned gift for you to receive. Stand firm. Don't give in to the yoke of slavery but renew your mind and your spirit in Christ. You are *alive* in Christ! You are *alive!*

---

*So, you too consider yourselves dead to sin but alive to God in Christ Jesus.*
—Romans 6:11

---

Further Scripture: Romans 6:16–18, 23; Ephesians 4:20–24

### *Week 19, Day 129: Romans 7*
Living Free from Sin

When you receive Jesus as your Savior and confess with your mouth, He is Lord, you are a new creation. You were released from the law, from your old ways, and from sin. Christ liberated you and set you free. Stand firm in Jesus. Stand firm! Don't go back to the old ways when you were a slave to the law, striving to work for your salvation. Don't go back to your old sin patterns. Don't live in that bondage again. You have been set *free*. You belong to Christ.

But it's hard, right? You want to do good, but you struggle and feel like a failure. Remember, walking with Jesus is not about keeping the law and striving to do good and be better. *It's about walking with Jesus and living in His Spirit.* He calls you to abide in Him. Spend time with Him. Allow His love to fill you up, and as you abide in Him, not the things of this world, you will begin to bear fruit—the fruit of the Spirit. Apart from Him, you will struggle, unable to produce the fruit of the Spirit on your own. Apart from Him, you will strive to keep the law. But your striving is not the freedom He has called you to live in. He has released you from the law so you can live in freedom. Today, abide in Him and walk in the Spirit, not in your flesh.

---

*Therefore, my brothers, you also were put to death in relation to the law through the crucified body of the Messiah, so that you may belong to another—to Him who was raised from the dead—that we may bear fruit for God. . . . But now we have been released from the law, since we have died to what held us, so that we may serve in the new way of the Spirit and not in the old letter of the law.* —Romans 7:4, 6

---

Further Scripture: John 15:4–5; Galatians 5:16–18, 22–23

### *Week 19, Day 130: Romans 8*
### No Condemnation Through Christ

The mind set on the Spirit of God brings life and peace, whereas a mind set on flesh brings death. Therefore, set your mind on the Spirit. Walk in the power of the Spirit. When afflictions and suffering come, as you walk in the Spirit, you will respond in the Spirit and not in your flesh. Even though you walk through pain, in the Spirit you will receive the fruits of peace and joy. You will walk in God's love for you. You will walk believing in God's faithfulness, allowing all things to work together for good for those who love God and are called according to His purpose. *This is walking in the Spirit.*

As believers, you live life in victory, not defeat! You are more than victorious through Christ who loves you and gave His life for you. As you walk in the Spirit, you walk believing nothing has the power to separate you from the love of God. *Nothing.* So do not live defeated. Live with your shoulders back, your eyes fixed ahead on Christ, and walk in the power of His Resurrection. You have victory in Christ. Walk in His peaceful, life-giving Spirit. Stand firm and remain in Christ's love.

---

*No, in all these things we are more than victorious*
*through Him who loved us.*
*For I am persuaded that not even death or life,*
*angels or rulers,*
*things present or things to come, hostile powers,*
*height or depth, or any other created thing*
*will have the power to separate us*
*from the love of God that is in Christ Jesus our Lord!*
—Romans 8:37–39

---

Further Scripture: Romans 8:5–6, 28; 1 Corinthians 15:57

## *Week 19, Day 131: Romans 9*
### God Fulfills His Promises

From the beginning, the Lord had a plan for the people of Israel—adoption by God, His presence with them, the covenants, the Law, the temple service, and the promises. The Lord has shown His faithfulness, justice, righteousness, and graciousness to the people of Israel. Even so, they stumbled over the stone, the living stone, Jesus. They missed Jesus as their Messiah. Consequently, they continue to live under the law and not in the grace the Lord had for them. Despite all that, God remains in control. God continues to pour out His mercy even when His people do not follow His will. He is in charge, and His character remains consistent—*He will fulfill His promises.*

God is working in ways beyond what you can see to display His greatness, both with Gentiles and Jews. What is the Lord doing through you today? Can you miss exactly what God wants to do? Perhaps, but by faith, believe in the God of mercy, love, justice, righteousness, and grace. His plan will come forth. As you walk with God, you can't mess up with Him. He has a patient love. He is with you and for you. Trust His plan will come forth.

---

*And what if He did this to make known the riches of His glory on objects of mercy that He prepared beforehand for glory—on us, the ones He also called, not only from the Jews but also from the Gentiles?*
—Romans 9:23–24

---

Further Scripture: Romans 9:4, 32–33; 2 Peter 3:9

### *Week 19, Day 132: Romans 10*
### The Jews Rejected Jesus

The message of the Gospel is for all people. If you call upon the name of Jesus as Lord, you will be saved. However, the people of Israel rejected this message. They did not receive it. So, what now? They still need to hear the truth in a way that creates jealousy and, perhaps, even causes them to *become angry that they lack understanding.*

People need to hear the message of the Gospel from your heart. Today, that's your job. You are to confess with your mouth, "Jesus is Lord," believing in your heart that God raised Him from the dead. How will people hear this truth unless your beautiful feet deliver it? How will they know the love of a Savior unless your life reflects His amazing, graceful love? Open your mouth and share this message. Share about the peace and freedom you found in Christ. Christ came for *all.* Pray for *all* to no longer reject the truth but receive God's love. May Christ's love compel you to share with someone today.

---

*For there is no distinction between Jew and Greek, since the same Lord of all is rich to all who call on Him. For everyone who calls on the name of the Lord will be saved.* —Romans 10:12–13

---

Further Scripture: Romans 10:8b–10, 14–15; 2 Corinthians 5:14

## Week 19, Day 133: Romans 11
### Provoke Jealousy

God is not done with His chosen people, the Jewish people. God will have mercy on all, both Gentiles and Jews. The Jewish people will come across the Cornerstone, Jesus, as the Gentiles make them jealous by portraying Christ's love. So there is a call for Gentiles—anyone who is not Jewish—*to live out their faith in a way that provokes the Jews to jealousy.* Allow them to see how amazing Jesus' grace and love is, how awesome His ways are, and the depth of His riches—both wisdom and knowledge. Today, live your life for Jesus in such a way the Jews will want to receive the Messiah as *their* Messiah.

There is more to consider regarding God's kindness. He has called His people to Himself; therefore, He is not done. May they see the one-and-only true Cornerstone, the Living Stone, Jesus, in their lives. For from Him and through Him and to Him are all things. *Live your life in Christ in a way that brings Him glory.* May Jesus' will be done until He returns.

---

*I ask, then, have they stumbled in order to fall? Absolutely not! On the contrary, by their stumbling, salvation has come to the Gentiles to make Israel jealous. Now if their stumbling brings riches for the world, and their failure riches for the Gentiles, how much more will their full number bring!* —Romans 11:11–12

---

Further Scripture: Zechariah 12:10; Matthew 23:37, 39; Romans 11:33, 36

### *Week 20, Day 134: Romans 12*
### A Living Sacrifice

God has been merciful to you through the death and resurrection of Jesus Christ. Because of Jesus, you are justified by faith. Just as you have received mercy from God, it is now your turn to pour mercy into others . . . not in your own strength but in the strength that comes from your daily worship of the Lord *and the renewing of your mind.* This means reading the Word, spending time in prayer, thanking and praising the Lord. As the Holy Spirit works in you, *your life will be transformed,* giving you the strength to show the Lord's mercy to others.

Ask yourself and be honest: Are you renewing your mind daily in worship to the Lord? If you are worn out and weary, it may be time to pause and worship the Lord. Love the Lord with all you have. It's a daily living sacrifice. Then you are able to discern God's will. Through this discipline, you will be filled with His power and His Spirit to walk out the mercy and love He wants to pour out through you into His people. Then the world will know of His great love.

---

*Therefore, brothers, by the mercies of God, I urge you to present your bodies as a living sacrifice, holy and pleasing to God; this is your spiritual worship. Do not be conformed to this age, but be transformed by the renewing of your mind, so that you may discern what is the good, pleasing, and perfect will of God.* —Romans 12:1–2

---

Further Scripture: Romans 12:9–12; 1 Corinthians 6:19–20; Hebrews 13:15–16

### *Week 20, Day 135: Romans 13*

## Our Relationship to Authorities; Putting On Christ

As a believer, you serve God—the ultimate authority over all. And as a believer, you must submit to governing officials because God has instituted them. If you respect God as your authority, then you should respect governing officials. As you follow the Lord, you put on Jesus Christ. In doing so, you put on truth, peace, and righteousness, just like putting on clothing. When people see you, they should see the attributes of Christ. You display love to all people, even those placed as authority in government.

Love your governing officials. Pray for them. God desires for *all* to know His love. What if your role is to love like Jesus and look like Jesus as you interact with governing officials so they know the truth of the Gospel through you? Don't let pride and fleshly desires get in the way. Trust God as your ultimate authority and humbly walk out the love of Christ. Be Jesus with skin on. *Love others, love your neighbors, and love those in authority as governing officials.* This is how the world will truly change—when they want to know the Jesus in you.

---

*Everyone must submit to the governing authorities, for there is no authority except from God, and those that exist are instituted by God.*
—Romans 13:1

---

Further Scripture: Romans 13:7, 14; 1 Timothy 2:1–2

### *Week 20, Day 136: Romans 14*
### Love in Unity Without Judgment

The Lord calls you to receive one another. Just as you would receive a gift or accept a compliment, *you are to receive one another.* This requires you to love like Christ loves. Do not be judgmental. Do not argue about opinions when others are weaker in faith. Do not criticize. Do not be a stumbling block or a pitfall in your brother's way. That's a lot of "don'ts." However, as a follower of Christ in the kingdom of God, you are called to righteousness, peace, and joy in the Holy Spirit. Therefore, as you walk in the power of the Holy Spirit, *you will bear these fruits demonstrating Christ's love.*

Righteousness, peace, and joy create unity and promote encouragement. God's not asking you to play umpire or referee in the kingdom of God. God alone holds authority and judgment. He simply asks you to bear His fruit of the Spirit, which will result as you abide in Him and His love. Today, don't get bogged down by all the differences in the body of Christ. Seek to love and receive one another. Then the peace, joy, and righteousness you desire will abound through the power of the Holy Spirit!

---

*For the kingdom of God is not eating and drinking, but righteousness, peace, and joy in the Holy Spirit. Whoever serves Christ in this way is acceptable to God and approved by men. So then, we must pursue what promotes peace and what builds up one another.* —Romans 14:17–19

---

Further Scripture: Romans 14:1, 13; Colossians 3:14

*Week 20, Day 137: Romans 15*
Hope in the Lord

What is hope? Hope is a desire or expectation for a certain thing to happen: "I hope you get better." "I hope surgery goes well." "I hope you get the job." It is the God of *hope* who fills you with all joy and peace as you believe in Him. If you are hoping for something, remain in the Lord, rest in Him, and abide in His love for you. Wait and trust the Lord. In Christ, you will have peace and joy while hoping. The Lord promises you will actually *overflow* with *hope* through the power of the Holy Spirit. Picture a kitchen sink overflowing with water and spilling all over a floor. That's how much *hope* the Holy Spirit will give you!

As you hope for unity in the body of Christ, walk in the power of the Holy Spirit. As you hope in the Lord for His future for your life, walk in the power of the Holy Spirit. Paul's travel plans were often altered even though he strongly desired and hoped to go to Rome. But God had another plan for him to travel to Jerusalem where He used Paul in a mighty way to serve the saints. When you focus on the hope found in Christ, you have peace and joy whatever the outcome may be, because you are aligned with God's will. Today, place your hope in the Lord alone!

*Now may the God of hope fill you with all joy and peace as you believe in Him so that you may overflow with hope by the power of the Holy Spirit.*
—Romans 15:13

Further Scripture: Psalm 33:20–22; Romans 15:22–25; Hebrews 10:23

## *Week 20, Day 138: Romans 16*
Paul's Final Greetings

Paul greeted many of the Roman Christians that he encountered along his journey while delivering the Gospel. He poured into these specific people and spent time in their homes. Paul shared the good news with them so they could take the Gospel even farther. Paul discipled all these people and invested in their lives.

You are called to do that same thing—to invest in the people around you with the message of the Gospel. When you do, those people can carry the Gospel to those around them, and the cycle continues. That was how Jesus did ministry and how Paul modeled Jesus' ministry by delivering the Gospel truth that transforms lives. The question remains: What does your list of names look like? *Who are you pouring into with the message of Jesus' grace?* Perhaps your children, your grandchildren, your neighbors, or coworkers? You will impact lives when you love people like Jesus and share about His grace in your life. It's not a complicated program or conference; *it's simply loving people according to the Gospel of Jesus Christ.* Today, go and love.

---

*Give my greetings to Prisca and Aquila, my coworkers in Christ Jesus, who risked their own necks for my life. Not only do I thank them, but so do all the Gentile churches. Greet also the church that meets in their home. Greet my dear friend Epaenetus, who is the first convert to Christ from Asia. Greet Mary, who has worked very hard for you.* —Romans 16:3–6

---

Further Scripture: Romans 16:19–20, 25; 2 Timothy 2:2

## Week 20, Day 139: 1 Corinthians 1
## Called into Fellowship with Jesus

Do you ever wonder if you are adequate to serve the Lord? Do you ever wonder what you are called to? Perhaps you wonder if God is even faithful in your life? When Paul addressed the church in Corinth, those who were sanctified in Christ, he knew the church was divided, and different views were surfacing. Therefore, Paul spoke these truths to the believers: *Christ is confirmed among you. You do not lack any spiritual gift as you rest in the Lord. God will strengthen you. It is okay to feel weak, because Christ will strengthen you daily to be blameless, fully forgiven from Jesus. God is faithful. Period. No questions. You are called by God into fellowship, into relationship, into friendship with Jesus Christ.*

What are you called to today? To walk with the Lord. To love Him. To seek to know Him. When you remember these truths that Paul reminded the Romans of, guess what? It's not about you anymore. Instead, it's all about the Lord and His justifying, sanctifying, redeeming power, and grace in your life. So, boast in the Lord and His faithfulness. Don't question yourself any longer. You are saved, and you have His power at work in your life.

---

*In this way, the testimony about Christ was confirmed among you, so that you do not lack any spiritual gift as you eagerly wait for the revelation of our Lord Jesus Christ. He will also strengthen you to the end, so that you will be blameless in the day of our Lord Jesus Christ. God is faithful; you were called by Him into fellowship with His Son, Jesus Christ our Lord.*
—1 Corinthians 1:6–9

---

Further Scripture: 1 Corinthians 1:30–31; 2 Thessalonians 3:3; 2 Timothy 2:13

### *Week 20, Day 140: 1 Corinthians 2*
## Mind of Christ

As a follower of Jesus Christ, you have the mind of Christ. You have the power of the Holy Spirit within you. As the Spirit dwells within you, He searches you, teaches you, and matures you so you may understand what has been feely given to you by God.

You may feel like a failure. You may feel weak, fearful, and tremble. You may not be a good speaker with lots of wisdom. However, your faith is not based on man's wisdom and strength but on God's power. You are a child of God, and you are able to do more than you can even imagine because God's power is alive within you. Paul shared the Gospel in his weakness, in fear, in trembling, and while feeling inadequate. But he didn't let that stop him. He went in the power of Spirit. So today, step out in faith and trust that still, small voice that says, "You can do this." *You have the mind of Christ—full of His strength, power, and wisdom.* Walk it out in faith and believe this powerful truth for your life.

---

*I came to you in weakness, in fear, and in much trembling. My speech and my proclamation were not with persuasive words of wisdom but with a powerful demonstration by the Spirit, so that your faith might not be based on men's wisdom but on God's power.* —1 Corinthians 2:3–5

---

Further Scripture: Exodus 4:10–12; 1 Corinthians 2:13, 16

### Week 21, Day 141: 1 Corinthians 3
## God Gives Strength

Just as Paul planted and Apollos watered, you have a role to play—displaying Christ's joy, peace, and righteousness in His kingdom. Remain responsible to your role. Don't worry about what others are doing. Rather, use the gifts the Lord has given you. Open your eyes to see what God sees and how the roles all work together for the same purpose—to give glory to the Lord.

If you catch yourself glorifying man or even boasting in yourself, then stop, humble yourself in the sight of the Lord, release your prideful thoughts, and give praise and honor to the Lord. As you faithfully carry out your role, you may feel frustrated at times as you plant seeds of the Gospel but do not see immediate growth. Remember, it's God who gives you power, God who gives you grace, and God who gives you wisdom. Ultimately, God gives the growth. *The kingdom belongs to God, and through Him it will grow.* Today, give thanks for your role, and let God focus on the growth!

---

*What then is Apollos? And what is Paul? They are servants through whom you believed, and each has the role the Lord has given. I planted, Apollos watered, but God gave the growth. So then neither the one who plants nor the one who waters is anything, but only God who gives the growth.*
—1 Corinthians 3:5–7

---

Further Scripture: Matthew 6:33; Luke 6:20; 1 Corinthians 3:21–23

### *Week 21, Day 142: 1 Corinthians 4*
### Fools for Christ

Like the apostle Paul, live as a fool for Christ. What does that mean? It means your life may not make sense to those looking in from the outside. It means others may judge and evaluate you, but you know the real evaluation only comes from the Lord. Being a fool for Christ may look like weakness, but you know you are strong in Him. It may look like you are dishonored, but you are a distinguished, royal priesthood before the Lord. You may be persecuted and knocked down, but you endure the pain, just like Jesus. Even though what is seen may be deteriorating, the Lord looks at what is unseen. For what is seen is temporary, and what is unseen is producing a weight of glory.

Look around you. Look for someone who is a fool for Christ. Someone who doesn't live to please man but rather *lives to please the Lord in confident humility*. When you find that person, seek to imitate them as they imitate Christ. You will find ultimate fulfillment and peace when you live as Christ lived and love as Christ loves. Today, step out as a fool . . . a fool for Christ.

---

*We are fools for Christ, but you are wise in Christ. We are weak, but you are strong! You are distinguished, but we are dishonored!*
—1 Corinthians 4:10

---

Further Scripture: 1 Corinthians 4:15–16; 2 Corinthians 4:16–18; Ephesians 5:1–2

### Week 21, Day 143: 1 Corinthians 5

## No Contamination!

If you knew something would contaminate your favorite refreshing beverage, you would stay away from it so you could enjoy the pure, intended taste. Who wants to drink iced tea with a little dish soap? Yuck! The Christian life is similar. The Lord advocates for you to flee from certain things: sexual immorality, malice, and evil. These things contaminate the purity of your walk with the Lord.

Christ intends for your life with Him to be filled with sincerity and truth. He desires for you to love Him passionately, fervently, and earnestly, while focusing on the truth of His Word. When you dabble with sexual temptation and sin, when you look at others with envy, or when you entertain thoughts of malice, *you contaminate your walk with the Lord.* The Lord longs for you to walk sincerely with Him so you can fully receive all He has for you. God is a God of love, grace, and mercy. Today, as temptations arise, ask yourself: "Do I want to contaminate this cup of iced tea?" Choose to stay strong, stand firm, and remain pure for Jesus. He promises He will give you strength as you walk by the Spirit.

*Therefore, let us observe the feast, not with old yeast or with the yeast of malice and evil but with the unleavened bread of sincerity and truth.*
—1 Corinthians 5:8

Further Scripture: 1 Corinthians 5:1–2; Galatians 5:16; 2 Timothy 2:21–22

### *Week 21, Day 144: 1 Corinthians 6*
### Permissible but Not Beneficial

As a believer, you were washed, sanctified, and justified in the name of the Lord Jesus Christ by the Spirit of God. You have freedom and peace in Christ. The Lord longs for you to walk in wisdom and truth through the power of His Holy Spirit. He equips you, He empowers you, and He strengthens you as you renew your mind in Him every day.

*You have been given freedom through Christ.* This does not mean you are free to choose a lifestyle of sin. Freedom in Christ does not give you permission to live in your flesh. Instead, you are to walk in the Spirit. So slow down. Think before you act. Think before you speak. Consider others and seek counsel. Focus on the Lord. Serve one another in love. Let some time pass before deciding to give in to a fleshly temptation such as sexual immorality, idolatry, adultery, greediness, or drunkenness. Think things through before you quickly give in. Then you will enjoy walking fully in the Lord's righteousness and grow in the kingdom of God.

---

*And some of you used to be like this. But you were washed, you were sanctified, you were justified in the name of the Lord Jesus Christ and by the Spirit of our God. "Everything is permissible for me," but not everything is helpful. "Everything is permissible for me," but I will not be brought under the control of anything.* —1 Corinthians 6:11–12

---

Further Scripture: Romans 6:1–2; 1 Corinthians 6:9–10; Galatians 5:13

### Week 21, Day 145: 1 Corinthians 7
## Honor the Lord in Marriage

Marriage is a covenant agreement between a man and woman who are joined together as one flesh in unity all the days of their lives. Joining together for all the days of your life is easier said than done, but God promises *nothing is impossible with Him!* Yes, even a strong, unified marriage is possible! Therefore, together in marriage, *keep your eyes on Christ and walk in the power of His Spirit.*

Marriage is one key to building up the kingdom of God. This is why the enemy seeks to destroy marriage. The enemy schemes to get through the crack in marriage to bring destruction. Therefore, don't withhold anything from your spouse. Don't withhold sharing information. Don't withhold serving one another. Don't withhold sexual intimacy. As you trust the Lord and walk in the Spirit, being open and vulnerable with your spouse creates strength in your marriage and eliminates opportunities for the enemy to creep through cracks. *Seek to have complete and pure devotion to Christ in every area of your marriage.* Christ will give you the strength and wisdom needed daily as you draw near to Him.

---

*Do not deprive one another sexually—except when you agree for a time, to devote yourselves to prayer. Then come together again; otherwise, Satan may tempt you because of your lack of self-control.* —1 Corinthians 7:5

---

Further Scripture: 2 Corinthians 11:3; Galatians 5:16; Ephesians 5:31–33

### Week 21, Day 146: 1 Corinthians 8
## Love Builds Up

Jesus taught His disciples the greatest commandment: *Love the Lord your God with all your heart, with all your soul, and with all your mind.* Then Jesus taught the second greatest commandment: *Love your neighbor as yourself.* The apostle Paul gave similar guidelines to the church in Corinth. First, if anyone loves God, he is known by Him. Second, knowledge inflates with pride, but *love builds up.*

What do you learn from Jesus and Paul as you walk through this life with Christ and with others? Keep it simple. It's not about knowledge, and it's not about works or keeping the law. *As you love God, you will know God, and He will know you.* More than teaching, more than sacrifice, *God desires for you to love Him.* Then the Lord's love will overflow from your life into those around you. You don't need to force knowledge, justice, or judgment on them. As you love God, He will fill you with wisdom and grace for others. They will feel Jesus's transforming love through your life and will hunger for the love you offer them. Today, focus on loving God and loving others, and then trust the Lord to transform your heart and theirs.

---

*About food offered to idols: We know that "we all have knowledge." Knowledge inflates with pride, but love builds up. If anyone thinks he knows anything, he does not yet know it as he ought to know it. But if anyone loves God, he is known by Him.* —1 Corinthians 8:1–3

---

Further Scripture: 1 Samuel 15:22; Matthew 22:36–39; Romans 12:2

## *Week 21, Day 147: 1 Corinthians 9*
### Enduring Everything

Paul did not take advantage or leverage his position to receive benefits from people he shared the Gospel with or did ministry alongside. He didn't make use of his rights; he did almost the opposite as he endured everything for the sake of the Gospel. He didn't rely on position, power, or rank. Rather *he relied on the power and provision of the Lord.* He became all things to all people, so by every possible means, people would hear and receive the Gospel.

Jesus said the pure of heart will see God, and the poor in spirit will inherit the kingdom of God. The Lord longs for your heart to praise Him and to trust Him in obedience. As your heart remains pure and as you live with humility, the Lord will allow you to hear from Him, to recognize His ways, and inherit the kingdom of God. You don't need to bend the rules, manipulate, lie, cheat, or take things under your own control. On the contrary, walk in obedience, no matter where the Lord has you go. The Lord will honor your obedience. He will meet every need. God promises He will be with you, and He will reward you. Whatever you do, do it in the name of the Lord Jesus, giving thanks to God the Father through Him.

---

*If others have this right to receive benefits from you, don't we even more? However, we have not made use of this right; instead we endure everything so that we will not hinder the gospel of Christ.* —1 Corinthians 9:12

---

Further Scripture: Matthew 5:3, 8; Ephesians 6:5–8; Colossians 3:17

### *Week 22, Day 148: 1 Corinthians 10*
### Flee Idolatry

Paul encouraged the Corinthian believers to flee from idolatry. Even in the church today, idolatry remains a temptation. The enemy schemes and lures people to worship other idols. You may think, *What? Idolatry? Me? I don't struggle with bowing down and worshipping other gods!* Worshipping other gods refers to anything in your life that commands more time, loyalty, or devotion over the one true God—your Savior, Jesus Christ. Perhaps your idol is security, wealth, health, success, achieving a fit body, or following a sports team. Even your children's activities or family time may become an idol if you find yourself placing this time before quality time worshipping the Lord.

The Lord says, "Glorify Me *with everything*." He didn't say to only worship the Lord with only half of you and worship other gods with your other half. If you are tempted in the area of idolatry, remember, the Lord is with you and will provide freedom. When you humble yourself and confess your sin of idolatry, the Lord will bless you with forgiveness and peace. He wants you to flee from all idolatry! So today, put on your running shoes and run after Jesus first and foremost and with everything you have!

---

*Therefore, my dear friends, flee from idolatry.* —1 Corinthians 10:14

---

Further Scripture: Exodus 34:14; 1 Corinthians 10:12–13, 31

### *Week 22, Day 149: 1 Corinthians 11*

## Imitate Christ

Paul told the Corinthians, "Imitate me, as I also imitate Christ." Paul walked as Christ walked. He humbly knew the example he set for believers on how to live their lives. God is not calling you to live a perfect life so others will imitate your perfection. No, Paul was the first one to say, "God's grace is sufficient as God's power is made perfect in my weakness." *Paul may have appeared strong, but it was God's grace and power made perfect in Paul's weakness.* That's just how God works.

Therefore, imitating Christ includes walking in His power in order to love others, forgive others, and humbly give up your life for others. It's Christ's love working in you as you abide in Him. As people imitate you, they don't need to see perfection without any cracks or broken pieces. Allow others to see your cracks and broken pieces. It's in the brokenness the love and light of Jesus shines through you. And it's God's amazing grace and Christ's power you long for others to see.

---

*Imitate me, as I also imitate Christ.* —1 Corinthians 11:1

---

Further Scripture: 2 Corinthians 12:9; Philippians 2:5–8; 1 John 2:6

### Week 22, Day 150: 1 Corinthians 12
### Gifts of the Holy Spirit

As a demonstration of the Holy Spirit, each person has been gifted to benefit the body of Christ and build up the kingdom of God. God activates gifts in each person through the Holy Spirit to produce what is beneficial for the body. He gifts His people with wisdom, knowledge, faith, healing, miracles, prophecy, discernment, tongues, and interpretation of tongues. God is the same yesterday, today, and tomorrow. Therefore, His Spirit empowers the body of Christ today, just as He did years ago!

You may wonder: *What is my gift for the body?* Just as every part of your body works together for the greater good of the whole, the body of Christ *works together* to build up the kingdom of God. All the gifts *work together* and are necessary. Child of God, you have a part in the body of Christ. Earnestly ask the Holy Spirit to empower you with gifts to do His will. Then walk in humble obedience to the Holy Spirit prompting you. Trust Him and step out in faith. Pray for *healing*. Ask the Lord *for discernment* or *wisdom* in a situation. You never know how the Lord's power and giftings will move unless you are willing to step out in faith.

---

*But one and the same Spirit is active in all these, distributing to each person as He wills. For as the body is one and has many parts, and all the parts of that body, though many, are one body—so also is Christ.*
—1 Corinthians 12:11–12

---

Further Scripture: Romans 12:4–5; 1 Corinthians 12:17–20; Ephesians 4:11–13

### *Week 22, Day 151: 1 Corinthians 13*
### Love: The Superior Way

You can have all the gifts of the Spirit and faithfully use them for the kingdom, but if you don't demonstrate love—*then you gain nothing.* Love is essential and greater than the gifts of the Spirit. If love is absent, then any gifts used are canceled out.

So how do you love? You love others out of the love you have been given from the heavenly Father. As you receive God's love, He will fill you up to love others as you walk in the Spirit. *Love is number one in the kingdom of God.* If you think, *I don't know the gift God has given me,* then start by loving others as Christ has loved you. Remember, God's greatest commandments are to love Him and love others. Today, take a deep breath and receive the love of your Father. Then go out and love others!

---

*If I have the gift of prophecy*
*and understand all mysteries*
*and all knowledge,*
*and if I have all faith*
*so that I can move mountains*
*but do not have love, I am nothing.*
*And if I donate all my goods to feed the poor,*
*and if I give my body in order to boast*
*but do not have love, I gain nothing.* —1 Corinthians 13:2–3

---

Further Scripture: Mark 12:29–31; 1 Corinthians 13:4–8a; Colossians 3:14

## Week 22, Day 152: 1 Corinthians 14
## The Priority of Prophecy

The Holy Spirit gives spiritual gifts for building up the body of Christ, such as speaking in tongues and prophesying. However, Paul warned the church, *everything must be done decently and in order.* Just like in today's church, Paul knew the gifts could easily cause division and confusion, which then voids and distracts from God's intended purpose. Paul instructed believers to walk in the Spirit and not despise prophecies, but he also instructed them to test them and hold on to what is good. The person who prophesies speaks to others for edification, encouragement, and comfort, *just as the gifts of the Spirit are used to build up the body of Christ, not tear it down.*

If you have what you believe is a prophetic vision or a word for another person, ask the Lord if it will edify, encourage, or comfort that person. Seek confirmation before you communicate. Trust the Holy Spirit, and as confirmation comes, communicate what you hear from the Lord. If you have a prophetic word that may bring fear, discouragement, or confusion, then perhaps you need to practice self-control and pray for the person, rather than release it immediately. Remember to pray at all times and give thanks, for this is the will of the Lord.

---

*Therefore, my brothers, be eager to prophesy, and do not forbid speaking in other languages. But everything must be done decently and in order.*
—1 Corinthians 14:39–40

---

Further Scripture: 1 Corinthians 14:3; 1 Thessalonians 5:17–21; 2 Peter 1:20–21

## *Week 22, Day 153: 1 Corinthians 15*
## Victory Through Jesus!

Paul reminded the church of the simple Gospel. Even today the Gospel message can get overly complicated or even lost. Remember this truth that sets you free: *Christ died for your sins. He was buried. He was raised on the third day. If you confess with your mouth and believe in your heart that God was raised from the dead, then you will be saved.* That's the bottom line of the Gospel. This simple truth will transform your life . . . and give you victory as you remain in Christ.

Yes! Because you believe Jesus was resurrected, then death has no sting. Jesus gives you victory over sin. Jesus gives you victory over death. Through your faith in Christ, you are victorious in all things! The world, the enemy, and the lies are all defeated because in Christ you have life, you have victory, and you have peace. Live today as an overcomer. Live today as a conqueror. Think about a stadium full of fans shouting after a sport team's victory over an opponent. Today, shout hallelujah, praise the Lord, and give thanks, honor, and glory to the Lord Jesus Christ because through Him, you have victory!

*Death, where is your victory?*
*Death, where is your sting?*
*Now the sting of death is sin,*
*and the power of sin is the law.*
*But thanks be to God, who gives us the victory*
*through our Lord Jesus Christ!* —1 Corinthians 15:55–57

Further Scripture: Romans 10:9–10; 1 Corinthians 15:3–6; 1 John 5:4

### Week 22, Day 154: 1 Corinthians 16
## Wide-Open Doors

Paul exemplified a life surrendered to God's will. Even as he discussed his travel plans, he held them loosely, acknowledging *only if the Lord wills*. He also looked for *open doors* for ministry. He didn't fear man as he learned of people opposing him, calling it a closed door. Rather he called it a wide-open door for effective ministry. He embraced the persecution and walked with boldness and confident fear of the Lord.

Sometimes you make plans, and no matter what red flags or closed doors come your way, you don't consider they may be God trying to get your attention to redirect you for His good purposes. However, the Lord encourages His people to pray, "Thy will be done," trusting Him to make the path clear and walk in humility, even when it means changing plans or direction. The key is to open your mind to the plans you have and trust them to the Lord. Release control and allow Him to take the reins. Ask the Lord to open doors, and only go *if He wills*. As you live a life surrendered to the Lord's will, it doesn't mean there won't be opposition or sufferings. But with Christ leading the way, remember, *you will be victorious.*

---

*I don't want to see you now just in passing, for I hope to spend some time with you, if the Lord allows. But I will stay in Ephesus until Pentecost, because a wide door for effective ministry has opened for me—yet many oppose me.* —1 Corinthians 16:7–9

---

Further Scripture: Proverbs 3:5–6; Matthew 6:9–10; James 4:13–15

## *Week 23, Day 155: 2 Corinthians 1*
## God of All Comfort

When you think of comfort, what do you think of? Perhaps being wrapped in a cozy, soft blanket while sitting by a fire, drinking your favorite cup of tea or coffee, being hugged by a loved one at the end of a hard day, or snuggling with a puppy. These are all wonderful but temporary comforts. As Paul told the Corinthian church, God is the God of *all comfort.*

When you feel sad or disappointed, depressed or grieving a loss, God's presence will comfort you. God is there for you and will never leave you because He is constant. Therefore, turn to God. Read His Word. Listen to worship music. Rest in His presence through prayer. Spend time with other people seeking the Lord together. Oftentimes you hurt when those you care for hurt. Pray for God to comfort them and for them to trust His promises for their lives. Each and every one of God's promises is a yes. This means every one of God's promises is fulfilled. *Every promise is a yes.* With this truth in mind, find comfort in the Lord. You can stand in His faithfulness and say, "Amen!" God loves you even when life feels as though it's falling apart. Today, may the Lord comfort you and help you.

---

*Praise the God and Father of our Lord Jesus Christ, the Father of mercies and the God of all comfort.* —2 Corinthians 1:3

---

Further Scripture: Psalm 23:4; 86:17; 2 Corinthians 1:20

### Week 23, Day 156: 2 Corinthians 2
Fragrance of Christ

Have you ever thought about how you smell? Not physically *but spiritually?* Paul called the Corinthians the "fragrance of Christ." Just like a clerk puts a bottle of perfume on display at the department store, God puts you on display as His child, His ambassador, His vessel, *His aroma*, in order for you to represent Christ to the world around you. What does your aroma smell like today? As you abide in Christ, your aroma could smell like unity, life, forgiveness, love, peace, or comfort. So many victorious combinations exist as you walk with the Lord!

Remember, Satan comes to kill, steal, and destroy the intentions of Christ. Satan schemes for your aroma to be death, disunity, unforgiveness, strife, and anxiety. *Therefore, stand guard!* Don't fall into the traps and schemes of the enemy. The people around you will be drawn to your pure, humble, and sincere aroma as your love of Christ is displayed for all to "smell." Abide in Christ, and you will have the fragrance of Christ.

---

*But thanks be to God, who always puts us on display in Christ and through us spreads the aroma of the knowledge of Him in every place. For to God we are the fragrance of Christ among those who are being saved and among those who are perishing.* —2 Corinthians 2:14–15

---

Further Scripture: John 10:10; 2 Corinthians 2:10–11; Ephesians 5:1–2

*Week 23, Day 157: 2 Corinthians 3*
Freedom in Christ

Paul emphasized to the Corinthian church the ministry of the Spirit versus living under the Law. He described the Jewish people as having a veil covering their hearts to the truth and freedom found in Jesus Christ. However, with faith, God can remove the veil over anyone's heart. And when He does, freedom is found. Jesus came with a new covenant of grace and love. The Spirit of the Lord gives freedom.

Have you thought about the freedom you have in the Lord? Or do you find yourself still striving to keep up, do better, and find competence in yourself? The truth is you don't have to do more for God. Your competence comes from Him. He came to set you free. Imagine a five-year-old child running freely in a field with a fence around it. The fence around the open space protects the child from harm. But inside the fence, the child can run, play, and spin in circles with freedom and enjoyment. That same picture is for you today. Child of God, *twirl around in the freedom you have in Christ.* Cease striving and know God's got you just as you are. Be confident in His love for you and the freedom you have in the Spirit of the Lord.

---

*Even to this day, whenever Moses is read, a veil lies over their hearts, but whenever a person turns to the Lord, the veil is removed. Now the Lord is the Spirit, and where the Spirit of the Lord is, there is freedom.*
—2 Corinthians 3:15–17

---

Further Scripture: John 8:36; Acts 13:38–39; 2 Corinthians 3:4–6a

### *Week 23, Day 158: 2 Corinthians 4*
### Treasure in Clay Jars

Paul encouraged the Corinthian church *to not give up*. He understood they were pressured in every way from the outside, and yet they weren't crushed. They were perplexed, persecuted, and struck down, but they were not in despair, abandoned, or destroyed. Yes, from the outside, their momentary troubles appeared devastating. But what the Lord saw on the inside was *the unseen work of the Holy Spirit*. The Lord was producing an absolutely incomparable eternal weight of glory.

Perhaps you feel like giving up today. Debt is mounting, your health problem seems incurable, you're facing devastation in your marriage, or you feel so much sadness and grief that you don't want to lift your head out of bed. *Don't give up, friend.* Press on. Keep going. Get up. God's power is at work *inside you*. You are His vessel. Yes, you have cracks, imperfections, and hardships, but you are beautifully and wonderfully made this way! These cracks enable the power of God, His strength and love, to shine through you to others. Hang on to the *hope* you have in Christ. God's power is at work within you! *Don't give up!* You will make it through!

---

*Therefore we do not give up. Even though our outer person is being destroyed, our inner person is being renewed day by day.*
—2 Corinthians 4:16

---

Further Scripture: 2 Corinthians 4:7–9, 17–18; Galatians 6:9

### *Week 23, Day 159: 2 Corinthians 5*
### Walk by Faith

Paul challenged the Corinthians believers to *walk by faith, not by sight.* Faith is complete trust or confidence in someone or something. As a believer, you can have 100-percent complete confidence and trust in God. This requires you to let go of control and accept you are not all-knowing. Imagine yourself with a blindfold on, taking steps forward, and trusting the ground will be there as you take each step. However, perhaps there are holes in the ground. Faith is believing you will have the help you need even in the midst of the holes. *You will have help to keep on walking.*

It is time for you, child of God, to *walk by faith and not by sight.* God promises He will be there. He will never leave you. Jesus says rest in Him because you can do nothing apart from Him. God promises by faith you will do even greater things than Jesus, above and beyond what you can even imagine. So today, what is one action of faith you can take a step forward in? It may feel scary and unsettling, but most likely, that is the step of faith you need to take today. Trust that the Lord will help you navigate the unknowns ahead. Let go and let God.

---

*For we walk by faith, not by sight.* —2 Corinthians 5:7

---

Further Scripture: John 14:12; 15:5; Hebrews 11:1

### Week 23, Day 160: 2 Corinthians 6
## God's Ministers

As a follower of Christ, you are a new creation, and your old ways have passed away. God's grace is upon you, and you have the Holy Spirit to empower you to walk in a new way of life. As you do, you serve as an ambassador for the Lord, representing Christ to others. As God's minister, *you have a responsibility to reflect Christ*, regardless of hardships and afflictions. Yes, the Lord says hardships will come, just as they did for Paul. But even through the hard, reflect Christ with patience, kindness, purity, knowledge, and wisdom as the power of the Holy Spirit works through you. Show sincere love and convey the message of truth.

This may seem like a list of things to do, but Christ doesn't intend for you to take on a checklist. Rather walk this out with thanksgiving and joy in the Lord. Why? Because you are a new creation! Walk and rejoice in the power of the resurrected Savior. Walk in His saving grace. No matter how hard life may get, and all the Lord calls you to endure—*remember the Lord will give you His power through the Holy Spirit*. As an ambassador of God, walk by faith, trusting His grace will carry you through each step.

---

*We give no opportunity for stumbling to anyone, so that the ministry will not be blamed. But as God's ministers, we commend ourselves in everything.*
—2 Corinthians 6:3–4

---

Further Scripture: 2 Corinthians 5:17, 20; 6:4b–7a; 1 John 2:4–5

## *Week 23, Day 161: 2 Corinthians 7*
### Express Your Encouragement

Paul wrote about the reality of the Corinthian lifestyle and how painful his visit with the Corinthians church had been. *Paul also expressed gratitude.* Even though watching the Corinthians had been painful at times, Paul's ministry had not been in vain. The Corinthians were similar to the church today—*sinners saved by grace who were learning how to live by the Spirit in faith and not by works.* The Corinthians were learning to live as broken vessels with God's powerful treasure inside. Therefore, Paul spent time affirming his gratefulness that grief leads to repentance.

There may be people in your life who need encouragement and guidance on how to walk with the Lord. These people could be peers, coworkers, neighbors, or even your children. Allow Paul's affirming and encouraging words to the church remind you to affirm others with your love for them. Perhaps today you need to encourage someone in your life, even in your own family. Even when frustrated, point out something positive, instead of dwelling on negatives or weaknesses. Build others up. Take a minute to love those in your life deeply, without any strings attached. The Lord is at work regardless of any fruit you may or may not see. The Lord is working all things out for His purposes.

---

*I have great confidence in you; I have great pride in you. I am filled with encouragement; I am overcome with joy in all our afflictions.*
—2 Corinthians 7:4

---

Further Scripture: Romans 1:8; 2 Corinthians 7:9–10; 3 John 1:4

## Week 24, Day 162: 2 Corinthians 8
### The Motivation of Giving

Paul testified about the Corinthian church's generous spirit, even in the midst of their affliction and poverty. In a similar way, God sacrificially gave the world His Son Jesus. Jesus also demonstrated selfless, abundant giving as He gave up His life for the world so you could be saved from death and have eternal life.

As an imitator of Christ, you are called to give as Jesus gave—selflessly and generously. As a believer, the Lord calls you to offer your whole life to Him. Give of your finances, even when it makes you uncomfortable. Give of your time, even when your schedule is full. Always give of your life for the sake of the Gospel. *Generous giving involves giving as the Spirit leads in faithful obedience*, even when it doesn't make sense or resemble what others around you are doing. The Lord calls you to follow Him and to not conform to the pattern of the world. How is the Lord calling you to give obediently today? Remember to trust in the Lord's faithfulness as you give from a place of obedience!

---

*During a severe testing by affliction, their abundance of joy and their deep poverty overflowed into the wealth of their generosity.* —2 Corinthians 8:2

---

Further Scripture: Ephesians 5:1–2; James 1:17; 1 John 3:16

## *Week 24, Day 163: 2 Corinthians 9*
Ministry of Giving

When the Holy Spirit prompts you to give, obey His voice. The Lord promises the person who sows sparingly will reap sparingly, and the person who sows generously will reap generously. If the Lord prompts your heart to give a specific amount of money, then follow through and give. If the Lord prompts your heart to bring a meal to a family, drive a carpool, spend time at the food pantry, or lead a discipleship group, but you don't think you have the energy, wisdom, time, or talent to make it happen, stop rationalizing and *instead walk it out in obedience.* Remember, the Lord is able to make every grace overflow to you so that in *every way,* you will always have *everything you need,* and you may excel in *every good work.*

The ministry of giving involves *a step of faith.* The ministry of giving *requires sacrifice.* The ministry of giving *takes obedience.* The ministry of giving *expects an extra measure of grace and power from the Holy Spirit.* The Lord promises that as you walk with Him in obedience, *He will make a way.* So, start walking in obedient giving. The more you let go of yourself and your things, the more room the Lord has to move in your life beyond what you can imagine! You can never out give God. His love, His grace, and His power will continue to *overflow* in your life.

---

*Each person should do as he has decided in his heart—not reluctantly or out of necessity, for God loves a cheerful giver. And God is able to make every grace overflow to you, so that in every way, always having everything you need, you may excel in every good work.* —2 Corinthians 9:7–8

---

Further Scripture: Romans 15:13; Philippians 4:13; 1 Timothy 1:14

## *Week 24, Day 164: 2 Corinthians 10*
## Battling Spiritual Warfare

As a follower of Christ, you must realize, just like the Corinthian church, you are in a spiritual battle. It's not a battle against flesh and blood *but a spiritual battle against rulers, authorities, world powers of this darkness, and spiritual forces.* What the Lord intended for good, the enemy wants to defeat.

To fight the battle, you must be aware of the war raging against you. Then the Lord says to renew your mind daily because you need the truth to stand firm, to resist the enemy, and to hear the voice of the Lord. The voice of the Lord speaks truth and life. The more you read His Word, the more you will recognize the Lord's voice in battle. The enemy speaks lies to you: "You aren't good enough. You aren't worthy. You are rejected. You can't succeed." Paul instructed the Corinthian believers to *take every thought captive.* This means that when these lies creep in, *stand and proclaim God's Word and the truth*: "You are perfectly and wonderfully made. You are clothed in righteousness. You are worthy. You can do all things through Christ who gives you strength." Believe the truth will set you free, and the enemy's voice will flee. Then you will find victory in the battle. Today, practice taking every thought captive and proclaim Jesus in the middle of your battle. He is with you, and He is freedom!

---

*Since the weapons of our warfare are not worldly, but are powerful through God for the demolition of strongholds. We demolish arguments and every high-minded thing that is raised up against the knowledge of God, taking every thought captive to obey Christ.* —2 Corinthians 10:4–5

---

Further Scripture: John 8:3; 10:10; Ephesians 6:12

## *Week 24, Day 165: 2 Corinthians 11*
## Press On in Ministry

Paul cared for those he ministered to, and this deep love motivated him to press on through the most difficult of times. He told the church in Corinth: *I love you, like God loves you. I am weak. I am beaten up, and I have suffered much for you, all for the simple Gospel and the truth that transforms lives. But it is worth it.* The pressure and alienation Paul experienced didn't stop him. He pressed on for the sake of the Gospel so believers would follow the truth and not become wayward. Paul boasted only in the Lord, and the love he had for others kept him going.

Paul serves as an example to press on through hard times of ministry. You may minister in your home to your children, by teaching a Sunday school class, through leading a small group, serving the homeless, teaching from a large stage, or praying for others from your closet. As you follow Christ, the Lord will put people around you to love deeply. This great love will drive you, as it did Paul, to press on in your weakness, press on in the pressure, and press on in your weariness *for the sake of the Gospel.* The Lord has you right where you need to be for a reason. Remember, you are not alone. Recall your great love for those around you and the desire within you for them to know Jesus. The Lord will give you the strength to press on in His great love.

---

*As the truth of Christ is in me, this boasting of mine will not be stopped in the regions of Achaia. Why? Because I don't love you? God knows I do!*
—2 Corinthians 11:10–11

---

Further Scripture: Acts 20:24; 2 Corinthians 11:27–30; Galatians 6:9

### Week 24, Day 166: 2 Corinthians 12

Sufficient Grace

Paul discussed the thorn in his flesh, the thing the Lord allowed so Paul would remain weak and not exalt himself. He asked the Lord to take it away three times, and yet it remained. It may have been a physical ailment, a temptation, a constant need, or even persecution. It was through Paul's weakness that he discovered and understood that strength comes from the Lord, and God's grace is sufficient.

The world says, "You have to be strong and have it all together." But the Lord says, "*When you are weak, then I am strong.*" Stop trying to have it all together. Resist the temptation to be self-sufficient, strong, and independent. You don't need to hide your weaknesses. When you are weak, Christ is able to be strong within you. In your weakness, you allow His presence, power, and grace into your life. In your weakness, *His power is perfected because there is actually room to work.* Others will see Christ's power in your life, instead of your own strength. Therefore, you boast in the Lord and not in yourself. The Gospel is all about Jesus and His grace working through you. Relax in your weaknesses. Just take a deep breath and inhale a little of God's grace for your life. Then expect the Lord's strength to shine through you.

---

*But He said to me, "My grace is sufficient for you, for power is perfected in weakness." Therefore, I will most gladly boast all the more about my weaknesses, so that Christ's power may reside in me. So I take pleasure in weaknesses, insults, catastrophes, persecutions, and in pressures, because of Christ. For when I am weak, then I am strong.* —2 Corinthians 12:9–10

---

Further Scripture: Romans 11:6; 2 Corinthians 4:7; 12:7–8

### Week 24, Day 167: 2 Corinthians 13

Examine Yourself

Not many people look forward to their regular exam at the doctor, the dentist, or even taking their car in for a regular tune-up. They may think, *It's going to cost me money I don't want to spend. I think I'm fine, so why do I need to even go? What if I find out something is wrong? Then I have to deal with it!* However, after you go, you are usually thankful and relieved! Similarly, your faith in the Lord needs regular exams and check-ups as well.

As Paul ended his letter to the Corinthian church, he encouraged them to *examine themselves in the faith.* Examining your faith may look like meeting with a friend once a week to discuss Scripture, praying consistently with a prayer partner, or asking a close friend to hold you accountable concerning an area of temptation in your life. It may also look like regularly quieting yourself before the Lord and asking Him to search your heart for anything not aligned with Him. The Lord desires for you to rejoice, become mature in Him, remain encouraged, and feel peaceful. In order to grow spiritually, diligently set these regular "exams," whether you feel like it to or not. Take time to make an "appointment" with a friend or ask the Lord to examine your heart today. Just do it!

---

*Test yourselves to see if you are in the faith. Examine yourselves. Or do you yourselves not recognize that Jesus Christ is in you?—unless you fail the test.*
—2 Corinthians 13:5

---

Further Scripture: 1 Corinthians 11:28; 2 Corinthians 13:11; Galatians 6:4

## *Week 24, Day 168: Galatians 1*
### Turning Away so Quickly

Isn't it interesting how people seem confident, filled with faith, and ready to be bold for Christ with the Gospel as you pour into them? Yet sometimes you find that confident, bold person will quickly turn away from the message of the Gospel and the truth. It's as though the seed of the Gospel was snatched away from them! Even Paul found this to be the case as he ministered to others. He struggled with understanding how they could turn away so quickly.

Remember, the Lord asks you to plant the seeds of the Gospel. The reality is that some seeds will grow strong; some seeds will struggle to grow; some seeds will get plucked away by the schemes of the enemy. The enemy, the deceiver, is on the prowl. Although your spirit may be willing, the flesh is weak. As a believer, continue to stay strong in the Lord. Continue to keep your eyes on the author of your faith. Remain steadfast in Him. Strength will arise as you keep your focus on the one true Son, Jesus Christ.

---

*I am amazed that you are so quickly turning away from Him who called you by the grace of Christ and are turning to a different gospel—not that there is another gospel, but there are some who are troubling you and want to change the good news about the Messiah.* —Galatians 1:6–7

---

Further Scripture: Matthew 13:19; John 10:10; 2 Peter 3:17–18

## *Week 25, Day 169: Galatians 2*
### Righteousness in Christ

Christ died and set you free from bondage, from laws, from performance, and from striving in your own strength to please God. Christ gave Himself *for you*. If Christ died but you still needed to keep the law for righteousness and abide by rules, then Christ would have died in vain. Rather, Christ died to set you free. *Your righteousness is found in Christ alone.* Your ego, your ways of keeping rules, and your attempts to appear perfect *died with Christ*. Your life is no longer about you. Doing things in order to earn God's approval are over and have been put to *death with Christ*. Now Christ lives in you, and you are righteous in Him.

Remember, Jesus died because He loves you and chose to give His life for you. Believe you are worthy for Him to love. When you feel as though you are failing and can't keep up, cease striving. Christ didn't come to earth and die so you would have to try to keep up. It's not about striving for perfection. Life in Christ involves *resting in Him alone*. It's about walking freely by faith in the grace Jesus gives abundantly. You are free from the law. Walk in that freedom. Praise the Lord!

---

*For through the law I have died to the law, so that I might live for God. I have been crucified with Christ and I no longer live, but Christ lives in me. The life I now live in the body, I live by faith in the Son of God, who loved me and gave Himself for me.* —Galatians 2:19–20

---

Further Scripture: Galatians 2:21; Ephesians 3:12; 1 Peter 2:16

## Week 25, Day 170: Galatians 3
### Faith in Christ

Paul continued to emphasize to the Galatians that *believers are saved by faith alone and the righteous live by faith.* This faith comes by hearing the Word of God. The law of sin and death is no longer necessary. There is no longer a distinction between Jew and Greek, slave and free, male and female. The law of the Spirit is found in Christ. *You belong to Christ.* So *put on Jesus* like a piece of clothing every day and *walk in His Spirit.* It's the Spirit who works miracles in your life.

Spend time in the Scriptures because faith comes from hearing God's Word. God's power will become great within you. The Word of God leads you to Jesus. The Word of God leads you to the Spirit. Remember, through your faith in Christ, you are a son or daughter of the Most High King. You belong to Christ, you have freedom in Christ, and you are one in Christ.

---

*For as many of you as have been baptized into Christ have put on Christ like a garment. There is no Jew or Greek, slave or free, male or female; for you are all one in Christ Jesus. And if you belong to Christ, then you are Abraham's seed, heirs according to the promise.* —Galatians 3:27–29

---

Further Scripture: Romans 10:17; Galatians 3:11; 3:26

## Week 25, Day 171: Galatians 4
### Children and Heirs

*You are an heir of God the Father.* God is your father, your *Abba,* your heavenly daddy. You are no longer a slave to the law. You are no longer a slave to this world. You are no longer a slave to fear. You are no longer a slave to performing. Dear one, no matter what your life was like before Christ, as you believe in Him, *you are His child and receive an inheritance from Him, your heavenly Father.*

You may think: *I don't deserve this.* That is a lie from the enemy. You are worthy of all the glorious riches from your heavenly Father. He has a great love for you, the love of a father. You are a child of God, adopted into His family. *You are wanted.* You are chosen. You are worthy. You are an heir through Christ. So, when you feel as though you are not enough, when you feel you have no family and are alone, remember to stand on this truth—*You are an heir of God the Father.*

---

*And because you are sons, God has sent the Spirit of His Son into our hearts, crying, "Abba, Father!" So you are no longer a slave but a son, and if a son, then an heir through God.* —Galatians 4:6–7

---

Further Scripture: 2 Corinthians 6:18; Galatians 4:1; 1 John 3:1–2

### *Week 25, Day 172: Galatians 5*

## Walk by the Spirit

Christ came to *set you free,* allowing you to *live in the Spirit, not the flesh.* The fleshly deeds include idolatry, strife, jealousy, outbursts of anger, dissensions, envy, and drunkenness. If your life shows any of these signs, then Paul says you are living in your flesh. You can't walk in both the Spirit and the flesh.

Imagine walking in the Spirit as a bumper car ride. Your bumper car connects by a metal bar to the power supply in the ceiling. As you drive your bumper car, the car is powered from above. The car won't move unless the power source and the bar are connected. In a similar way, your power to bear the fruit of the Spirit comes from the Holy Spirit. As you keep in step with Him, *His power flows through you* to produce fruit: love, joy, peace, patience, kindness, goodness, faithfulness, gentleness, and self-control. Ask yourself: *Am I connected to the power source and bearing fruit? Or am I striving on my own and continuing to produce the deeds of the flesh?* Today, stay connected to the power of the Holy Spirit and begin to watch the flesh fade away while His fruit remains in your life.

---

*But the fruit of the Spirit is love, joy, peace, patience, kindness, goodness, faith, gentleness, self-control. Against such things there is no law. Now those who belong to Christ Jesus have crucified the flesh with its passions and desires. Since we live by the Spirit, we must also follow the Spirit.*
—Galatians 5:22–25

---

Further Scripture: John 15:4–5; Galatians 5:1; Ephesians 5:18–20

## *Week 25, Day 173: Galatians 6*
### Spiritual Restoration

When you see a brother or sister in Christ sin, it can make you uncomfortable. Most people don't like others holding them accountable or confronting them in their sin pattern. However, as a follower of Christ, you are called to do this. So what do you do? When you feel led to confront a brother or sister in sin and help them seek restoration, ask yourself: *Am I fearing God or fearing man in this situation? Am I walking in the Spirit or walking in the law?*

As you walk in the Spirit, the Spirit will supernaturally lead *you to restore others with gentleness and love in just the right timing.* Walk with courage, and allow the Spirit to lead you, never quenching His influence in your life. Your role in the kingdom of God involves *holding others accountable and bearing their burdens with the love of Christ.* Can you imagine the difference gentle and loving accountability could make in the kingdom of God? Don't be afraid. If the Spirit is leading you, then most likely He is also preparing the other person's heart. That's the supernatural work of the Spirit and God's abundant grace producing unity.

---

*Brothers, if someone is caught in any wrongdoing, you who are spiritual should restore such a person with a gentle spirit, watching out for yourselves so you also won't be tempted. Carry one another's burdens; in this way you will fulfill the law of Christ.* —Galatians 6:1–2

---

Further Scripture: Psalm 56:4; Galatians 6:9–10; James 5:19–20

## *Week 25, Day 174: Ephesians 1*
### The Work of the Trinity

God sent Jesus Christ into the world as a free gift for you to receive. Your heavenly Father is the giver of every good and perfect gift. When you believe in Jesus, you receive redemption through His blood, forgiveness of your trespasses, and the indwelling of the Holy Spirit. Because God—as Father, Son, and Holy Spirit—is rich in grace, He *lavishes grace after grace upon you.* Today, you need to believe the truth that you are worthy to receive His lavish grace. Lavish means *amazingly rich, elaborate, or luxurious.* Many parents desire to lavish their children with good gifts of all types and sizes. Your heavenly Father *is able* to do abundantly more than you can even imagine. He chooses to lavish you with what He knows you need most of all—grace with all wisdom and understanding.

Stand and receive this truth today. Your heavenly Father delights in showering you with gifts. He gushes over you with grace, wisdom, and understanding. Lift up your hands and receive His wonderful gifts!

---

*We have redemption in Him through His blood, the forgiveness of our trespasses, according to the riches of His grace that He lavished on us with all wisdom and understanding.* —Ephesians 1:7–8

---

Further Scripture: John 1:16–17; Ephesians 3:20; 2 Peter 1:2

## *Week 25, Day 175: Ephesians 2*
Jesus Is Peace

God, who is rich in mercy and lavish in His grace, is also your peace. Christ came to be peace to those who believe by faith. When you rest in the Lord alone, when you cease striving, when you take a deep breath and humbly surrender your will with thanks, then *Christ will be your peace*. Open your hands and lift them up. Pray to the Lord: "*I believe in You. I receive Your mercy. I receive Your grace. I receive Your love.*"

God has everything in His hands—the issues, the worries, the problems, and the heartaches. Christ came so you may have peace. He is the one and only true assurance for peace in your life, the only authentic peace found in this world. Only Jesus. Nothing else will bring you peace. Nothing. Therefore, stop searching and receive Him. Then slow down long enough to rest in His peace. Give Him thanks at all times for His peace.

---

*For He is our peace, who made both groups one and tore down the dividing wall of hostility.* —Ephesians 2:14

---

Further Scripture: Psalm 85:8; John 16:33; Ephesians 2:17

## Week 26, Day 176: Ephesians 3
Kneeling Prayer

Paul knelt before God the Father and prayed for believers to be strengthened with power through the Holy Spirit. He wanted them to understand and comprehend God's vast love for them and be filled with the fullness of God. Paul cared for the spiritual health of the believers in Ephesus. He knew they could easily become discouraged, so he pressed in, got on his knees, and cried out honestly for believers.

Have you ever knelt while praying? If Paul modeled praying on his knees for those he cared about, then it may be wise to try it the next time you pray. Kneeling involves humility. It may make you physically uncomfortable or even self-conscience in a public setting. You are to give *everything* to Christ—*even do the uncomfortable things*. Kneel before the Lord and pray to Him, believing He is able to do above and beyond what you can ask or think according to His power at work within you. Bring Him all your worries for the day and ask Him to fill you with power through the Holy Spirit. Perhaps make kneeling prayer a new routine!

---

*For this reason I kneel before the Father from whom every family in heaven and on earth is named.* —Ephesians 3:14–15

---

Further Scripture: Psalm 95:6; Ephesians 3:20–21; Philippians 2:9–11

## *Week 26, Day 177: Ephesians 4*
## Worthy of the Calling

As a believer, God desires you to live a life worthy of the calling you have received. You may think to yourself, *I don't even know my calling!* In general, Jesus instructed believers to seek first the kingdom of God as you love God and love others. God may have other specific callings and tasks of obedience for you along the way, but begin with first seeking the kingdom of God daily. Jesus says the world will know of His great love as Savior when believers live in unity. Unity is a key in the kingdom of God.

A supernatural power and beauty ignite in the kingdom when believers walk out their specific gifts with humility and love. So how do you foster and uphold unity of the Spirit? *Walk in humility, gentleness, and patience, accept each other with love, and be diligent to keep peace.* It's as though Paul gave believers a recipe for unity. With humility, recognize you can't walk this out in your own strength. Ask the Lord to fill you up with the power of the Holy Spirit, and see what happens. There is no way to have unity of the Spirit without walking in humility.

---

*Therefore I, the prisoner for the Lord, urge you to walk worthy of the calling you have received, with all humility and gentleness, with patience, accepting one another in love, diligently keeping the unity of the Spirit with the peace that binds us.* —Ephesians 4:1–3

---

Further Scripture: 2 Chronicles 7:14; 1 Corinthians 1:10; 1 Peter 5:5–6

## *Week 26, Day 178: Ephesians 5*
## Walk in Love and Light

Have you ever seen a little child wear a pair of their daddy's shoes and attempt to walk around, pretending to be his or her daddy? It can look kind of clumsy and funny, but the *heart of the child longs to walk like his or her daddy.* In a similar way, as a follower of Christ, you are to *imitate your heavenly Father.* You are to walk in love and light just as Christ the Messiah loved you and sacrificed His life as a fragrant offering to God. What does it look like for you to walk selflessly in love and light? Be wise, not unwise. Think about others first, not just what's best for you. Don't be foolish but understand what God's will is. Be filled with the Spirit. Give thanks and praise to the Lord. Fear the Lord, not man. Walk in the light of Christ, not in darkness.

Today, imagine putting on the shoes of your heavenly Father, and, as you walk in His shoes, *imitate His love.* It may feel clumsy at first, but with time as you grow, it will feel more natural, and the love of your heavenly Father will overflow from your life. *Walk in His love* so you can *walk out His love.*

---

*Therefore, be imitators of God, as dearly loved children. And walk in love, as the Messiah also loved us and gave Himself for us, a sacrificial and fragrant offering to God.* —Ephesians 5:1–2

---

Further Scripture: Ephesians 5:15–21; 1 Peter 1:14–16; 1 John 1:6–7

## *Week 26, Day 179: Ephesians 6*
Put on the Armor of God

Remember you are in a spiritual battle as a follower of Christ. This battle is not against flesh and blood but against the spiritual forces of evil in the heavens. The devil schemes against you to steal, kill, and destroy everything in your life as you seek to bring glory to the Lord. He wants your time, your joy, your unity, your strength, and your thoughts.

In the midst of the battle, the Lord calls upon you to *stand strong* against the schemes of the devil. The Lord gives you spiritual armor to protect against the tactics of the devil. When the enemy goes after your marriage or your parenting, your children, or your ministry, walk with the sandals of readiness and the gospel of peace. When fiery darts of doubt enter your mind, hold up your shield of faith. The Lord your God is mighty within you. Walk in the power of the Spirit. You have victory! Don't get discouraged and give in! *Instead, be strengthened by the Lord and keep your armor on.* When you forget to put on your armor, or when you don't invite the Lord into your battle, you will grow weary. Therefore, *set your mind on Christ.* The enemy's schemes are defeated in Jesus' mighty name.

---

*Finally, be strengthened by the Lord and by His vast strength. Put on the full armor of God so that you can stand against the tactics of the Devil. For our battle is not against flesh and blood, but against the rulers, against the authorities, against the world powers of this darkness, against the spiritual forces of evil in the heavens.* —Ephesians 6:10–12

---

Further Scripture: 2 Corinthians 10:3–5; Ephesians 6:4; 6:13–17

## *Week 26, Day 180: Philippians 1*
Partnership in the Gospel

The church of Philippi encouraged and supported Paul during his ministry. As Paul wrote to them, he remembered them with joy and gave thanks to the Lord for them because of their partnership in the Gospel.

Today, think back over your walk with the Lord. Remember those people in your life who encouraged and supported your growth in the Lord. You don't have to be a full-time missionary to have people partner with you in the Gospel. Perhaps a youth pastor, a teacher at school, a friend from work, or an older sibling encouraged your walk with the Lord. *Take time today to thank the Lord for their partnership in your life.* Next pray for them. Pray for their love to continue to grow in knowledge and discernment so that they can continue to approve the things that are superior, pure, and blameless. Pray they are filled with the fruit of righteousness that comes through Jesus Christ. Then, take time to write them a note or send a quick text letting them know you give thanks to God every time you remember them and the impact they had on your life.

---

*I give thanks to my God for every remembrance of you, always praying with joy for all of you in my every prayer, because of your partnership in the gospel from the first day until now.* —Philippians 1:3–5

---

Further Scripture: Philippians 1:9–11; 2 Timothy 2:1–2; Titus 2:3–4

## *Week 26, Day 181: Philippians 2*
## Humility Like Jesus

"Consider others as more important than yourselves." These words from Paul are pretty countercultural. Everything in today's culture says: me first, bigger, more, better, improve yourself, help yourself, and strengthen yourself. And yet the Lord says, *make your attitude like Jesus.* Jesus humbled Himself. He submitted to walk in obedience to the point of death, something He certainly didn't earn or deserve. He put the needs of the entire world above His own life and gave everything up. That's the attitude of Jesus—completely surrendered in humility.

As you go through your day, ask yourself: *Am I considering others more important than myself? Am I walking in humility? Am I looking out for others' interests and not just my own?* It can be convicting. However, this perspective puts people and tasks in proper alignment. Hold the door open for someone or be the last person to get in line. Pause before you speak and listen to hear the heart of a person. Act in obedience, even if it means giving up your schedule. Do something without being recognized. The Lord says to humble yourself, and in due time, the Lord will lift you up. Rest in this promise.

---

*Do nothing out of rivalry or conceit, but in humility consider others as more important than yourselves. Everyone should look out not only for his own interests, but also for the interests of others.* —Philippians 2:3–5

---

Further Scripture: Philippians 2:5–8; James 4:6; 1 Peter 5:6–7

## Week 26, Day 182: Philippians 3
### Reaching for the Goal

Are you a person with goals? After Jesus transformed Paul, his life was no longer about his accomplishments and achievements. He considered those a loss compared to knowing Jesus Christ his Lord. Paul clearly stated his life goals: *knowing Jesus personally, experiencing the power of the resurrection, partnering with Jesus' suffering, and being conformed even to His death.*

As you go through life, the world may entice you to set goals for your career, to achieve a certain lifestyle, to travel with your family, or even for retirement. However, Paul emphasized, none of "the stuff" really mattered to him for his own life. He had one thing on his mind and that was *to know Jesus Christ fully*—even if knowing Christ fully meant suffering, dying to himself daily, or physically dying. Paul desired to live out the resurrected power of Jesus every day of his life. He didn't look back but focused on the future instead. Today, ask the Lord to reveal to you a goal for your life. As you fix your eyes on Jesus, *what's your one thing?* Write it down, post it where you will see it, and then ask the Lord to help you go after it.

*My goal is to know Him and the power of His resurrection and the fellowship of His sufferings, being conformed to His death, assuming that I will somehow reach the resurrection from among the dead.*
—Philippians 3:10–11

Further Scripture: Psalm 27:4; Matthew 6:33; Philippians 3:13–14

## *Week 27, Day 183: Philippians 4*
Worry About Nothing

Peace comes from Jesus. You can search the entire world, but only Jesus' peace will satisfy. To paraphrase Paul's words, "Don't worry. Pray. Give thanks. Make your requests known to God." Then begin to praise and thank the Lord. It's from this place of humility, surrender, and gratefulness that the God of peace will come upon you. Is it a formula? No. Is it law? No. It's a promise. Paul says, "*Do what you have learned, received, heard and seen in me, and the God of peace will be with you.*"

Each day may bring new things to worry about—the "what ifs" and "I don't knows" of life. But remember, nothing good comes from worrying. Really. So just stop. Make your requests known to God. From that moment on, just give thanks. Focus your thoughts on whatever is true, honorable, just, pure, lovely, commendable, and morally excellent. Don't waste your time thinking about the junk you worry about! As you focus on what is lovely and true, Jesus' peace will come. Try it today, and witness the Lord transform your mind and your heart.

---

*Don't worry about anything, but in everything, through prayer and petition with thanksgiving, let your requests be made known to God. And the peace of God, which surpasses every thought, will guard your hearts and minds in Christ Jesus.* —Philippians 4:6–7

---

Further Scripture: Matthew 6:34; Ephesians 5:20; Philippians 4:8–9

### Week 27, Day 184: Colossians 1

## He Holds It All Together

Sometimes in this crazy world where truth becomes blurred, *you need to refocus.* What is actual truth? Go back to God's Word to strengthen and establish what you believe. Paul went back to the basics with the church in Colossae. He emphasized Christ is supreme over creation because *He created everything.* Yes, God created everything in heaven and on earth, the invisible and the visible—thrones, dominions, rulers, and authorities. Truth to remember: *God created everything.*

When things in your life seem overwhelming, remember, as the firstborn over all creation, *Christ is before all things, and by Him all things hold together.* Truth to remember: *Jesus holds all things together.* He is there in the mess. He is there in the joy. Jesus is holding all things together at all times. He holds things together because He loves you, He cares for you, and *He created it all.* Try to picture God holding all things together in your life. Trust God to be the superglue and rubber band for your life. He's with you, holding all things together in your life because His love for you will never fail.

---

*For everything was created by Him,*
*in heaven and on earth,*
*the visible and the invisible,*
*whether thrones or dominions*
*or rulers or authorities—*
*all things have been created through Him and for Him.*
*He is before all things,*
*and by Him all things hold together.* —Colossians 1:16–17

---

Further Scripture: John 1:2–3; Romans 8:28; Hebrews 1:1–3

## *Week 27, Day 185: Colossians 2*
### Walk with Jesus

After you receive Christ, you begin to walk with Him and grow in the mystery of the Gospel. Like a student studying to become a teacher, a doctor, or a hairstylist, the time comes when you need to walk out what you have learned. Though you will never stop learning, it's time to start using your skills. As a believer who has accepted Christ as Lord and Savior, *start walking in faith as the Lord leads, trusting the Holy Spirit to fill you with all wisdom and knowledge.*

The more you walk in Christ's strength and not your own, *the deeper your roots grow in Him.* The storms may come, but they won't blow you over! You will not be shaken because you are established in your faith. Abide in Christ's presence in order to nourish your roots in Him. Walk with an attitude of praise and thanksgiving, worshipping the Lord your Savior. As you worship the Lord, the peace of Christ will be with you, providing what you need for what lies ahead.

---

*Therefore, as you have received Christ Jesus the Lord, walk in Him, rooted and built up in Him and established in the faith, just as you were taught, overflowing with gratitude.* —Colossians 2:6–7

---

Further Scripture: Jeremiah 17:7–8; Romans 10:9–10; Colossians 2:2

### *Week 27, Day 186: Colossians 3*
## Put on Love

Child of God, you are chosen. You are holy. You are loved. Let that soak in just a minute. Receive these promises over your life today. You don't have a reason to doubt or question. The enemy will put lies in your mind but take those thoughts captive. Believe this today: *You are chosen. You are holy. You are loved.*

Now because you walk with these promises over your life, you have a responsibility to represent Christ's love—to be His hands and feet to others. Therefore put on *compassion, kindness, humility, gentleness, patience,* and *forgiveness.* Put them on like clothing each day! And above all this, *put on love, which binds everything in unity. Above all, love.* Love others just as you have been loved. Remember, you received Christ's love as a gift. Jesus received you just as you are with an unconditional love. He modeled how you are to love others. No matter what you face today, *put on love,* remembering you walk as a chosen, holy, and loved child of God.

---

*Therefore, God's chosen ones, holy and loved, put on heartfelt compassion, kindness, humility, gentleness, and patience, accepting one another and forgiving one another if anyone has a complaint against another. Just as the Lord has forgiven you, so you must also forgive. Above all, put on love—the perfect bond of unity.* —Colossians 3:12–14

---

Further Scripture: 1 Corinthians 13:1; Ephesians 2:8–9; 1 John 5:2–3

## *Week 27, Day 187: Colossians 4*
Walk with Teammates

Paul wrote this letter to the Colossian believers while imprisoned for declaring the Gospel message. As he concluded the letter, Paul mentioned several of his coworkers in ministry. Paul was not alone; he had other people alongside him, walking out their faith and using their gifts as ambassadors for the Gospel. For example, Tychicus and Onesimus were sent with news about Paul as encouragement. And Paul's teammate, Epaphras, continued to pray for the believers. Paul cared deeply for the believers and gathered like-minded people to help him in his calling.

No matter how you serve the Lord with the gifts He has given you, *surround yourself with others to help walk out your calling.* If you don't have anyone, ask the Lord to provide someone to help you, someone to pray for you, and someone to sharpen you. Just as iron sharpens iron, the Lord created you to work with others to sharpen your own faith. Devote yourself to prayer and continue to give thanks for open doors for the message of Jesus Christ.

---

*I have sent him to you for this very purpose, so that you may know how we are and so that he may encourage your hearts. He is with Onesimus, a faithful and dearly loved brother, who is one of you. They will tell you about everything here.* —Colossians 4:8–9

---

Further Scripture: Colossians 4:12–13; 1 Peter 4:10; 3 John 1:8

## *Week 27, Day 188: 1 Thessalonians 1*
## Gospel Comes with the Holy Spirit

When you share the Gospel with others, you don't share with just words and methods. You testify with the Holy Spirit's power and passion. Christ's power transforms lives. As the Lord leads you to share the Gospel, remember it's not about you or how well you articulate the message. It's the passion, it's the testimony, and it's the Holy Spirit's presence and power *working through you and working in the lives of those listening* to the good news. *The Holy Spirit touches hearts*, not the fancy words.

It's in the moments when the Holy Spirit's power moves that lives will change. Therefore, live out your testimony to others. When you walk in obedience—when you walk in the power of the Holy Spirit, the message of your faith in God will travel. If you want to see change in your community, in your family, or in your marriage, then walk in the power of the Holy Spirit with deep conviction, in humility, in faith, in love, and in hope. As you endure all things, the Holy Spirit's power will touch and transform lives!

---

*For our gospel did not come to you in word only, but also in power, in the Holy Spirit, and with much assurance. You know what kind of men we were among you for your benefit. . . . For the Lord's message rang out from you, not only in Macedonia and Achaia, but in every place that your faith in God has gone out.* —1 Thessalonians 1:5, 8

---

Further Scripture: 1 Corinthians 2:4; 1 Thessalonians 1:3; 2 Timothy 1:7–8

*Week 27, Day 189: 1 Thessalonians 2*

Entrusted to Speak the Gospel

Just as the Lord led Paul to share the Gospel, the Lord will lead you to share the Gospel with others. As you go, remember to walk in obedience to the Lord. Don't focus on pleasing others. Don't worry about what others will even think of you. Rather, follow the voice of the Lord. If He is nudging you to share truth, to love someone with His love, to be His hands and feet in a specific way, *then follow that voice.* Fear the Lord, not others.

Oftentimes you feel a nudge to say or do something, but all kinds of "what ifs" and "I don't knows" pop into your mind discouraging you. Press on and *listen to the voice* of the Lord, which will always align with the Word of God. Walk obediently with pure motives, and you will see the Lord. God wants to move in your life and in others' lives in ways you can't imagine! Have a heart that cares enough for others to walk obediently to the Lord's voice!

---

*For our exhortation didn't come from error or impurity or an intent to deceive. Instead, just as we have been approved by God to be entrusted with the gospel, so we speak, not to please men, but rather God, who examines our hearts.* —1 Thessalonians 2:3–4

---

Further Scripture: Proverbs 29:25; Isaiah 30:21; 1 Thessalonians 2:8, 11–12

### Week 28, Day 190: 1 Thessalonians 3
## Encouraging and Praying for the Church

Paul and Silas intentionally sent Timothy to the Thessalonian church to help strengthen and encourage the believers there out of care and concern for them and their faith. Timothy returned with great reports of their strong faith, even amidst expected persecution. Paul continued to pray for them and encouraged them to stand firm in the Lord.

As believers, speaking words of encouragement is critical. How often do you take time to encourage a missionary or a pastor, a spouse, child, friend, or coworker? Encouragement brings life to a person's soul. As a believer, stand firm and speak life, hope, and encouragement to others. Today, take a few minutes to encourage and pray for someone the Lord puts on your heart. Call them or write them a note. As a guide, follow Paul's prayer for the Thessalonian church: *"May the Lord cause* [insert person's name here] *to increase and overflow with love for one another and for everyone, just as you also do for* [insert person's name here]. *May He make* [insert person's name here]*'s heart blameless in holiness before our God and Father at the coming of our Lord Jesus with all His saints. Amen."*

---

*But now Timothy has come to us from you and brought us good news about your faith and love and reported that you always have good memories of us, wanting to see us, as we also want to see you. Therefore, brothers, in all our distress and persecution, we were encouraged about you through your faith.*
—1 Thessalonians 3:6–7

---

Further Scripture: 1 Thessalonians 3:12–13; Hebrews 3:13; 10:24–25

## *Week 28, Day 191: 1 Thessalonians 4*
## Call to Sanctification and Comfort of Christ's Coming

Paul cared deeply about the church and encouraged them to walk and please God and to live a life of sanctification, not of impurity. He encouraged them because Jesus will return one day, and *Paul longed for the church to live ready for Jesus' return.*

The same is true today! Are you living ready for Jesus' return? As a believer, God called you to *grow in Him,* which is the process of sanctification. As a believer, you are set apart, you are righteous, you are holy, you are forgiven, and your sins have been removed. But even as a follower of Christ, temptations come your way. Sexual impurity and immorality remain rampant in today's culture, just as it was in Paul's. Even still, you are called to resist and flee from impurities, stand firm, and run toward growing in Christ. Don't mess with things in the flesh. Don't mess with momentary satisfaction. Abstain from sexual immorality. *Seek sanctification. This is God's will for your life.* In doing so, you will be ready for Jesus' return. Make today matter for the kingdom by not giving into impure temptations. His return is coming. *Be ready.*

---

*For this is God's will, your sanctification: that you abstain from sexual immorality, so that each of you knows how to control his own body in sanctification and honor, not with lustful desires, like the Gentiles who don't know God.* —1 Thessalonians 4:3–5

---

Further Scripture: Luke 12:40; 1 Thessalonians 4:7, 15–17

### *Week 28, Day 192: 1 Thessalonians 5*
### Live Ready

Jesus is returning. That is a fact. You just don't know exactly when. Paul thought it would be in his lifetime. You may think it will be in your lifetime. The question to ask is . . . *are you living as though Jesus could return today?* You are called to *live ready* for His return. Are you walking in the light or the darkness? Are you awake or sleeping as a follower of Christ? Are you filled with the Spirit or drunk and unaware? Are you equipped for the battle that wages war around you? Paul made it pretty clear: *Live in the light. Stay awake and be serious for Jesus. Put on the armor of faith. You are in a battle.* It's real, and it's happening. If you had a houseguest arriving tonight, wouldn't you get ready? The same is true for Christ's return. *Live ready!*

How do you live ready? God longs for you to pursue what is good for one another. God's will is for you to rejoice always, pray constantly, and give thanks in everything. As you prepare yourself for Jesus' return, focus on these things: rejoicing, praying, and giving thanks. By doing so every day, you will be ready for His return and others will see the light of Christ in you. Live ready!

---

*For you are all sons of light and sons of the day. We do not belong to the night or the darkness. So then, we must not sleep, like the rest, but we must stay awake and be serious. For those who sleep, sleep at night, and those who get drunk are drunk at night. But since we belong to the day, we must be serious and put the armor of faith and love on our chests, and put on a helmet of the hope of salvation.* —1 Thessalonians 5:5–8

---

Further Scripture: Matthew 24:27; Romans 13:12; 1 Thessalonians 5:16–18

## *Week 28, Day 193: 2 Thessalonians 1*
Well Done!

Paul validated the faith of the Thessalonian church and the persecution and afflictions they endured. He boasted and testified about their faith to others. Paul also continued to pray and encourage the church to press on and do the work of the Lord because eternity was at stake.

You may be facing persecution right now from family members who don't understand why you are walking by faith and following Christ. You may face insults from friends who want you to join the crowd or do perverse or impure actions. Yet you choose to remain pure in your body and in your thoughts. You need to hear . . . *well done!* Even in the midst of this culture, *stay strong, friend.* Remember you are worthy of your calling. The Lord will strengthen you with power so you can press on in faith, sharing the good news with those around you. Christ is glorified in and through you. *Do not give up.* God's judgment is coming; therefore, press on, go, and share His love with others in the strength of Jesus Christ!

---

*We must always thank God for you, brothers. This is right, since your faith is flourishing and the love each one of you has for one another is increasing. Therefore, we ourselves boast about you among God's churches—about your endurance and faith in all the persecutions and afflictions you endure.*
—2 Thessalonians 1:3–4

---

Further Scripture: Matthew 5:11–12; Acts 1:8; 2 Thessalonians 1:11–12

### *Week 28, Day 194: 2 Thessalonians 2*
### Stand Firm

Paul continued to warn believers about the end times. He specifically cautioned about the coming of the antichrist—the lawless one, based on Satan's working, who would come with all kinds of false miracles, signs, and wonders. When you hear of the antichrist, the lawless one, or false miracles, signs and wonders, *do not fear.* Don't worry. Don't question the power or the working of Jesus, the Resurrected Savior. Fear is the reaction Satan wants you to have, the place he wants to deceive you to stay in.

As a believer, stay informed and alert about the end times and the types of deception, lawlessness, and evil on the horizon. *But do not fear.* Rather, continue to thank God for His love for you. *Stand firm and hold on to the truth you have been taught.* God chose you for salvation through sanctification by the Spirit and through believing in the truth. Walk out your calling. The Lord's presence and power will never leave you as you walk with Him. He will give you everything you need for the day the lawless one comes. You will find victory in God alone! Therefore, walk in that victory!

---

*For the mystery of lawlessness is already at work, but the one now restraining will do so until he is out of the way, and then the lawless one will be revealed. The Lord Jesus will destroy him with the breath of His mouth and will bring him to nothing with the brightness of His coming. The coming of the lawless one is based on Satan's working, with all kinds of false miracles, signs, and wonders.* —2 Thessalonians 2:7–9

---

Further Scripture: Luke 12:25; Romans 8:38–39; 2 Thessalonians 2:13–15

## *Week 28, Day 195: 2 Thessalonians 3*
### But the Lord Is Faithful

"But the Lord is faithful." No matter what evil men do, no matter what life brings, no matter when the Lord returns, Paul reaffirmed this message to the Thessalonian church: The Lord is faithful. God is faithful to strengthen you and guard your heart from the evil one.

You may need to be reminded today of this simple yet powerful truth: But the Lord is faithful. You may be facing an outstanding medical bill you just don't know how you will pay—*but the Lord is faithful.* You may have a child whose heart seems to be swept away by culture and lies from the enemy—*but the Lord is faithful.* You may be dealing with a marriage, a relationship, a business, or a dream that seems to be failing—*but the Lord is faithful.* As you press on and seek the Lord in all your ways, the Lord will be faithful. He has promised that He will be faithful for a thousand generations! Whatever the weight on your shoulders may be, remember God's promise—*He is faithful.* God will walk with you. God will give you strength. God will guard you as you go. God will direct your heart to love and grant you endurance to press on. Hold on to His faithfulness through it all. *He is faithful.*

---

*But the Lord is faithful.* —2 Thessalonians 3:3

---

Further Scripture: Deuteronomy 7:9; 1 Corinthians 1:9; 2 Thessalonians 3:3b–5

### Week 28, Day 196: 1 Timothy 1

## You Have a Testimony

In this letter of advice to Timothy, Paul remembered his life before Christ. He remembered his days as a blasphemer, a persecutor, and an arrogant man. He shared his testimony so others would know about the grace and mercy he received from Jesus Christ, his Lord. *Because Paul testified to others*, his testimony of God's mercy *impacted and transformed* others' lives for eternity, bringing honor and glory to God.

If you have received Jesus as your Savior, then like Paul, you have a testimony. You have a story about who you were before Christ and who you are now after Christ. Not everyone has the same story. You may think, *My story isn't as dramatic as Paul's.* Don't compare! Guess who wrote your story? Jesus. He's the author and perfecter of your faith. If you question your testimony, you are questioning God's story in your life. Fill in the blanks to help you begin: "I give thanks to Christ Jesus my Lord who has strengthened me, because He considered me faithful—I was formerly a [fill in the blank] and [fill in the blank] person. But I received mercy. I am a new person in Christ." Now, *go and share your story* with at least one other person! Share from your heart the story the Lord has written and the mercy He has had on your life.

---

*I give thanks to Christ Jesus our Lord who has strengthened me, because He considered me faithful, appointing me to the ministry—one who was formerly a blasphemer, a persecutor, and an arrogant man. But I received mercy because I acted out of ignorance in unbelief.* —1 Timothy 1:12–13

---

Further Scripture: Psalm 66:16; Mark 5:19; 1 Timothy 1:16

## Week 29, Day 197: 1 Timothy 2
### Instructions for Prayer

Paul instructed Timothy on how to fight the spiritual battle the church faced as it followed Christ. He told Timothy to pray—petitions, prayer, intercession, and thanksgiving. Paul said to pray every kind of prayer. Paul urged the church to pray for everyone: authorities, outsiders, family, friends, enemies, and those who persecute others. You have the responsibility to pray for everyone. Why? Because it is good, and it pleases God.

Today, *take time to pray for others.* Try setting a timer for ten minutes and commit to pray during that time. Ask the Lord to bring specific people to your mind and make a list of names. Then pray all kinds of prayers.

**Petitions**: Ask in bold confidence from God's Word.

**Prayer**: Communicate to the Lord, your heavenly Father.

**Intercession**: Lift up the needs of others before the Lord.

**Thanksgiving**: Thank the Lord for everyone, even recalling His mighty attributes and answered prayers.

Pray for others as you press on in the spiritual battle. Prayer pleases God as He longs for all to be saved and know the truth.

---

*First of all, then, I urge that petitions, prayers, intercessions, and thanksgivings be made for everyone.* —1 Timothy 2:1

---

Further Scripture: Matthew 5:44; Ephesians 6:18; 1 Timothy 2:3–4

### *Week 29, Day 198: 1 Timothy 3*
### Household of Peace

God is a God of order and peace. Therefore, Paul instructed the church regarding the order and expectations for church leadership—the elders and deacons. At first glance it may appear like a checklist of how to behave and conduct yourself so you can become a church leader. Paul spoke frankly when he said those who can't manage their own households can't be expected to lead and manage a church body. Even so, Paul's heart reflected God's heart—*to maintain peace in God's household, the church of the living God, the pillar and foundation of truth.*

When your life possesses the qualities Paul listed for church leadership, it's an outward sign of your inward relationship with the Lord. Your life reflects your love and devotion to following Christ. This is important for church leadership because the God of peace and order understands a leader in the church must be strong in the Lord in leading his own household. As you follow God with everything in you, He gives you all you need to lead a godly life. Your household will actually reflect God's peace and order. Today, ask yourself: *Does my life, my character, and my household reflect my love for the Lord?*

---

*I write these things to you, hoping to come to you soon. But if I should be delayed, I have written so that you will know how people ought to act in God's household, which is the church of the living God, the pillar and foundation of the truth.* —1 Timothy 3:14–15

---

Further Scripture: 1 Corinthians 14:33; 1 Timothy 3:5; 2 Peter 1:3

*Week 29, Day 199: 1 Timothy 4*
The Characteristics of Godly Ministers

Paul was honest with Timothy, advising that as Timothy dealt with church life, some people would depart from their faith. They would be deceived and lured by hypocrisy. Timothy, even though he was a young man, needed to continue to live as an example to believers in speech, in conduct, in love, in faith, and in purity, thus reflecting his own devotion and strength in the Lord.

Like Timothy, no matter how young or old you may be, the Lord calls you to live as an example to others through your speech, conduct, love, faith, and purity. Do you have to be perfect? No! God does not ask for perfection. Instead, as you *daily seek* the Lord's presence and His Word, *God's grace will transform your speech, conduct, love, faith, and purity.* Your transformed life will serve as a godly example to others by the way you talk with patience and self-control, the way you show undeserved kindness, or the way you choose purity over immodesty. You represent God's love as you live your life. Today, *spend time with Jesus.* Time in His presence transforms your life and will serve as an example for others, spurring them on in their own faith in the Lord.

---

*Command and teach these things. Let no one despise your youth; instead, you should be an example to the believers in speech, in conduct, in love, in faith, in purity.* —1 Timothy 4:11–12

---

Further Scripture: John 13:35; Romans 12:2; 1 Timothy 4:1–2

### Week 29, Day 200: 1 Timothy 5
## The Widows

Paul advised his co-laborer Timothy as an older man pours into a younger man in the ministry, giving instructions on the characteristics for the church and the church's responsibility to care for widows and elders.

The heart of our heavenly Father is to look after His children. Specifically here, Paul discussed widows. God the Father has a caring and nurturing heart. As God's ambassador, you are called to care for widows. Take a minute to think about your community, your neighborhood, your family, or even your workplace. Ask the Lord how you can care for widows as a follower of Christ. Check in on them from time to time. Ask them to dinner. Mow their grass. Take them to doctors' appointments. Yes, it means going out of your way to care for someone else. Yes, it means setting aside your own agenda for someone else. But that is the heart of your heavenly Father! He loved you so you could unselfishly love and care for others. He will give you strength, wisdom, and joy as you trust Him to obediently care for widows. Open your eyes to see the widows in your life. It's what you are called to do.

---

*Support widows who are genuinely widows.* —1 Timothy 5:3

---

Further Scripture: Psalm 68:5; Ephesians 6:20; James 1:27

### *Week 29, Day 201: 1 Timothy 6*

Fight the Good Fight

So many worldly things fight for your attention, your love, and your focus: beauty, sports, fame, money, success, knowledge, trends, social media influence . . . you name it. They continue to add up but still leave you feeling as though you don't have enough. And then the lie creeps in that *you* are not enough.

God says to flee from these harmful desires, cravings, and love for things of this world. They can skew your mindset and draw you away from the Lord. Paul instructed Timothy to run from these things and follow God by pursuing righteousness, godliness, faith, love, endurance, and gentleness. Keep it simple—*run from the worldly things and pursue God.* As you intentionally abide in God's love day after day, you will hunger to know Him, you will desire to look like Him, and you will enjoy the things of the Lord more than the things the world offers you. You will find satisfaction in Him, and strength will arise for the spiritual battle you fight daily. The enemy is fighting to be your first love. But press on and stand firm in your faith in the Lord. Run away from worldly things and pursue God. Victory comes with Jesus by your side as you fight the good fight for the faith. Walk in that promise today.

---

*But you, man of God, run from these things,*
*and pursue righteousness, godliness, faith,*
*love, endurance, and gentleness.*
*Fight the good fight for the faith;*
*take hold of eternal life*
*that you were called to*
*and have made a good confession about*
*in the presence of many witnesses.* —1 Timothy 6:11–12

---

Further Scripture: Jeremiah 29:13; 1 Timothy 6:6; James 4:7

*Week 29, Day 202: 2 Timothy 1*

## Be Not Ashamed of the Gospel

In Paul's final letter to Timothy, he encouraged Timothy to continue sharing the Gospel of Jesus Christ with a spirit of power, love, and a sound mind, not being ashamed of his testimony from the Lord. Paul instructed Timothy to *rely on the power of God.*

As you seek to share the Gospel, to live your life for Christ, to be bold in your faith, you may feel fearful, even embarrassed, ashamed, or awkward. Ask yourself: *Am I relying on my own strength and knowledge or fully relying on the power of God?* Imagine a water skier trying to stand up on the water. If the skier tries to force himself out of the water in his own strength and muscle, he'll never get up. But when the skier focuses on positioning his body, aligning his eyes to focus on the boat, and allowing the power of the boat for the strength, that's when he is successful to get up on the water.

In a similar way, as you share your testimony, keep your eyes and heart focused on the power from the Lord. Let go of your agenda and control. As you align yourself with the Lord, relying on the power of God, sharing the Gospel will flow out from you supernaturally. Fear will fade away, and power will arise!

---

*So don't be ashamed of the testimony about our Lord, or of me His prisoner. Instead, share in suffering for the gospel, relying on the power of God.*
—2 Timothy 1:8

---

Further Scripture: John 14:26; Philippians 4:13; 2 Timothy 1:7

## *Week 29, Day 203: 2 Timothy 2*
## Commit to Discipleship

When you hear the word *discipleship*, what comes to your mind? Do you think, *I don't know how,* or *I don't have time for that,* or *that's only for people who work in the church?* Paul instructed Timothy to commit himself to discipling faithful men the things that Timothy heard from Paul. Paul desired for Timothy to continue to pass on the truth of the Gospel to others.

Like Timothy, the Lord calls you to make disciples. Pray and ask the Lord *who* to pour into with the love of Christ. The Lord calls you to commit to faithful men and women who are willing to grow in their walk with the Lord. It may look like meeting for coffee once a week and intentionally discussing what you are learning in the Word, doing life together, and praying for one another. Discipleship is committing to a relationship with the purpose of spurring one another on to grow in your walk with Jesus Christ. Let go of all the "what ifs" and "I don't knows." Remember, the Holy Spirit gives you the power, strength, and wisdom. He will fill you up and equip you. Today, ask the Lord to lead you to someone to disciple.

---

*And what you have heard from me in the presence of many witnesses,*
*commit to faithful men who will be able to teach others also.*
—2 Timothy 2:2

---

Further Scripture: Matthew 28:19–20; John 1:45; Titus 2:3

***Week 30, Day 204: 2 Timothy 3***

## Continue in God's Truth

Do you ever feel unequipped for the path the Lord has called you to? Perhaps you wish someone would hold your hand and guide and help you along your way? Timothy must have felt this way as Paul warned him about the difficult times ahead: growth of deception, increasing lack of godliness, and certainty of persecution.

Paul reminded Timothy he was equipped for these difficult days. In the same way, *you are equipped.* You have all you need in the Word of God because *all Scripture is profitable for teaching, rebuking, correcting, and training in righteousness so that you may be complete and equipped for every good work.* Therefore, read Scripture every day. Seek the Lord for wisdom while studying God's Word. Discuss it with friends. As you press on to know the Lord, He will *equip* and *empower* you to be ready and will *give you everything required for the work He calls you to.* You don't need to fear hard or troubling times, because the Lord, your loving Shepherd, promises to never leave you. Today, spend time in the Word so you will be equipped and complete for the journey ahead.

---

*All Scripture is inspired by God and is profitable for teaching, for rebuking, for correcting, for training in righteousness, so that the man of God may be complete, equipped for every good work.* —2 Timothy 3:16–17

---

Further Scripture: 2 Timothy 3:12–14; Hebrews 13:20–21; 2 Peter 1:3

*Week 30, Day 205: 2 Timothy 4*
A Well-Lived Life

As Paul's time on earth neared the end, he never gave up and continued to proclaim the good news of Jesus so others would hear. Paul fought the good fight, he finished the race, and he kept the faith. Paul poured his life out as a drink offering for the sake of the Gospel. Paul shared a promise from the Lord in his final words to his disciple, Timothy, *Even when everyone deserted me, the Lord stood with me, the Lord strengthened me, and the Lord rescued me.*

Following Christ may be lonely, scary, and tiring as you press on, hold on, and go on sharing the Gospel while living your life on the narrow path. However, even when friends turn their backs, when evil and temptations come your way, even when hardships and heartaches arise, *the Lord will stand with you. The Lord will strengthen you. The Lord will rescue you.* Dear friend, it is worth the cost to live for the sake of Jesus Christ. So even when you look around and see no one standing near, *do not fear.* The Lord is standing near. He hasn't left your side, and He will bring you safely into His heavenly kingdom. Go on . . . fight the good fight, finish the race, keep your faith, and share the good news!

---

*But the Lord stood with me and strengthened me, so that the proclamation might be fully made through me and all the Gentiles might hear. So I was rescued from the lion's mouth. The Lord will rescue me from every evil work and will bring me safely into His heavenly kingdom. To Him be the glory forever and ever! Amen.* —2 Timothy 4:17–18

---

Further Scripture: Isaiah 41:10; Mark 16:15; 2 Timothy 4:6–7

### *Week 30, Day 206: Titus 1*
## God Our Savior

Paul wrote to encourage Titus, who was serving on the island of Crete. Paul described the people of Crete as detestable, disobedient, and disqualified for any good work. They professed to know God, but they denied Him by their works. The Lord called Titus to rebuke them and encourage them to remain strong in their faith.

Ever feel like Titus? As you live your life for the Lord, do you feel surrounded by people who say they believe in God with their lips, but their actions and words display something different? If the Lord has led you to this place, *rest assured that the Lord will strengthen you with the wisdom needed to care for those around you.* Be a light as you live your faith authentically. Share about the Lord's grace and mercy in your own life. Open up about your struggles and temptations and testify about the power of the risen Savior. His power gives strength when your flesh is weak. His power gives hope when your spirits are down. His power provides for your needs when you have nothing. Today, pray for those who profess to know God but whose words and actions do not affirm the same. May the power of God in your life encourage others to live their lives for Him.

---

*They profess to know God, but they deny Him by their works. They are detestable, disobedient, and disqualified for any good work.* —Titus 1:16

---

Further Scripture: Isaiah 29:13; Mathew 15:8; Titus 1:5

### *Week 30, Day 207: Titus 2*

## Sound Teaching and Christian Living

Paul told Titus to continue to instruct, encourage, and rebuke with authority while remaining consistent to the sound teaching of the Gospel of Jesus Christ. Paul reminded Titus, *it is only because of the grace of God, through His Son Jesus, that you and I are redeemed from all lawlessness and cleansed as God's people.* Because of the grace and mercy they received, it encouraged others to eagerly do good works for the world to see.

God calls you to speak this consistent Gospel message, encourage others, and rebuke with authority from the truth of His Word. You have a responsibility to remain true to the call, to remain pure, to remain honest, and to take time to encourage young women and young men. As you live your life for Christ, open your eyes to see people around you. Share the truth consistent with sound teaching. Always encourage others. As the Spirit moves in your heart, ask the Lord for His timing to rebuke when necessary. Today, be eager to do this good work because of the love you first received from Jesus. May His great love motivate you as you go out in His name.

---

*He gave Himself for us to redeem us from all lawlessness and to cleanse for Himself a people for His own possession, eager to do good works. Say these things, and encourage and rebuke with all authority. Let no one disregard you.* —Titus 2:14–15

---

Further Scripture: Matthew 28:19–20; 2 Timothy 4:2; Titus 2:1

## *Week 30, Day 208: Titus 3*
## Encourage Others on Their Journeys

Every believer has a story of Christ's love and redemption changing his or her life. *Your story of God's saving grace can encourage others on their journeys.* Paul encouraged Titus to live his life through the power of the Holy Spirit with kindness and gentleness. Paul not only poured this truth into Titus, he then challenged Titus to diligently pour into others, like Zenas and Apollos, on their own journeys. The Lord also calls you to share your journey with others.

Pray and ask the Lord for someone you can diligently pour into and help on their journey with Christ. They may have a different occupation from you, they may have a different calling, but one thing remains the same: You are *all* called to live for Jesus through the power of the Holy Spirit. God wants you to live in community and diligently help one another pursue Christ. Don't isolate yourself. Pray and ask the Lord to bring someone into your life to help. The Lord hears your prayers and will answer you. *Just start praying.* Remember, as you pursue Christ, He promises to provide help along the journey.

---

*Diligently help Zenas the lawyer and Apollos on their journey, so that they will lack nothing.* —Titus 3:13

---

Further Scripture: 2 Corinthians 5:17; Titus 3:3–5; James 1:4

***Week 30, Day 209: Philemon 1***
Perhaps This Is Why

While in prison, Paul witnessed Onesimus, Philemon's runaway slave, give his life to Christ. Therefore, Paul wrote a letter to his friend and fellow believer, Philemon, requesting he grant freedom to Onesimus as a slave, since they were now brothers in Christ. Paul understood the big picture of God's grace, explaining *perhaps* God allowed Onesimus to go to prison, *so that* he'd receive the Gospel and become a dearly loved brother in Christ.

If you trust God as your Master in life and live fully submitted to Him, then He promises to work all things together for good. Even if you end up in prison, even if you go through a health crisis, or even if you give in to the temptation to sin. Yes, these times bring difficulty and pain, but *perhaps* you go through them *so that* you can return, no longer a slave to the world, no longer a slave to sin, but as *a brother or sister in Christ*. Free from sin. Free from bondage. Free to dance in the grace and victory found in Jesus. *Perhaps this is why.* With Christ as your master, fully surrendered to Him, you can see all things work together for good. Today, ask yourselves: *What is my "perhaps this is why" moment?* God is a God of providence. Live surrendered to His will so you can find grace and victory in the midst of each situation.

---

*For perhaps this is why he was separated from you for a brief time, so that you might get him back permanently, no longer as a slave, but more than a slave—as a dearly loved brother. He is especially so to me, but even more to you, both in the flesh and in the Lord.* —Philemon 1:15–16

Further Scripture: Psalm 103:19; Romans 6:22; 8:28

### *Week 30, Day 210: Isaiah 1—2*
### Repent or Rebel

In Isaiah's vision concerning Judah and Jerusalem, the Lord clearly gave His people two options: *repent and obey* or *rebel and disobey*. Obedience would lead to good things in the Lord, whereas disobedience would lead to destruction.

In the same way, if you confess your sins, Jesus is faithful and righteous to forgive you and cleanse you from all unrighteousness. Jesus came so you may receive mercy and grace if you choose to believe in Him as the risen Savior of the world. Once you repent, the Lord asks you to turn away from your old ways and walk obediently in the newness of Christ. When you wake up each day, *ask the Lord to help you obey His voice.* The Lord will be with you as you turn to the right or to the left, following His lead. It's a daily obedience as you abide in Him and *follow His voice.* Otherwise, you can wake up each day, choose to turn away from Christ, and just do your own thing. You may hear God's voice, but like a disobedient child, you choose to do whatever you want, whenever you want. You ignore counsel and walk in disobedience. Today, the choice is yours: *repent and obey* or *rebel and disobey.* How will you choose to walk with Christ?

---

*"Come, let us discuss this," says the* LORD.
*"Though your sins are like scarlet, they will be as white as snow;*
*though they are as red as crimson, they will be like wool.*
*If you are willing and obedient, you will eat the good things of the land.*
*But if you refuse and rebel, you will be devoured by the sword."*
*For the mouth of the* LORD *has spoken.* —Isaiah 1:18–20

---

Further Scripture: Psalm 119:9–11; Proverbs 28:13; 1 John 1:9

### *Week 31, Day 211: Isaiah 3—4*
## Revealing God's Glory

Just as Judah and Jerusalem were in the midst of judgment and wrath when God granted mercy, *God willingly grants you mercy.* You may feel as though you have messed up with everything and everyone. Perhaps anything or anyone you looked to for security has disappeared. Remember, no matter what, *God remains.* He offers you grace and mercy. He is the God who forgives. He is the God who loves in the midst of darkness. It's in this place of mercy and grace that *God reveals His glory.*

Imagine a dark, dreary day on the beach. Just when you think there's no hope for the sun to shine, brightness peeks out from behind a cloud! With your head up, you joyfully walk into the sunlight and find hope for a beautiful day ahead. The day feels redeemed. In a similar way, when you think you've lost all hope in your life, when you feel your destiny is doomed, *remember God shines grace and mercy in the midst of your darkness.* God hasn't given up on you. Open your eyes and receive His redeeming love for your life through His Son Jesus Christ. Jesus will set you free from bondage. He will be your refuge and shelter from the storms of life. You are loved in His eyes. Today, open your eyes and receive His light and glory in your life!

---

*On that day the Branch of the* LORD *will be beautiful and glorious, and the fruit of the land will be the pride and glory of Israel's survivors. Whoever remains in Zion and whoever is left in Jerusalem will be called holy—all in Jerusalem who are destined to live.* —Isaiah 4:2–3

---

Further Scripture: Psalm 130:3–4; Isaiah 3:1a; Ephesians 1:7–8

## Week 31, Day 212: Isaiah 5—6
Isaiah's Call and Mission

God called upon the prophet Isaiah to communicate a message of judgment to Judah and Jerusalem. God needed someone to go and speak to the people who had turned away from Him. The Lord called out, "Who should I send? Who will go?" Isaiah heard the voice of the Lord and replied, *"Here I am. Send me."*

The Lord calls people for specific assignments. When God calls, He desires a response to His voice. First, ask yourself, *Am I listening to God's voice?* Then, *Am I responding to His voice?* If you are willing, respond to God's voice, *Here I am. Send me!* The Lord doesn't need your perfection. He doesn't need your strength or perfect résumé of past experiences. *The Lord needs your willingness.* He works best with weakness, with humility, and with insufficiencies. He creates, He makes, He strengthens, and He increases through His power! If you hear the same thing repeat over and over in your mind, or if you feel burdened about something or someone in your heart, just say to the Lord, *"Here I am Lord. Send me."* He will provide the next steps once He hears *you are willing.*

---

*Then I heard the voice of the LORD saying:*
*Who should I send?*
*Who will go for Us?*
*I said:*
*Here I am. Send me.* —Isaiah 6:8

---

Further Scripture: Exodus 35:5; 1 Chronicles 29:9; 2 Corinthians 8:12

### *Week 31, Day 213: Isaiah 7—8*
## The Immanuel Prophecy

King Ahaz found himself in an intense political situation. His heart *trembled like trees shaking in the wind.* Do you know that feeling? Have you ever been nervous about a situation or wondered how you would overcome the battle you faced? Isaiah consistently spoke hard instructions to King Ahaz and the people: *Don't be afraid or act cowardly.* If you do not stand firm in your faith, then you will not stand at all. Do not fear or be terrified of man's power. Regard the Lord of hosts as holy. God should be feared and held in awe (*not* man). God will be your sanctuary. Finally, Isaiah said: "The Lord Himself will give you a sign: The virgin will conceive, have a son, and name him Immanuel."

Isaiah foreshadowed God the Father sending His Son Jesus from heaven to the world to *be with* the people. Immanuel means "God with us." Therefore, the people had no need to tremble or fear man. They needed to trust the God of the impossible. The same is true for you. Think about whatever has you trembling like a tree in the wind in your own life. Remember and take heart—*God is with you.* He's the God of the impossible. Stand firm in your faith. God's got you!

---

*Therefore, the Lord Himself will give you a sign: The virgin will conceive, have a son, and name him Immanuel.* —Isaiah 7:14

---

Further Scripture: Isaiah 7:2, 4; 8:12b–14a; John 5:23

*Week 31, Day 214: Isaiah 9—10*

## The Prince of Peace

God's people weakened as Assyria sought their destruction, and yet the Lord continued to give Isaiah a message of hope. *Isaiah foretold of the coming Savior,* Immanuel—a child born for the people, a royal son who would carry the government on His shoulders. As the child reigned on David's throne, His name would be: *Wonderful Counselor, Mighty God, Eternal Father, Prince of Peace.* The people, although in despair, again had hope.

The son's name is Jesus, the Savior, the Son of God. The One God sent to save the world from death and give eternal life. Therefore, keep your eyes on Jesus in the midst of despair. Hold on to the hope found in Jesus. Even when your situation looks uncertain, even if you feel as though you are failing and alone, remember, God sent His Son for you—*the Wonderful Counselor, the Mighty God, the Eternal Father, the Prince of Peace.* Get to know Him. Seek His heart as a counselor. Trust in His might. Believe in His eternal love. Rest in His peace. Seek the One who came, lived, and died so you may have eternal life and everlasting hope. Seek Christ alone.

---

*For a child will be born for us,*
*a son will be given to us,*
*and the government will be on His shoulders.*
*He will be named*
*Wonderful Counselor, Mighty God,*
*Eternal Father, Prince of Peace.* —Isaiah 9:6

---

Further Scripture: Psalm 72:17; Isaiah 9:7; Matthew 1:23

### Week 31, Day 215: Isaiah 11–13
## A Branch Will Be a Fruit

Isaiah prophesied Jesus would come forth from the line of Jesse as part of the Davidic Covenant. The people thought the line of Jesse had ended, yet Isaiah foretold a "shoot would grow from the stump of Jesse, and a branch from his roots will bear fruit." The shoot referred to Jesus, and He would be different from other descendants of David. Jesus would carry out His work on earth with the Spirit of wisdom and understanding, the Spirit of counsel and strength, the Spirit of knowledge, and the fear of the Lord.

As a child of God, you have the mind of Christ and the Spirit of the Lord to carry out the work of the kingdom of God. You may feel as though your strength is gone. This is a lie from the enemy! You can do so much more than you think because the Lord's power is great within you. Therefore, press on! Keep your eyes on Christ. Today, take your mind off yourself, and ask the Lord, "What do You want me to do for Your kingdom?" Trust the Lord for *the Spirit of wisdom and understanding*. Make your attitude that of Christ Jesus, remembering you have *the Spirit of counsel and strength*, as well as *the Spirit of knowledge* and *fear of the Lord*. The Spirit of the Lord is upon you. Walk it out with confidence in Christ.

---

*Then a shoot will grow from the stump of Jesse,*
*and a branch from his roots will bear fruit.*
*The Spirit of the Lord will rest on Him—*
*a Spirit of wisdom and understanding,*
*a Spirit of counsel and strength,*
*a Spirit of knowledge and of the fear of the Lord.* —Isaiah 11:1–2

---

Further Scripture: 1 Corinthians 2:16; 12:6–8; Philippians 2:5

### *Week 31, Day 216: Isaiah 14–16*
### God Sits on the Throne

Satan, the shining morning star, arrogantly proclaimed: "I will ascend to the heavens; I will set up my throne," along with other "I will" statements. A battle rages. Satan has always and will always attempt to elevate himself above God. But God is not the great "I will." *God is the great I Am—the One who is and the One to come.* He's the author and the creator. He's the first and the last. He is the name above all other names. He reigns victorious. Others will attempt to say they will be higher and greater, but only God will sit on the throne. Only God will reign victorious.

The great I Am is on your side. The great I Am is with you, and He fights your battles. You are never alone. Satan, full of pride, will attempt to gain ground in your life, but the I Am is greater because the One who is in you is greater than the one who is in the world. Arrogance and pride will gain zero ground for Satan, just like arrogance and pride in your own life will lead to defeat. Walk in humility as Christ walked in humility, and in due time, you will be lifted up. You have a choice—pride or humility. Choose humility, and you will be victorious.

---

*Shining morning star, how you have fallen from the heavens!*
*You destroyer of nations, you have been cut down to the ground.*
*You said to yourself:*
*"I will ascend to the heavens;*
*I will set up my throne above the stars of God."*
. . . . . . . . . . . . . . . .
*But you will be brought down to Sheol*
*into the deepest regions of the Pit.* —Isaiah 14:12–13, 15

---

Further Scripture: Exodus 6:2; Isaiah 41:10; 1 Peter 5:6

## *Week 31, Day 217: Isaiah 17–18*
## Look to the Lord

Isaiah delivered an oracle against the ancient city of Damascus, a prophetic word about destruction in their lives. Yes, they repented and *looked to the Lord,* but they still faced consequences for the choices they made. They did not receive the fullness of God's goodness that He intended for them to enjoy.

Dear child of God, *the Lord wants you to look to Him* in everything you do. The Lord wants you to include Him in your plans. The Lord created you. He is your maker. He has a destiny for you. He desires you to live in the fullness of His love, His grace, and His mercy. You can choose to do your own thing. You can choose to walk in sin, and you can choose to seek temporary pleasures. The Lord will not leave. He is Immanuel God, God who is with you. He has so much more for you than the world will ever offer. Therefore, seek Him in all things. Look to Him, and He will help you through the hard times. Today, wake up and commit your day, your relationships, and your goals to the Lord. Ask Him for wisdom and strength, and He will answer. Don't compromise with the world. Include the Lord moment by moment—He will bless you, and His hand will be upon you.

---

*On that day people will look to their Maker and will turn their eyes to the Holy One of Israel. They will not look to the altars they made with their hands or to the Asherahs and incense altars they made with their fingers.*
—Isaiah 17:7–8

---

Further Scripture: Proverbs 16:3; Acts 17:26–27; Ephesians 3:19

### Week 32, Day 218: Isaiah 19—20
## Radical Obedience

The Lord needed to get Egypt's attention *again*—to remind the people to trust in God *alone*. Again, God called upon the prophet Isaiah and gave him clear instructions: Go naked and barefoot for three years as a symbol representing disgrace and need in Egypt. Isaiah *radically obeyed* the Lord by going naked and barefoot for the sake of others turning to the Lord.

Like Isaiah, the Lord calls you to *radical obedience*. This often means setting aside your agenda, your pride, even your entire life. Jesus said to follow Him you must deny yourself and pick up your cross. *Is there something radical the Lord has put on your heart to do for the sake of the Gospel?* The prophet Joshua gathered the people to walk around Jericho's walls for six days, and then on the seventh day, they gave a mighty shout. Just as God promised, the city walls came tumbling down after their obedience. Perhaps you sense the Lord asking you to prayer walk around your home, seek reconciliation and forgiveness, fast from lunch at the office for a month, or give up your home or even your job. Don't dismiss what's on your heart. As you walk in this radical obedience like Isaiah, it could foster a change in someone's life, or even an entire country. Don't miss out on what the Lord wants to do in and through you!

---

*During that time the LORD had spoken through Isaiah son of Amoz, saying, "Go, take off your sackcloth and remove the sandals from your feet," and he did so, going naked and barefoot—the LORD said, "As My servant Isaiah has gone naked and barefoot three years as a sign and omen against Egypt and Cush." —Isaiah 20:2–3*

---

Further Scripture: Joshua 6:2–5; Matthew 16:24; 2 John 1:6

## *Week 32, Day 219: Isaiah 21—22*

Consider the One

As Jerusalem tried to defend itself from the Assyrian army's attacks, Isaiah questioned Jerusalem's defense approach. Again, they staged their own defense, built their own weapons, and independently collected water in reservoirs. It was all pretty impressive, *but they never looked to God. They never considered God in their plans.*

As you go through the day, the Lord desires for you to commit your works to Him. He created you with gifts and talents and personality for such a time as this. Seek Him. Delight yourself in Him and consider Him in all you do. *Don't just do things on your own and consider your own interest.* Isaiah the prophet asked Jerusalem: "What's the matter with you?" Today, if you are *not considering the Lord in your plans,* ask yourself: *What's the matter with me?* The Lord wants to surprise you with all He has in store for you! It's beyond your comprehension. Therefore, *stop focusing on just you.* In all your ways acknowledge the Lord, and He will direct your path!

---

*You made a reservoir between the walls for the waters of the ancient pool, but you did not look to the One who made it, or consider the One who created it long ago. —Isaiah 22:11*

---

Further Scripture: Proverbs 3:6; Jeremiah 29:11–12; Colossians 3:17

### *Week 32, Day 220: Isaiah 23—25*
### Living with the End in Mind

Isaiah prophesied about the day Jesus will return. Although many people will not wait for the Lord or seek His ways, *a remnant will remain faithful.* The remnant will stand before Jesus and state: "Look, this is our Lord, we have waited for Him! Let us rejoice and be glad in His salvation."

Will the Lord find you faithful? Will He see you and say: "Well done, good and faithful servant"? Or is your life built around worldly and temporary pleasures? Are you just living your own life and not seeking the Lord's ways? The Lord longs for you to be ready for His return. Therefore, rejoice in the Lord always. Give thanks at all times, for your salvation is found in Him! Prepare yourself for eternity with Jesus as you spend time on earth loving Him with all your heart, soul, mind, and strength. The time to repent and turn to the One who created you is *now.* God doesn't need your perfection. He doesn't require your strength. God wants to have your whole heart in humility. As you give your heart to Him, He will raise you up, allowing you to live in the fullness He has for you. He is waiting for you today. Will you be waiting for Him?

*On that day it will be said,*
*"Look, this is our God;*
*we have waited for Him, and He has saved us.*
*This is the LORD; we have waited for Him.*
*Let us rejoice and be glad in His salvation."* —Isaiah 25:9

Further Scripture: Psalm 27:13–14; Matthew 25:21; Romans 13:11

## *Week 32, Day 221: Isaiah 26—27*

## Waiting on the Trumpet

Isaiah prophesied that on the day Jesus returns—when the "great trumpet will be blown"— the Israelites will be gathered *one by one*. Yes, even in the final days, the Lord will go after the *one*. The Lord is a God who loves, a God who sees, a God who knows, and a God who provides. You are the *one* He goes after.

Everyone wants to belong, to be known, to be cared for, and above all, to be loved. You are no different. Don't deny it! Today, rest in the promise that no matter what is swirling around you—*you are loved*. The Lord would leave everything to gather *you*. Just as He cares for lilies of the field, He cares for a simple sparrow, and, yes, the Lord cares for you. He provides for you. He sees you and pursues you. Trust Him with your burdens. Trust Him with your pain. Trust Him with your loneliness. The Lord promises perfect peace to those whose mind is dependent on Him. Allow the Lord to be your rock, your refuge, and your stronghold. Depend on Him alone—not the things of this world, which only lead to temporary satisfaction. Seek the Lord alone, and you will find peace.

---

*On that day*
*the LORD will thresh grain from the Euphrates River*
*as far as the Wadi of Egypt,*
*and you Israelites will be gathered one by one.* —Isaiah 27:12

---

Further Scripture: Isaiah 26:3–4; Matthew 6:30; Luke 15:4–6

### *Week 32, Day 222: Isaiah 28—29*
### No Lip Service

Isaiah prophesied a great battle that would include all nations when Jesus returns. Jesus will be victorious in that battle. He will be there for the people. Jesus knows everything about everyone. He knows the ones walking with Him. He knows the ones whose hearts have gone astray. Even if they look like strong Christians on the outside, the Lord knows what they do behind closed doors and, most importantly, *in their hearts.* The Lord knows and the Lord sees. You cannot escape His presence.

Hiding from God is not worth the grief it brings on you. It's not worth the agony of lying, cheating, and faking who you are. The world does fake: fake nails, fake leather, fake news, and fake tans. Eventually fake wears off, and the truth is revealed. The Lord sees your heart. Child of God, come before the Lord and repent of any fakeness or lip-service in your life. Be real and vulnerable before the Lord, just as you were created to be. Seek His face, and you will have joy and peace. Peace does not exist in the darkness. Joy is not found in the darkness. Walk into the light of Christ where grace and mercy abound. You were created to live victoriously. Now is the time to step into His great love for you.

---

*The Lord said: Because these people approach Me with their mouths*
*to honor Me with lip-service—*
*yet their hearts are far from Me,*
*and their worship consists of man-made rules*
*learned by rote. —Isaiah 29:13*

---

Further Scripture: Psalm 139:7–12; Isaiah 29:15; Hebrews 4:13

## *Week 32, Day 223: Isaiah 30—31*

The Lord Is Waiting

Even after judgment, even after destruction, Isaiah continued to encourage the people of Israel with this truth—*the Lord is waiting for you.* He is waiting to show you mercy and compassion. He cares for you.

God's mercies never end. Just as sure as the sun rises, the Lord's mercies are new each day. Wait patiently through the hardship you may be going through, and you will be happy. Your life may feel shattered in millions of pieces, you may feel broken beyond repair, but friend, God is the God who will make beauty from the ashes, beauty from the broken pieces. He will turn them into something beautiful for His glory. Don't rush the work of the Lord. Most of the time, it's not a fast fix. But God's mercy *is* coming. Draw near to the Lord today, and the next day, and the day after that. No matter what situation you have fallen into, the Lord wants to *shower you with His mercy and His compassionate love.* Wait for Him. Wait patiently, and you will be happy.

---

*Therefore the LORD is waiting to show you mercy,*
*and is rising up to show you compassion,*
*for the LORD is a just God.*
*All who wait patiently for Him are happy.* —Isaiah 30:18

---

Further Scripture: Isaiah 30:12–15; Joel 2:13; James 4:8

## *Week 32, Day 224: Isaiah 32—33*
## Hope in the Lord

God's people sought everything but the Lord. After being destroyed and betrayed by other nations, *their only hope was to wait on the Lord* to restore them, to save them, and redeem this time of defeat and destruction. The Lord was their judge, lawgiver, and king. Even those who had been far away from the Lord sought His goodness. And those who had walked closely with the Lord knew He was their strength.

When you seek success, attempt to find your worth in people, strive in your own strength and then fail . . . where do you turn for hope and help? You can choose to sit in a pit of despair. Or you can humble yourself and *find hope in the Lord.* The Lord will always be there during your time of trouble. You are never too far gone, too great in sin, or too messed up to turn back to the arms of your loving Father. He is Immanuel. He is the God who is with you. His love stretches from the east to the west, and nothing will ever separate you from His vast love. You can always go back to Him. Therefore, *wait for Him in the morning.* Wait for Him to lift you up with strength.

---

*Lord, be gracious to us! We wait for You.*
*Be our strength every morning*
*and our salvation in time of trouble.* —Isaiah 33:2

---

Further Scripture: Isaiah 33:13, 22; Hebrews 13:5

### *Week 33, Day 225: Isaiah 34—36*

## A Turnaround God

Through the prophet Isaiah, God declared He would save, transform, and redeem His people from ungodliness. *God is a turnaround God.* He redeems all things. He will turn the desert into a blossoming garden. He will turn dry land into flowing rivers. He strengthens weak hands and steadies shaking knees. He gives courage to the cowardly and sight to the blind. He satisfies the thirsty and fills the hungry. He is the God of redemption for those who trust in *His name.*

From the east to the west, from the north to the south, the Lord loves you, and He desires to bring redemption to your life. Right now you may be going through hardship after hardship. Suffering, grief, temptation, and unknowns spin around you. Yet God is with you even in that place. He may not change the situation immediately, but *He will change and redeem you.* Turn to Him. Ask Him for eyes to see how He sees. Ask Him to steady your knees and strengthen your hands. He will answer you when you call upon Him. The Lord will equip you as a mighty warrior. Trust in His name above all other names. Trust in God alone.

*But the redeemed will walk on it,*
*and the redeemed of the LORD will return*
*and come to Zion with singing,*
*crowned with unending joy.*
*Joy and gladness will overtake them,*
*and sorrow and sighing will flee.* —Isaiah 35:9–10

Further Scripture: Psalm 107:2–3, 8–9; Isaiah 35:1–4; Ephesians 1:7–8

## *Week 33, Day 226: Isaiah 37—38*
How to Deal with Enemies When Walking in the Will of God

King Hezekiah received a letter from King Sennacherib telling Hezekiah not to trust in Yahweh because Jerusalem would be handed over to the Assyrians. Hezekiah received the letter, read it, and then immediately went into the Temple of the Lord. He *spread the letter out* before the Lord and prayed: "LORD of Hosts . . . You are God—You alone—of all the kingdoms of the earth. . . . LORD our God, save us from his power so that all the kingdoms of the earth may know that You are the LORD—You alone."

If you find yourself facing a problem, surrounded by enemies, and fighting a battle, immediately go and *spread it out* before the Lord God Almighty. He is God alone. He will fight your battles. He will give you what you need and will bring victory in His name. In King Hezekiah's situation, the Lord sent an angel and, in one night, He struck down the enemy camp. The Lord fought the enemy for King Hezekiah after Hezekiah *spread it out* before Him. Today *spread your life before the Lord.* Allow the Lord to have control of your life and ask Him to fight your battles. In Christ, you will have victory!

---

*LORD of Hosts, God of Israel, who is enthroned above the cherubim, You are God—You alone—of all the kingdoms of the earth. You made the heavens and the earth. Listen closely, LORD, and hear; open Your eyes, LORD, and see. Hear all the words that Sennacherib has sent to mock the living God.*
—Isaiah 37:14—17

---

Further Scripture: Deuteronomy 3:21–22; 2 Chronicles 32:7–8; Isaiah 37:20

*Week 33, Day 227: Isaiah 39—40*

God's People Comforted

Isaiah prophesied that God would deliver the people of Israel. God was in the midst of their despair. God is the everlasting God and the creator of the whole earth. God does not grow tired, and His understanding is limitless. He gives strength and power to the weak and powerless. Even during their exile and hardship, *the people of God needed to trust Yahweh to deliver them and give them strength.*

God still desires for you to trust in His name. He promises to give you strength. Isaiah wrote that as you trust the Lord, you will "soar on wings like eagles." Just picture yourself on the wings of an eagle. An eagle soars through the sky effortlessly and smoothly. An eagle isn't frantic or fatigued. The Lord wants your life with Him to feel like that picture. He wants you to believe that no matter what hardship you find yourself in, you can trust Him in your weariness, in your weakness, and in your waiting. Through it all, *allow God to be your eagle wings and rest.* He will strengthen you to press on without getting tired or growing faint. Today, rest in the Lord, and He will deliver you.

---

*Do you not know? Have you not heard?*
*Yahweh is the everlasting God, the Creator of the whole earth.*
*He never grows faint or weary;*
*there is no limit to His understanding.*
*He gives strength to the weary and strengthens the powerless.*
*Youths may faint and grow weary, and young men stumble and fall,*
*but those who trust in the LORD will renew their strength; they will soar*
*on wings like eagles; they will run and not grow weary;*
*they will walk and not faint.* —Isaiah 40:28–31

---

Further Scripture: Psalm 62:5–8; Matthew 11:28–30; Hebrews 13:8

## *Week 33, Day 228: Isaiah 41—42*
## God Chose You

Isaiah reaffirmed God's promise made in the covenant with Abraham that Israel was His chosen nation. God chose them—He had not rejected them. Israel did not need to fear. God proclaimed, "I am with you," as He reminded them of His covenant with them. God promised protection, stating He would hold on to Israel with His mighty, righteous right hand.

God chose Israel, but then as Isaiah prophesied, God also sent His Son Jesus, His servant, Savior and Redeemer for the world, so all may be saved through His love. Walk in your identity as God's chosen one. You may feel rejected, unwanted, or unloved. These are all lies from the enemy. Focus on the promises of Christ: *You are chosen.* You are welcomed. You are deeply and tenderly loved. You may face fears, concerns, and worries. Let them go. Grab ahold to the Lord's righteous right hand. He holds you. He knows you. He will strengthen you. He will help you. Just focus on today. The Lord promises to be with you. Hang on to that promise, *chosen child of God.*

---

*I brought you from the ends of the earth*
*and called you from its farthest corners.*
*I said to you: You are My servant;*
*I have chosen you and not rejected you.*
*Do not fear, for I am with you;*
*do not be afraid, for I am your God.*
*I will strengthen you; I will help you;*
*I will hold on to you with My righteous right hand.* —Isaiah 41:9–10

---

Further Scripture: Psalm 34:17–19; Isaiah 41:13–14; Romans 3:23–24

## *Week 33, Day 229: Isaiah 43—44*

## Restoration of Israel

Isaiah boldly declared that the Lord would restore the Israelite people and bring them back to their land. The Lord confirmed to them: *I love you; I have called you by name; you are precious and honored in My sight.* He reminded them: *Do not fear, I will be with you.* The people would walk through the things in life that naturally bring destruction, like fires and floods, *unharmed because God was with them.*

This God is unlike any other god or idol. This God saves. This God redeems, and this God restores. This Savior God will do a new thing and make a way when there seems to be no way. There is no other God like Yahweh, your rock, refuge, deliverer, and salvation. No matter where you are today, the Lord is with you. He loves you, and He longs to restore you back to Him. He is there as you walk through the fire and through the high waters. He will protect you and restore you. Today, just receive this truth for your life—*the one and only Savior God loves you. He calls you precious in His sight, and He is with you.*

*Now this is what the LORD says—*
*the One who created you, Jacob,*
*and the One who formed you, Israel—*
*"Do not fear, for I have redeemed you;*
*I have called you by your name; you are Mine.*
*I will be with you when you pass through the waters,*
*and when you pass through the rivers, they will not overwhelm you.*
*You will not be scorched when you walk through the fire,*
*and the flame will not burn you." —*Isaiah 43:1–2

Further Scripture: Isaiah 43:4a, 10–12; John 3:16

### *Week 33, Day 230: Isaiah 45—46*
God of Plans and Promises

The Lord proclaimed through His prophet Isaiah, "I formed the earth and made it. I established it, to be inhabited and not empty." God made the earth. God established the earth. God formed you. He knows everything about the earth and about you. *He is Yahweh.* There is no other god like this God. And this God who created everything *called you by name.*

Do you hear the questions? How was the world created? How did man and woman come into existence? If you believe in the Word of God, then believe and know this truth: *God created the earth, and God created you.* There is no other god like Yahweh. His plan will take place, and He will accomplish His will. You are in His plans. He has plans just for you because He calls you by name. Think about the people in your life who call you by name: your family, your friends, coworkers, and neighbors. These people truly know you. God says He calls you by name. Yes, the creator of the world says He has *called you.* He has appointed you for this time, for this season. He says, "I have made you, I will carry you, I will bear and save you." You are important to the creator of this world.

---

*For this is what the LORD says—*
*God is the Creator of the heavens.*
*He formed the earth and made it.*
*He established it;*
*He did not create it to be empty,*
*but formed it to be inhabited—*
*"I am Yahweh, and there is no other."* —Isaiah 45:18

---

Further Scripture: Genesis 1:1, 26–28; Isaiah 45:4; 46:4

*Week 33, Day 231: Isaiah 47–49*

Born with Purpose

Isaiah foretold about a coming servant—the Savior of the world, Jesus. The Lord formed Jesus in His mother's womb to serve the world as a servant and to restore Israel back to God. This coming Savior would be despised, abhorred by people, and a servant to rulers. Even so, when kings saw Him they would stand up and princes would bow down because of the Lord.

Today, remember, you were formed in your mother's womb. You are called, you have purpose, and you have a destiny on your life. You are not here by chance. God has a plan for your life. You are honored in the sight of the Lord. The Lord will be your strength. Whether you are praying for your own child or are seeking the Lord as His child, believe this truth: *You are perfectly and wonderfully made. You were formed in your mother's womb for such a time as this.* Concerns and uncertainties may arise, but remember, *the Lord has called you and those you love by name.* The Lord will redeem your lives for His glory. His hand is on you. So, get out of bed with shoulders back and eyes fixed ahead on Jesus. Press on in prayer and walk in God's truth because He has plans for you today! You were born with a purpose!

---

*And now, says the LORD,*
*who formed me from the womb to be His Servant,*
*to bring Jacob back to Him*
*so that Israel might be gathered to Him;*
*for I am honored in the sight of the LORD,*
*and my God is my strength.* —Isaiah 49:5

---

Further Scripture: Psalm 139:13–16; Isaiah 49:1, 7

## Week 34, Day 232: Isaiah 50—52

Proclaim His Name

God's people turned away from the Lord, received the punishment and consequences for their sin, and then found restoration in the Lord. In time God would set them free from captivity. Because of God's redeeming power in their lives, *they proclaimed His name*. People heard about God, the Great I Am, the only God who reigns. Yes, He is the God who frees captives and brings peace for today and hope for a future.

As Jesus departed the earth, He left His followers with this task: *go* and *proclaim* His name and *bring* Him glory as witnesses of His redeeming power. God even calls your feet *beautiful* when you proclaim His name and share the good news of Jesus Christ! The world promises beauty through products, workouts, and even surgeries. But God says: "You are beautiful when you proclaim My name!" Today, put on your walking shoes for Jesus. Proclaim the good news of Jesus giving life rather than death, peace in place of anxiety, freedom instead of bondage, and hope for the future. So get up, beautiful child of God— you've got some walking to do!

*Therefore My people will know My name;*
*therefore they will know on that day*
*that I am He who says:*
*"Here I am."*
*How beautiful on the mountains*
*are the feet of the herald,*
*who proclaims peace,*
*who brings news of good things,*
*who proclaims salvation,*
*who says to Zion, "Your God reigns!"* —Isaiah 52:6–7

Further Scripture: Matthew 28:19–20; Romans 10:15; 2 Corinthians 4:15

*Week 34, Day 233: Isaiah 53—55*

Healed by His Wounds

Generations before Mary gave birth to Jesus, Isaiah prophesied God would send Immanuel—*God with us*. This Immanuel would be the suffering servant. Immanuel, Jesus, bears your sickness and carries your pain. He was struck down and afflicted, pierced for your transgressions, and crushed for your iniquities. *His wounds healed you.* Ultimately, Jesus came to the earth to live and die for you. He suffered for you.

Jesus called Himself a shepherd and you the sheep of His pasture. Yes, as God's sheep, you wandered away. Therefore, God sent Jesus to suffer and *die as a sacrifice* for you so you wouldn't have to bear the pain and death of your sin. Jesus came so you may have eternal life in Him. Today, receive this truth, rest in this gift of life, and rejoice in the Lord. Lift your head up and spend time in a posture of thankfulness. Give thanks to the Lord for His mercy and grace, for finding you and placing you in the green pastures of His love. He is the Good Shepherd, and *His love for you is unconditional.* Receive His unconditional love today.

> *But He was pierced because of our transgressions,*
> *crushed because of our iniquities;*
> *punishment for our peace was on Him,*
> *and we are healed by His wounds.*
> *We all went astray like sheep;*
> *we all have turned to our own way;*
> *and the LORD has punished Him*
> *for the iniquity of us all.* —Isaiah 53:5–6

Further Scripture: Isaiah 53:11–12; John 17:3–4; 1 Peter 2:24–25

## *Week 34, Day 234: Isaiah 56—58*
Gather

Isaiah prophesied that the Lord would gather His people back to Jerusalem. God, the Great Shepherd, cares for all His sheep and gathers them until they are all together, even those deserving punishment and discipline. The Lord will bring them back.

As a follower of Christ, if you love like God loves, others will know the love of Jesus. One way Jesus showed His loved was as a *gatherer*. A gatherer *brings people together into one group.* Gather people like Jesus gathered people—as one. Gather people into your home. Gather people at a park. Gather people at a coffee shop. Go out and find people in the outside spaces and love them. As you gather people together, ask the Holy Spirit to lead and guide you. Coffee, ice cream, tacos, or a Wiffle ball game help connect people as you gather together. *But ask the Lord to help you go deeper.* Go beyond food and activity and *ask the Lord to connect hearts to the heart of Jesus* and His great love. His love will impact lives for eternity—the ultimate gathering of them all!

---

*This is the declaration of the Lord God,*
*who gathers the dispersed of Israel:*
*"I will gather to them still others*
*besides those already gathered."* —Isaiah 56:8

---

Further Scripture: Jeremiah 23:3; Zechariah 10:8; Matthew 23:37

## *Week 34, Day 235: Isaiah 59—61*
Messiah's Jubilee

Isaiah's prophecy of the Messiah, the Suffering Servant, in Isaiah 61 is known as the Messiah's Jubilee. He shares the Messiah would bring good news to the poor, heal the brokenhearted, and proclaim liberty to the captives and freedom to the prisoners. In Luke 4:18, Jesus quoted Isaiah from the scrolls in the Synagogue: "The Spirit of the Lord is on Me, because He has anointed Me to preach good news to the poor. He has sent Me to proclaim freedom to the captives and recovery of sight to the blind, to set free the oppressed, to proclaim the year of the Lord's favor." After quoting the prophet Isaiah, Jesus said: *"Today as you listened, this Scripture has been fulfilled."*

As a believer, anointed and dearly loved, *you walk in the Spirit of the Lord.* Jesus instructs you to go and share His truth with others. He calls you to reach out to the poor, the captives, the blind, and the oppressed. Share your story of redemption and restoration through the grace and mercy found in Jesus. With confidence in the Lord, share your story of beauty from ashes, festive oil from mourning, and splendid clothing from despair. As you rest in the Lord day and night, His living water will bring you life, enabling you to share with others!

*The Spirit of the Lord God is on Me,*
*because the Lord has anointed Me*
*to bring good news to the poor.*
*He has sent Me to heal the brokenhearted,*
*to proclaim liberty to the captives*
*and freedom to the prisoners.* —Isaiah 61:1

Further Scripture: Psalm 1:2–3; Isaiah 61:2–3; Luke 4:18–21

### Week 34, Day 236: Isaiah 62—64

Zion's Restoration Excitement

Have you ever had some crazy fun news you just couldn't keep quiet? Maybe someone's expecting a baby or the Lord healed a friend or provided in a miraculous way? Isaiah announced he *would not keep silent about all the Lord did for Jerusalem.* The righteousness of God shone like a bright light—like a flaming torch. Picture the Olympic torch. You can't hide that kind of bright light!

As the Lord moves in your life, *His light will shine brightly in you—* like a big, flaming torch. Yes, it may take some molding, some walking through the fire, or even having your life reduced to ashes and brokenness. But it's in this place, where His light from the fire is the hottest, that the Lord promises to restore, rebuild, rename, and refresh you as He molds and moves in your life. His light will shine brightly for all to see His great love and righteousness. Proclaim His goodness to all! Shine your light. God has given you a new name, a new heart, a new righteousness, and a new love. The Lord delights in you. He rejoices over you. Today, don't stay silent!

---

*I will not keep silent because of Zion,*
*and I will not keep still because of Jerusalem,*
*until her righteousness shines like a bright light*
*and her salvation, like a flaming torch.*
*Nations will see your righteousness*
*and all kings, your glory.*
*You will be called by a new name*
*that the Lord's mouth will announce.* —Isaiah 62:1–2

---

Further Scripture: Isaiah 63:7–8; 64:8; Matthew 5:15–16

## *Week 34, Day 237: Isaiah 65—66*

### The Established People

The prophet Isaiah ended his prophetic word to the people by speaking forth declarations from the Lord. Yes, the Lord's hand was upon Jerusalem. Yes, the Lord judged the nations and punished those who did not walk with Him. But ultimately, *the Lord's heart is to bring hope to the nations for His glory so all will know His name.* God looks for people who walk humbly and submissively in their spirit, who fear the Word of the Lord. People will notice a heart turned to the Lord proclaiming God's glory among the nations.

Today, ask yourself three questions. (1) Am I seeking the Lord in humility? (The opposite of humility is pride.) (2) Am I yielded to God's voice? (Or do I listen to the voice of culture, the world, or the enemy?) (3) Do I fear the Word of the Lord?

To grow in the Lord, read the Word of God and display a reverence for His Word. The Lord looks favorably on humility, submission to the Him, and fear of the Word. Then you will bring Him glory and all will know His great name. Draw near to the Lord, and He will draw near to you.

---

*Knowing their works and their thoughts, I have come to gather all nations and languages; they will come and see My glory. I will establish a sign among them, and I will send survivors from them to the nations—to Tarshish, Put, Lud (who are archers), Tubal, Javan, and the islands far away—who have not heard of My fame or seen My glory. And they will proclaim My glory among the nations. —Isaiah 66:18–19*

---

Further Scripture: Genesis 15:5–6; Psalm 96:1–3; Isaiah 66:2

### *Week 34, Day 238: Jeremiah 1–2*
### God Chose You

The Lord called Jeremiah to be a prophetic voice for Judah. Jeremiah gave every excuse to the Lord, but God had chosen him. Therefore, the Lord would be with Jeremiah, help him, and never leave him. God promised to give him the words to say.

Don't you do the same as Jeremiah? When you sense the Holy Spirit say, for example, *go and talk to that person, leave or change jobs*, or *go in humility and ask for forgiveness*, do you give excuses? *No, Lord, I'm too young. No, Lord, I have no experience. No, Lord, there are others who could do it. No, Lord, I've messed up too many times.* However, the truth is that *when the Lord calls you to something, no matter if it is a big life event or an everyday conversation, it is important to God, His plan, and His people.* Remember, He chose you. He appointed you. He set you apart for such a time as this. Therefore, obey Him. Believe He will be with you. The Holy Spirit will put the words in your mouth to speak forth. It will be good and bring Him glory. Trust in the Lord.

---

*The word of the Lord came to me:*
*I chose you before I formed you in the womb;*
*I set you apart before you were born.*
*I appointed you a prophet to the nations.* —Jeremiah 1:4–5

---

Further Scripture: Psalm 139:13–16; Jeremiah 1:6–9; Luke 12:12

## *Week 35, Day 239: Jeremiah 3—5*
## Unfaithful Israel

Jeremiah declared the Lord's words to Judah: "Return, unfaithful Israel." Then God reminded them: "I will not look on you with anger, for I am unfailing in my love." The Lord longed for His people to return back to Him. Although they had worshipped false gods and looked to idols for hope, He would not be angry. God loves with an unfailing love.

Friend, the Lord longs for you to seek His ways. If you have turned to other gods, if you have idols, or if you have wandered away from the faith you once knew in your youth, *the time to turn back to Him is now.* He will welcome you back. He will forgive you. He will love you with a redeeming, everlasting, never-failing love. Humble yourself, repent, turn to the Lord, and His fresh living water will wash over you. His love *never fails.* Today, turn away from life-stealing addictions, turn away from deception, turn away from overspending, turn away from gossip . . . and *turn to Jesus.* He loves you!

---

*Go, proclaim these words to the north, and say:*
*Return, unfaithful Israel.*
*This is the LORD's declaration.*
*I will not look on you with anger, for I am unfailing in My love.*
*This is the LORD's declaration.*
*I will not be angry forever.*
*Only acknowledge your guilt—*
*you have rebelled against the LORD your God.*
*You have scattered your favors to strangers under every green tree*
*and have not obeyed My voice.*
*This is the LORD's declaration.* —Jeremiah 3:12–13

---

Further Scripture: Psalm 109:26–27; Jeremiah 4:1–2; Acts 3:19–20

### *Week 35, Day 240: Jeremiah 6–8*
## Jeremiah Continued to Call Out God's Judgment

Jeremiah tried to reach the people of Judah, urging them to repent and turn back to the Lord. And yet it was as though the people's ears had been cut off from the Word of God. They no longer paid attention. They found no pleasure in the voice of the Lord. They were so far removed that they didn't even feel a conviction when they sinned and acted in disobedience.

The more you live in sin without repentance or spending time with the Lord and His Word, the more insensitive you become to feeling guilty and the deafer you are to hear the Lord's voice saying, "Turn this way and follow Me." You have a decreased hunger for God's Word. Therefore, you go further and further into a pattern of sin without feelings of angst or guilt. Today, ask yourself: *Is there something in my life I have done for so long that I no longer feel convicted by it?* You may not feel the *weight of your sin* anymore, but the Lord feels the *loss of His child.* His love for you never ends. Humble yourself and confess your sin to the Lord. Then receive His love and forgiveness. He will wipe away your guilt and pain. It is never too late to turn back to the Lord. Today, listen to that still, small voice calling you to return to the Lord.

---

*Who can I speak to and give such a warning*
*that they will listen?*
*Look, their ear is uncircumcised,*
*so they cannot pay attention.*
*See, the word of the* LORD *has become contemptible to them—*
*they find no pleasure in it.* —Jeremiah 6:10

---

Further Scripture: Jeremiah 6:15; Matthew 13:13–15; Acts 28:27

## *Week 35, Day 241: Jeremiah 9–11*
## Boast in the Lord

The Lord used Jeremiah's voice as an instrument to draw the people back to His love and obedience to His ways. Jeremiah reminded them to *boast in the Lord* alone. He told the wise man, the strong man, and the wealthy man not to boast in their own wisdom, strength, or wealth but rather to *boast in the Lord*. Boast in the Lord's faithful love, understanding, justice, and righteousness. The Lord created the heaven and earth. There is no one like Yahweh.

As you grow in wisdom, strength, or wealth, who do you boast in? Do you give the Lord praise and glory for His work in your life? Remember, He is your rock and your power. Apart from God, you can do nothing. He is your creator. He has plans for you. He is in all things and above all things. He is the author of your faith. He alone is worthy of your praise. Don't boast in yourself but *boast in the Lord*. As you boast in the Lord, others will witness His great love. Today, think about your life with thanksgiving, and give Him praise and glory for the great things He has done.

*This is what the LORD says:*
*The wise man must not boast in his wisdom;*
*the strong man must not boast in his strength;*
*the wealthy man must not boast in his wealth.*
*But the one who boasts should boast in this,*
*that he understands and knows Me—*
*that I am Yahweh, showing faithful love,*
*justice, and righteousness on the earth,*
*for I delight in these things.*
*This is the LORD's declaration.* —Jeremiah 9:23–24

Further Scripture: Jeremiah 10:6–7; Psalm 20:7; 1 Corinthians 1:30–31

## *Week 35, Day 242: Jeremiah 12—14*
## Jeremiah and Undergarments

God called all His prophets to humble, radical obedience in order to deliver a message to His people. The Lord instructed Jeremiah to buy a linen undergarment, wear it without washing it, and later hide it in a rocky crevice. Jeremiah followed the Lord's instructions, and the Lord used Jeremiah's obedience to deliver a word to His people—*He would ruin the great pride of His people in Judah and in Jerusalem.* Because of pride, Judah was about to be ruined and removed, just like Jeremiah's underwear.

The Lord despises pride. He exalts and lifts up the humble. Today, ask the Lord where you need to repent of pride in your life. Whether you realize it or not, pride creeps into everyone's lives—at work, in parenting, in marriage, even in getting dressed in the morning. Examine your heart. *Do you care more about what others think than following the Lord in obedience?* Radical obedience requires you to *walk in humility.* Don't worry about what others think. If the Spirit of the Lord is leading and prompting you, just do it. The Lord will use your obedience for His glory.

---

*This is what the LORD said to me: "Go and buy yourself a linen undergarment and put it on, but do not put it in water." So I bought underwear as the LORD instructed me and put it on.* —Jeremiah 13:1–2

---

Further Scripture: Isaiah 20:3–4; James 4:10; 2 John 1:6

## Week 35, Day 243: Jeremiah 15–17
### Eat God's Words

As Jeremiah asked the Lord for vengeance, he found God's words and "ate them." Jeremiah described God's words as "a delight and the joy of my heart." Even in the midst of hardship, Jeremiah knew the Lord's hand was on his life. He sat alone rather than being with people who were not seeking after the Lord.

Seeking the Lord and growing in your walk with Him does not just happen. *You have to make the choice* to draw close to the Lord. *You have to make the choice* to put your phone down and read God's Word. *You have to make the choice* to sit in His presence. *You have to make the choice* to resist temptation from the world, even if it means being alone. The choice you make to spend time with the Lord, in His Word, and in His presence will always be worth it—His Word brings direction and clarity, His presence brings joy, and in Him you have peace. His hand rests on your life as you follow Him. As you chose to spend time delighting in Him, you will find victory and freedom. Make the choice today!

*Your words were found, and I ate them.*
*Your words became a delight to me*
*and the joy of my heart,*
*for I am called by Your name,*
*Yahweh God of Hosts.*
*I never sat with the band of revelers,*
*and I did not celebrate with them.*
*Because Your hand was on me, I sat alone,*
*for You filled me with indignation.* —Jeremiah 15:16–17

Further Scripture: Psalm 16:11; 119:105; Hebrews 4:12

## Week 35, Day 244: Jeremiah 18–19
### Shattered Pottery

The Lord instructed the prophet Jeremiah to go down to the potter's house and buy a clay jar. Then God commanded Jeremiah to take the potter's jar and proclaim the words that He gave to Jeremiah. In summary, God would shatter the people like pieces of a broken vessel. In obedience, Jeremiah stood where the Lord instructed, shattered the jar in the presence of the people, and then spoke forth this word from the Lord: *I am bringing destruction to you, your people, and your land because of your disobedience.*

It's never easy to call out disobedience in others. But what if the Lord instructs and leads you to address sin in someone's life and the destruction that he or she has brought upon themselves? *Have you even been so bold? Would you be so bold?* Sometimes your obedience to the Lord is for someone else's own good. Perhaps God has instructed you to talk to a friend about his or her sin issues or poor decisions. The Lord takes sin and walking obediently pretty seriously. Today, ask yourself: *Am I walking obediently to what God has asked me to do? Is there something I know I need to do but haven't because of fear?* Overcome your fear and be bold in obedience. The Lord will give you strength and grace as you walk one step at a time. Choose to be obedient.

---

*This is what the LORD of Hosts, the God of Israel, says: "I am about to bring on this city—and on all its dependent villages—all the disaster that I spoke against it, for they have become obstinate, not obeying My words."*
—Jeremiah 19:15

---

Further Scripture: Deuteronomy 29:29; Jeremiah 19:10–11; 1 John 2:5–6

# September 1

*Week 35, Day 245: Jeremiah 20–21*

Surrender Your Life

The priest Pashhur ordered Jeremiah beaten and put in the stocks. After enduring pain and humiliation, Jeremiah was released. He warned Pashhur about the consequences Pashhur would soon receive from the Lord. But then the time came for Jeremiah to *stop talking to the people and just turn to the Lord.* Jeremiah laid it all out before the Lord—his every concern, every care, and every heartbreak. And at the end of his honest cry to the Lord, Jeremiah still *believed* God was with him through the pain and that God would fight for him.

No matter what pain you are facing, *turn to the Lord.* Bring Him your whole heart. Write it out in a journal or get on your knees and lift your hands in the air. Bring every care, every burden, every disappointment, every failure, every thought to the Lord as you cry out to Him. Ask the Lord to heal you, ask the Lord to reveal truth to you, and ask the Lord where He is in the midst of your pain. Then listen to Him. Listen to the Lord whisper His love to you. You are a warrior. God is fighting for you. The Lord is in your midst. Cry out honestly before the Lord, allowing Him to carry you through this painful season. You will endure.

---

*For I have heard the gossip of many people,*
*"Terror is on every side! Report him; let's report him!"*
*Everyone I trusted watches for my fall.*
*"Perhaps he will be deceived so that we might prevail against him*
*and take our vengeance on him."*
*But the Lord is with me like a violent warrior.*
*Therefore, my persecutors will stumble and not prevail.*
*Since they have not succeeded, they will be utterly shamed,*
*an everlasting humiliation that will never be forgotten.*
—Jeremiah 20:10–11

---

Further Scripture: Psalm 34:17–18; Jeremiah 20:7, 12; Zephaniah 3:17

### *Week 36, Day 246: Jeremiah 22—23*
### The Righteous Branch of David

In the midst of warning the people of Judah about judgment and destruction, Jeremiah prophesied about the Righteous Branch of David, saying: *This Branch will reign wisely as king, administer justice and righteousness in the land. All of Judah will be saved, Israel will dwell safely. And this Branch will have a name: Yahweh Our Righteousness.* Through Jeremiah, the Lord foretold of the coming Messiah—Jesus, our righteous Savior.

Perhaps *righteousness* is a word you quickly read over, moving on to the next sentence, never giving much thought. Righteousness is a standard to live by. It's God's holiness in action. Some refer to God's righteousness as God's justice. But then what does "Yahweh Our Righteousness" really mean? It means God's character always guides Him to do the right thing. *So, what does this mean for you?* In Christ, He sees you as righteous, justified, and whole. You don't have to look elsewhere for completion, and you don't have to do more to earn righteousness. In Christ you are enough. Rest in Him, and through faith, receive His unconditional love that brings security in "Yahweh Our Righteousness." Just rest in Him today.

---

*In His days Judah will be saved,*
*and Israel will dwell securely.*
*This is what He will be named:*
*Yahweh Our Righteousness.* —Jeremiah 23:6

---

Further Scripture: Psalm 116:5; Romans 1:16–17; Revelation 16:5

*Week 36, Day 247: Jeremiah 24—26*

## But You Have Not Obeyed

For twenty-three years Jeremiah spoke prophetic words from the Lord that shared a common theme: judgment, destruction, and exile were all coming to the nations that would not obey God. But the people simply did not listen. Because of their disobedience, the Lord would come like a roaring lion, a wine press, a refuge, broken pieces of pottery, a lawsuit, a cup of wrath, and slaughtered flock. God even eliminated joy and gladness. *If only they had turned back to Him and obeyed.*

The same truth is for you today—receive the Lord and obey His words. That's all the Lord asks when you follow Him. Maybe you make excuses. You say: "Oh, I'll follow Jesus when I have kids, when my kids move out, when my finances are steady, or when I feel better about myself." Life moves on. Stop. Just stop. *Obey Jesus today.* It may seem hard to turn the ship you've been sailing around, but when you turn into Jesus, His grace will guide you. His power will help you. His love will comfort you. So turn around. *Turn around and obey God's words today.* Jesus said the greatest commandment is to love Him with all your heart.

---

*From the thirteenth year of Josiah son of Amon, king of Judah, until this very day—23 years—the word of the LORD has come to me, and I have spoken to you time and time again, but you have not obeyed. The LORD sent all His servants the prophets to you time and time again, but you have not obeyed or even paid attention.* —Jeremiah 25:3–4

---

Further Scripture: Deuteronomy 28:1–2; Jeremiah 25:8, 10–11; Mark 12:30

---

### *Week 36, Day 248: Jeremiah 27—29*
### God Has Plans for You

God exiled His people. They were living out some very dark, unwanted days. And yet the prophet Jeremiah continued to speak into their lives. He encouraged them to live in the place the Lord sent them. He told them not to be idle in this dark, difficult season. *Instead* they were to build houses, plant gardens, and even get married and have families. Jeremiah affirmed that even in this unwanted season of captivity and exile, *the people could still live because God had plans for them.* Jeremiah encouraged the people to pray and seek the welfare of the city. If they would seek the Lord, He would be found.

You may be in an unwanted, unexpected, or unknown season. You may be wondering: *What am I doing here? This is hard, this is unwanted, and this feels like captivity.* Even in this dark, difficult season, *keep on living.* Take your eyes off yourself. Seek the Lord and His kingdom. Don't worry. Plant seeds, pour into those seeds, and seize the day! Today, take the first step and *seek the Lord.* Why? Because He keeps His promises, and He has promised—*He will be found by you.*

---

*"For I know the plans I have for you"—this is the LORD's declaration—*
*"plans for your welfare, not for disaster, to give you a future and a hope.*
*You will call to Me and come and pray to Me, and I will listen to you.*
*You will seek Me and find Me when you search for Me with all your heart.*
*I will be found by you"—this is the LORD's declaration.*
—Jeremiah 29:11–14

---

Further Scripture: Proverbs 8:17; Jeremiah 29:5–7; Matthew 6:33–34

## Week 36, Day 249: Jeremiah 30–31
### The New Covenant

The Lord declared through Jeremiah a new covenant was coming. This new covenant referred to the Messiah, Jesus Christ. Jeremiah declared hope and forgiveness of sins for every person, from the least to the greatest. The Messiah would turn weeping to dancing and restore what was once lost. God had this hope coming for His people through the new covenant!

*God has made this new covenant,* Jesus the Messiah, *available for you.* Jesus came to earth as God's Son. He died and was buried, and three days later, He rose from the grave. He did all this for you. Yes, Jesus came with an unfailing love to save you. And because Jesus came, you have hope. Even if you have wandered far away from the Lord, Jesus welcomes you back to Him. Receive Him into your life. Jeremiah prophesied this truth long ago, and *now you get to live it out in victory.* The new covenant is not about doing good or being good enough. Jesus came as a free gift of forgiveness and grace. In Christ, you have freedom and righteousness. Today, receive this new covenant for your life and be set free from captivity forever.

---

*"Instead, this is the covenant I will make with the house of Israel after those days"—the LORD's declaration. "I will put My teaching within them and write it on their hearts. I will be their God, and they will be My people. No longer will one teach his neighbor or his brother, saying, 'Know the LORD,' for they will all know Me, from the least to the greatest of them"—this is the LORD's declaration. "For I will forgive their wrongdoing and never again remember their sin."—Jeremiah 31:33–34*

---

Further Scripture: Jeremiah 31:3, 17; Mark 14:22–24

## *Week 36, Day 250: Jeremiah 32—33*
## Call on the Lord

By faith and obedience, Jeremiah bought land in Israel from his cousin. Jeremiah believed *nothing was too difficult for the Lord*. He remembered God's faithfulness and praised the Lord for His eternal love. He believed when he called upon the Lord, God would answer and tell him great and incomprehensible things Jeremiah did not know. Jeremiah trusted the Lord to bring healing, rebuilding, and cleansing to the people.

Today, believe *nothing* is too difficult for the Lord. Right now what is the "difficult mountain" in front of you? It is *not* too difficult for the Lord. Instead of spending time staring at the mountain in front of you, recall the faithfulness of God in your life. And like a child calls upon his parents for help, *call on the Lord*. He promises *He will answer*. He will share with you His heart, His words, His truth, and He will tell you great and incomprehensible things you do not know. God is able to move in your life. Walk with Him, talk with Him, listen to Him, and live obediently to His words by faith. Today, call upon the Lord, and believe He will answer you. *Nothing is too difficult for Him.*

---

*Call to Me and I will answer you and tell you great and incomprehensible things you do not know.* —Jeremiah 33:3

---

Further Scripture: Psalm 136:1; Jeremiah 32:11, 17

## *Week 36, Day 251: Jeremiah 34—36*
### God's Word Will Prevail

The prophet Jeremiah dictated the Word of the Lord to Baruch, a scribe who wrote all the words on a scroll. Then Jeremiah instructed Baruch to read the words to the people inside the temple. The people asked Baruch to read the words to the officials who then communicated the words to King Jehoiakim. King Jehoiakim ordered the scrolls to be burned and then commanded that Jeremiah and Baruch be seized. However, *the Lord hid them.* Jeremiah delivered an unwanted messaged in obedience and *the Lord protected him.* Then the Lord instructed Jeremiah to take another scroll and have Baruch *rewrite the words on them.* And so, he did.

The Word of the Lord cannot be destroyed. It will not fade. It will not disappear. It will never go void. *God's Word will prevail.* As He calls you to walk by faith and be bold about your faith and about His Word, *trust the Lord will protect you.* The time is *now* to go and live out in faith all that the Lord has commanded! Preach His Word. Declare the truth. Be bold in love. *Stand confidently in God and in His Word.*

---

*Then Jeremiah took another scroll and gave it to Baruch son of Neriah, the scribe, and he wrote on it at Jeremiah's dictation all the words of the scroll that Jehoiakim, Judah's king, had burned in the fire. And many other words like them were added.* —Jeremiah 36:32

---

Further Scripture: Proverbs 19:21; Isaiah 40:8; Jeremiah 36:26

## *Week 36, Day 252: Jeremiah 37—39*
By Faith

Three times Jeremiah delivered the Word of the Lord to King Zedekiah. Each time he proclaimed the same message: *Surrender to the Lord, and you will be saved from harm.* The king had a choice—to function in faith by surrendering or to function in fear by fleeing. The king functioned in fear and died. Jeremiah declared the Word of the Lord obediently by faith and experienced freedom.

You face the same choice: *function in fear or function in faith? Functioning in fear* may look like holding onto control, worrying, doing what seems easiest, what you feel adequate for, or what you have done before. *Functioning in faith* may look illogical, out of your control, something you don't feel equipped for, but you feel peaceful and almost excited for the adventure. So, you do it. By faith you surrender and take the first step. He calls you to walk by faith, not by sight. *Take one step of faith at a time.* As you walk by faith, the Lord will grant you freedom and victory in ways you never imagined! Take the first step today!

---

*Jeremiah therefore said to Zedekiah, "This is what the LORD, the God of Hosts, the God of Israel, says: 'If indeed you surrender to the officials of the king of Babylon, then you will live, this city will not be burned down, and you and your household will survive. But if you do not surrender to the officials of the king of Babylon, then this city will be handed over to the Chaldeans. They will burn it down, and you yourself will not escape from them.'"* —Jeremiah 38:17–18

---

Further Scripture: Joshua 1:9; Jeremiah 38:19–20; 2 Corinthians 5:7

## *Week 37, Day 253: Jeremiah 40–42*

### Hypocritically Seeking God's Will

The remnant that remained in Judah approached Jeremiah for a word from the Lord. The people promised they would certainly obey God's word. After ten days Jeremiah delivered a message from the Lord instructing the people to remain in the land and not flee to Egypt. But once again they completely disregarded God's directive and went with their own plan.

Perhaps you have sought the Lord for advice or insight but chose to keep your own plan. You say you included God in the planning, but *when He tried to stop you or change direction, you didn't obey.* The Lord calls you to heed His word and promises He has plans for you—plans not to harm you but to prosper you. If you hear from the Lord, obediently do what He says. If you say you believe in the Lord with your mouth but don't listen to Him with your ears, then you aren't living out what you honestly believe. Follow the voice of the Lord. Otherwise, over time, your ears will grow dull and your life will lead to destruction.

---

*For I have told you today, but you have not obeyed the voice of the Lord your God in everything He has sent me to tell you. Now therefore, know for certain that by the sword, famine, and plague you will die in the place where you desired to go to live for a while.* —Jeremiah 42:21–22

---

Further Scripture: Isaiah 42:20; Jeremiah 42:5–6; 2 Timothy 4:3–4

### *Week 37, Day 254: Jeremiah 43–45*

## The Lord Removes His Hand

The Lord attempted over and over to turn the people of Judah around from its idolatrous behavior, but they would not listen. They were filled with pride and *did not pay attention to the Lord*. They continued on burning incense and presenting drink offerings to other gods. Therefore, the Lord removed His hand from Judah and watched as disaster struck them.

If you declare Jesus as Lord and Savior of your life, take time to listen and obey Him. Walk in humility and recognize your need for Him. Look for ways the Lord is speaking to you through His Word, through others, through dreams, and through the Holy Spirit. You will begin to see He is with you. He will either confirm the steps in your life or give you warnings to turn away from idols, false gods, pride, or other issues that have gotten in the way of your love for God. Ask the Lord to search your heart. Also slow down and seek the Lord. He will be found when you search for Him with all your heart. Think about how often you seek the things of the world, and yet how much do you seek the Lord? Today, put your screens away for thirty minutes, and spend that time in God's Word or in prayer. *Don't ignore the Lord God of your life.*

---

*So I sent you all My servants the prophets time and time again, saying: Don't do this detestable thing that I hate. But they did not listen or pay attention; they did not turn from their evil or stop burning incense to other gods.* —Jeremiah 44:4–5

---

Further Scripture: Psalm 119:10; Jeremiah 44:10, 26–28

*Week 37, Day 255: Jeremiah 46–47*

Turn Back

The Egyptians sinned and turned away from the Lord, and so the Lord handed them over to the Babylonians. But even after this time of war and punishment, the Lord declared through Jeremiah that people would one day inhabit the land again. In the same way the Lord would bring punishment and discipline to the people of Israel, *if they turned back to Him, He would save them.*

The Lord forgives, offering grace and mercy every single day. God loves you with unconditional love, which means His love is not determined by what you do or who you are. God simply and powerfully loves you. If you sin, wander away, or mess up, He never leaves you. God will wait for you to repent and turn away from your evil ways. Therefore, humble yourself and turn back to Him. Today, pray for that person who needs to turn back to the Lord. He is the God of hope, the God of healing, and the God of miracles. Pray for a miracle today. He is the God who saves, *if only* people humble themselves and turn back to Him.

---

*The LORD of Hosts, the God of Israel, says: "I am about to punish Amon, god of Thebes, along with Pharaoh, Egypt, her gods, and her kings— Pharaoh and those trusting in him. I will hand them over to those who want to take their lives—to Nebuchadnezzar king of Babylon and his officers. But after this, it will be inhabited again as in ancient times." This is the LORD's declaration.* —Jeremiah 46:25–26

---

Further Scripture: 2 Chronicles 7:14–15; Jeremiah 46:28; Luke 17:3–4

## *Week 37, Day 256: Jeremiah 48—49*

### Restoration Through the New Covenant

Jeremiah prophesied against many nations: Moab, Ammon, Edom, Damascus, Kedar, Hazor, and Elam. They had sought their own ways, formed their own gods, and boasted in themselves, not in the Lord. The Lord saw everything and brought about the judgment and punishment they deserved. *Nevertheless*, for some of the nations, the Lord would *restore their lives in the last days.*

God sees, and God restores. He is the loving, gracious Father. Today, the Lord sees your pride, your selfishness, your arrogance, your haughty heart, and the things you treasure. He sees. You cannot hide from the Lord. He will try to draw you back to Him with His everlasting love. Turn back to the Lord. Ask Him to search your heart to see if there is any offensive way in you. As the Lord reveals areas in your heart that need repentance, humility, or forgiveness, obey His leading. *The Lord will restore you.* The Lord will renew your heart. Make today the day you stop wandering away from Him. That thing you need to cease doing—stop it. That person you know you need to forgive—call them. That possession you need to sell—let it go. The Lord wants to restore you beyond what you can imagine.

---

*Yet, I will restore the fortunes of Moab in the last days. This is the LORD's declaration. The judgment on Moab ends here.* —Jeremiah 48:47

---

Further Scripture: Psalm 26:2–3; 139:23–24; Jeremiah 48:29–30

## *Week 37, Day 257: Jeremiah 50*

### Persia Overthrowing Babylon

Babylon destroyed Jerusalem and the land of Judah. And God declared He would demolish the Babylonian cites. Just like in Sodom and Gomorrah, no one would remain. God called the Israelites *His redeemed, His beloved, His chosen people.* He protectively watched over His people, and He saw those who harmed them. God sought judgment on the Babylonian nation who harmed His beloved. He opened His armory of weapons and brought turmoil to Babylon.

The Lord sees your life. He calls you *His beloved, His redeemed, His chosen.* His hand rests on you. God says He will hide you in the shadow of His wings and protect you. He watches over you by day and by night. He is with you and never leaves you or forsakes you. He sees those who harm you, who hurt you, and who mistreat you. Run to Him. He will protect you and watch over you with His strength. The God of Hosts promises to open His armory and bring out His weapons of wrath. He *promises to fight your battles for you.* Today, allow the Lord of Hosts to fight for you. Be still and rest in His love.

---

*This is what the Lord of Hosts says:*
*Israelites and Judeans alike have been oppressed.*
*All their captors hold them fast;*
*they refuse to release them.*
*Their Redeemer is strong;*
*Yahweh of Hosts is His name.*
*He will fervently plead their case*
*so that He might bring rest to the earth*
*but turmoil to those who live in Babylon.* —Jeremiah 50:33–34

---

Further Scripture: Psalm 78:35; Jeremiah 50:24–25, 40

*Week 37, Day 258: Jeremiah 51—52*

The Fulfillment of God's Promises

Judgment and destruction came to the land of Judah just as Jeremiah had prophesied. And yet, even in the midst of these dark times, Jeremiah highlighted Jehoiachin, king of Judah, in the line of David, the lineage of Christ. After the destruction, King Jehoiachin remained alive in prison. And yet Judah's King Jehoiachin received a pardon by King Evil Merodach. King Jehoiachin received new robes and a place at the king's table, in the presence of the king, for the remaining days of his life.

The same is available for you. No matter the disaster you are in, the captivity you face, or the destruction all around you, *the King of kings and Lord of lords invites you to join Him at His table in the kingdom of God.* When you receive His invitation, He will clothe you in new white robes of righteousness. You will enter into a royal priesthood as a chosen one. You are a possession of your heavenly Father, the Lord God Almighty, who was and is and is to come. Will you say yes to your invitation? Will you humbly receive the invitation from Jesus to sit at His table and wear robes of righteousness? He wants you to have a seat because He loves you.

---

*He spoke kindly to him and set his throne above the thrones of the kings who were with him in Babylon. So Jehoiachin changed his prison clothes, and he dined regularly in the presence of the king of Babylon for the rest of his life.* —Jeremiah 52:32–33

---

Further Scripture: Zechariah 3:4; Luke 12:37; Revelation 22:14

## *Week 37, Day 259: Lamentations 1—2*
Jeremiah's Laments

Jeremiah wrote Lamentations from Jerusalem's perspective as a hurting and struggling city following Judah's destruction and punishment. The city felt alone. She wept during bitter nights and found no comfort from others because all her friends had betrayed her. There were only feelings of anxiety. No rest could be found. Jerusalem had sinned greatly and now experienced the consequences. She felt humiliated and admitted her rebellion. At last Jerusalem's heart broke.

Sometimes you may feel lonely, humiliated, or shamed, regretting your past, your sin, and the consequences you now face. It hurts when no one cares to comfort you. You may feel naked and exposed or simply broken. Today, *allow yourself to embrace what you feel.* Feeling can be a first step toward healing and lead you to see the Lord in the midst of your pain. Give yourself permission to tell the Lord how you feel, and let the tears fall. Remember the Lord loves you. The Lord is near to the brokenhearted. Allow His love and grace to pour over you today.

*LORD, see how I am in distress.*
*I am churning within;*
*my heart is broken,*
*for I have been very rebellious.*
*Outside, the sword takes the children;*
*inside, there is death.* —Lamentations 1:20

Further Scripture: Psalm 34:18; Lamentations 1:2; Romans 8:18

## Week 38, Day 260: Lamentations 3
### Mercy for the One Who Suffers

The prophet Jeremiah cried out to the Lord in distress. He clearly articulated his feelings: "My soul has been deprived of peace; I have forgotten what happiness is. . . . My future is lost . . . I . . . have become depressed." And *yet*, in the midst of his lament, he recalled the promises of God: "*Because of the LORD's faithful love we do not perish, for His mercies never end. They* are new every morning; great is Your faithfulness! I say: The LORD is my portion; therefore I will put my hope in Him."

If you have ever gone through a dark, difficult season, feeling depressed, grieving, lonely, or like a failure, then you can relate to Jeremiah's words. Remember, it is okay to express your feelings to the Lord. Tell Him you are sad. Tell Him you are angry. Tell Him you are hurt. And *yet*, in the midst of feeling this way, *turn to Him and wait for Him*. He promises His love never ends. *He promises new mercies each morning*. Great is His faithfulness. Put your hope in the Lord, and when you rise up in the morning, give thanks for hope, give thanks for faithfulness, *give thanks for new mercies*, and give thanks for unfailing love. Take the day one step at a time and trust the Lord's faithfulness will go with you.

---

*Yet I call this to mind, and therefore I have hope:*
*Because of the LORD's faithful love*
*we do not perish, for His mercies never end.*
*They are new every morning; great is Your faithfulness!*
*I say: The LORD is my portion;*
*therefore I will put my hope in Him.* —Lamentations 3:21–24

---

Further Scripture: Psalm 16:5; 73:26; Lamentations 3:17–21

## Week 38, Day 261: Lamentations 4—5
## Prayer for Restoration

God's people spent years rejecting Him, worshipping false gods, and living in complete defiance and disobedience to the ways of the Lord. As a result, God gave them consequences and punishment. The people knew they had rejected God, and yet the question remained: *Had God completely rejected His people? Or would He grant mercy and grace; would He restore and renew them so they could return to Him?* They cried out with the ultimate cry for revival: "LORD, restore us to Yourself, so we may return."

You know the end of the story. And you know the Lord's character is rich in mercy, abounding in love, and gracious beyond measure. Years later God would send His Son Jesus, who died for the sin of the world. All who believe in Jesus will never perish but have everlasting life. Not because you earn it or deserve it, but because God loves you. He redeems you. From the east to the west, God has removed your sin and forgiven you. Nothing will ever separate you from His great love.

---

*LORD, restore us to Yourself, so we may return;*
*renew our days as in former times,*
*unless You have completely rejected us*
*and are intensely angry with us.* —Lamentations 5:21–22

---

Further Scripture: Psalm 103:12; John 3:16; Romans 8:37–39

### Ezekiel's Vision

The Lord revealed His glory to Ezekiel in a vision. In the presence of the Lord, Ezekiel fell facedown as he listened to the Lord's voice. In that moment Ezekiel received his divine assignment: *to speak to the Israelites who had rebelled against God.* They may listen or refuse to listen, but they would know the Lord sent a prophet to be among them. The Lord promised the prophet Ezekiel if he would just open his mouth, He would provide the words.

Ezekiel's unique calling as a prophet parallels your role as a follower of Christ in one important way. Jesus calls you to a similar assignment: *to proclaim the glory and good news of Jesus Christ to the ends of the earth.* Yes, even to those who may not listen or obey. As you go into all the nations, remember the first moment the Lord called you to follow Him. May the fire within you be rekindled to go forth in boldness, not with a spirit of timidity but of power, love, and sound mind. The Lord created you for this. Walk in confidence because the Lord's hand rests upon you. He promises to provide every word, every answer, everything you need to proclaim His name. Wait, listen, and trust His voice. He will show up and reveal Himself to you. Rely on His power.

---

*He said to me: "Son of man, I am sending you to the Israelites, to the rebellious pagans who have rebelled against Me. The Israelites and their ancestors have transgressed against Me to this day. The children are obstinate and hardhearted. I am sending you to them, and you must say to them, 'This is what the Lord GOD says.' Whether they listen or refuse to listen— for they are a rebellious house—they will know that a prophet has been among them." —Ezekiel 2:3–5*

---

Further Scripture: Ezekiel 1:28; 2:7; 2 Timothy 1:6–8

*Week 38, Day 263: Ezekiel 3*

## Messenger, Sufferer, Watchman, and Sign

The Lord called Ezekiel to serve and communicate to His people in different ways and promised to put words, sweet as honey, in Ezekiel's mouth. Then he would deliver a message the people did not want to hear. Ezekiel would be a watchman over the house of Israel, delivering messages of warning, regardless of the cost to himself. Through all of this, *Ezekiel followed obediently what he heard from the Lord.*

Obedience means you do what you've been told to do. *Nevertheless how can you walk out obedience to the Lord if you don't take the time to listen and hear His instructions for you?* It's like a child not taking time to listen to a parent's directions. You must posture yourself in a place of availability to hear from the Lord. As you walk with the Lord, you will go, do, and say what the Spirit leads you to do for His kingdom. Keep in mind, you are responsible to the Lord for *your obedience* (not the obedience or response of others). Listen to the Lord. Then obediently open your mouth as the Lord gives you words to speak. Remember, the Lord has plans for you as you walk in His Spirit.

---

*Then the hand of the LORD was on me there, and He said to me, "Get up, go out to the plain, and I will speak with you there." So I got up and went out to the plain. The LORD's glory was present there, like the glory I had seen by the Chebar Canal, and I fell facedown.* —Ezekiel 3:22–23

---

Further Scripture: Ezekiel 3:10–11, 27; Galatians 5:25

## Week 38, Day 264: Ezekiel 4–5

### A Remaining Remnant

Ezekiel proclaimed that the Lord's anger toward Israel would soon reveal itself. Jerusalem, the center of the nations, had rebelled against the Lord, His ordinances, and His statues, and had rejected Him. The Lord's plan would come forth: a third of the people would die by sword, a third would die by plague and famine, and a third would be scattered and die as the sword chased after them. But even in the judgment, the scattered would *develop a remnant*—a few surviving people from Israel, thus ensuring God would never completely wipe out His chosen people. As the Lord instructed him, Ezekiel symbolically demonstrated God's promise as he tucked a few pieces of his beard under the folds of his robes.

Even today the Lord searches for those believers in Christ who truly follow His ways. Yes, you are saved by grace, *but are you living your life fully surrendered to the Lord?* As you follow Him, you will experience the goodness of the fullness of the Lord. Just as Ezekiel tucked a few pieces of hair and hid them in the folds of his robe, as you follow the Lord surrendered to His will, He will hide you in the shadow of His wings. He will protect you and care for you. He is the Good Shepherd, and He loves you.

---

*But you are to take a few strands from the hair and secure them in the folds of your robe.* —Ezekiel 5:3

---

Further Scripture: Isaiah 1:9; Ezekiel 5:11–12; Ephesians 3:17b–19

## *Week 38, Day 265: Ezekiel 6–7*
Announcement of the End

Ezekiel announced the end was coming. Doom was on the horizon. The people had their high places. They had sought wealth over the Lord. They had worshipped idols before worshipping the God Almighty. And now the Lord was going to bring judgment and destruction. When destruction finally came, the people would know that *God is Yahweh. He is the One and Only True God.*

Whom do you worship? Whom or what do you seek with all your heart? Do you seek to find peace and hope in the things of this world? Idols? Perfectionism? Wealth? Identity? *The one and only thing worth attaining is hope and peace from the Lord.* Other things only bring temporary satisfaction. They will leave you discontented and searching for even more. The things of this world are stumbling blocks and may ultimately lead you to destruction. However, if you fall to the bottom, it's often then you realize the truth—*God is Yahweh.* He is the God who brings complete satisfaction. Today, worship Him with all your heart, and *let the other things of this world fade away.*

> *So I will bring the most evil of nations*
> *to take possession of their houses.*
> *I will put an end to the pride of the strong,*
> *and their sacred places will be profaned.*
> . . . . . . . . . . . . . .
> *The king will mourn; the prince will be clothed in grief;*
> *and the hands of the people of the land will tremble.*
> *I will deal with them according to their own conduct,*
> *and I will judge them by their own standards.*
> *Then they will know that I am Yahweh.* —Ezekiel 7:24, 27

Further Scripture: Ezekiel 7:19; Matthew 5:6; 1 John 2:15

## Week 38, Day 266: Ezekiel 8–10

The Departure of the Shekinah Glory of God

In Ezekiel's vision from the Lord, he saw people committing terrible and detestable things inside the temple. The place intended for God's glory and worship was being used as a place to worship false idols, and detestable things were engraved all over the walls. Ezekiel saw the vision of the Lord's wrath slaughtering Jerusalem. He also saw a man going through the city and marking the people who groaned and sighed at the detestable practices committed in the temple. The Lord discerned the hearts of those not pleased with the detestable practices, and the Lord would save them from the slaughter. Ultimately, the Lord removed the presence of His glory from the temple.

When you see people doing evil, what do you do? Walk away? Sigh and groan? Join in and experiment? Seek the Lord and ask for His wisdom and discernment? The Lord calls you to walk in His ways and to discern His good, pleasing, and perfect will. He says: *Flee from evil. Do not conform to the patterns of the world. Do not love the things of this world, which is filled with pride and lust. Love without hypocrisy. Cling to what is good.* Even if you think it's lonely to be the "only one" clinging to good, God is there with you. As you cling to the Lord, the Lord promises to watch over you all the days of your life.

---

*He called to the man clothed in linen with the writing equipment at his side. "Pass throughout the city of Jerusalem," the LORD said to him, "and put a mark on the foreheads of the men who sigh and groan over all the detestable practices committed in it."* —Ezekiel 9:3–4

---

Further Scripture: Ezekiel 9:6; Romans 12:9; 1 John 2:15–17

*Week 39, Day 267: Ezekiel 11–13*

## Ezekiel Dramatizes the Exile

The people of Israel lived rebelliously and did not believe in the Lord's messages through the prophet Ezekiel. However, the Lord made it clear the *fulfillment of every vision would come to pass.*

The Word of God says Christ will return. You just don't know when. As a follower of Christ, you are to live ready for His return. Don't live life exhausted and sleepy. Wake up and live by the power of the Holy Spirit. Believe in Jesus, surrender your life to Him, and allow His Spirit to transform you. Don't delay turning to Jesus, thinking you have time to do your own thing, ignoring God's call on your life. Don't resist coming to Jesus, believing you need to get clean or get your life in order before you turn to Him. He wants you to *receive His love and grace in your life.* Then He will transform you and equip you with strength and grace each day. With His power flowing through you, you will live ready for His return. No fear, no pain, no worry—just the peace of Jesus.

---

*Son of man, what is this proverb you people have about the land of Israel,*
*which goes:*
*The days keep passing by,*
*and every vision fails?*
*Therefore say to them: This is what the Lord* GOD *says: I will put a stop to this proverb, and they will not use it again in Israel. But say to them: The days draw near, as well as the fulfillment of every vision.*
—Ezekiel 12:22–23

---

Further Scripture: Ezekiel 12:25; Matthew 25:10–13; 2 Peter 3:3–4

## Week 39, Day 268: Ezekiel 14—15
### Divided Hearts of Worship

Elders of Israel sat before the prophet Ezekiel acting religious. The Lord told the elders, "Repent and turn away from your idols; turn your faces away from all your detestable things." If they chose not to, Yahweh would turn against them and cut them off from His people. God could see the idols they had set up, *not just on the outside but also in their hearts*. He recognized their divided hearts of worship. The elders knew they disobeyed God but still chose not to turn away from evil.

Like the elders of Israel, you may say the right things and be at all the right Christian events, making you look like a great Christ-follower. However, you haven't fooled God. God sees your heart. He knows your heart—even the parts you've worked hard to keep hidden. The Lord desires that you worship no other gods beside Him. Today, ask the Lord, *"Is there anything in my life You want me to repent and turn away from?"* Don't let a false god or an idol become the stumbling block for your relationship with Jesus. He has more for you than you can imagine. He has gifts and goodness beyond what you can see right now. But to see or enjoy His blessings, first you need to *make time* and *make space* to experience the one true God in your life.

---

*Therefore, say to the house of Israel: This is what the Lord GOD says: Repent and turn away from your idols; turn your faces away from all your detestable things.* —Ezekiel 14:6

---

Further Scripture: Ezekiel 14:4–5; 1 Corinthians 10:14; Revelation 9:20

# September 25

*Week 39, Day 269: Ezekiel 16—17*

The Parable of the Adulterous Wife

The Word of the Lord spoken through Ezekiel symbolically described the nation of Israel as an adulterous wife and eventually as a prostitute. In the beginning Israel received and sought the Lord for help and life. However, ultimately, Israel became self-sufficient, indulged in idols, and turned away from the Lord. Because they turned away, Israel deserved and received wrath and judgment. Even still God offered hope through the everlasting covenant and granted atonement for all Israel had done. These were His chosen people.

The Lord chose you as His child. The Lord longs for you to embrace the abundant life found in Him. Although you are self-sufficient, although you seek other gods, and although you walk in the ways of this world, *Jesus continues to love you.* God sent His Son to die for you. Jesus died as atonement for your sin so you may receive salvation and have eternal life. God is faithful to keep His everlasting covenant. You just have to receive it. Say, "*Yes,* I believe Jesus saves me from my sin." Say *yes* and you will have eternal life. Say *yes* to walking with Christ. He said *yes* to you long ago and *loves* you so much!

---

*"I will establish My covenant with you, and you will know that I am Yahweh, so that when I make atonement for all you have done, you will remember and be ashamed, and never open your mouth again because of your disgrace." This is the declaration of the Lord GOD.*
—Ezekiel 16:62–63

---

Further Scripture: Ezekiel 16:6–7; John 3:16; Romans 5:8–9

## *Week 39, Day 270: Ezekiel 18—19*
### Individual Responsibility for Sin

God made it clear to the people of Israel that He could free them from bondage—*if only they turned to Him.* Their family didn't define them nor did the past. The Lord longed to give them life! God is just and will judge His people according to their ways, but God also finds pleasure in setting His people free when they turn from their wicked ways and live with Him.

Even today the Word of the Lord remains the same. *Your family doesn't define you nor does your past.* You can break free from the generational sins of your family. Your alcoholic grandparent does not define who you are today. Your parents' debt does not make you who you are. The generations of divorce in your family *can stop* with you through the power of Jesus. His blood covers all sin. The Lord came to set you free from sin and guilt. The Lord can break the bondage of generational sin. If this is your desire, *then you must turn and seek Him.* Repent, turn from your transgressions, and seek the Lord. You will be set free, and a new chapter will begin in your family's history.

---

*"Therefore, house of Israel, I will judge each one of you according to his ways." This is the declaration of the Lord GOD. "Repent and turn from all your transgressions, so they will not be a stumbling block that causes your punishment. Throw off all the transgressions you have committed and get yourselves a new heart and a new spirit. Why should you die, house of Israel? For I take no pleasure in anyone's death." This is the declaration of the Lord GOD. "So repent and live!"* —Ezekiel 18:30–32

---

Further Scripture: Ezekiel 18:23; 1 Timothy 2:3–4; 2 Peter 3:9

## *Week 39, Day 271: Ezekiel 20–21*

### Elders Consult God

The elders of Israel came to consult God. In response God brought to their attention all the ways they had turned away from Him and lived only for themselves. The Lord had such great plans and promises for His chosen people. *When the elders inquired of God, He saw right into their rebellious hearts.* They sought everything except the Lord, and now they wanted to inquire a fresh word from Him. He responded confidently through the prophet Ezekiel: "As I live, I will not be consulted by you!"

Like Israel's elders, you may come to the Lord longing for Him to give you a fresh word. You may wonder *why you don't seem to hear or see Him.* However, if you are living a double-sided life, attempting to walk one foot with Jesus and one foot caught up in the ways of the world, then you may stumble and fall down. God longs to have your whole heart turned toward Him, not just parts of it. It may be time to humble yourself and purify your heart so you can see and hear Him more clearly. With humility in your heart, walk worthy of God's calling. He knows you, He sees you, and He loves all of you. He just wants your humble, honest, whole-hearted devotion as you come before Him.

---

*"When you offer your gifts, making your children pass through the fire, you continue to defile yourselves with all your idols to this day. So should I be consulted by you, house of Israel? As I live"—this is the declaration of the Lord GOD—"I will not be consulted by you!"* —Ezekiel 20:31

---

Further Scripture: Romans 13:11–14; Colossians 1:10–11; 1 Peter 5:5–6

## *Week 39, Day 272: Ezekiel 22—23*

Be the One

The Lord searched for just *one* man to stand in the gap and stand before the Lord on behalf of all in the land. *Just one righteous person.* The Lord could not find even one. Therefore, God poured out His indignation and consumed Israel with the fire of His fury.

The Lord longs for His people to stand in the gap between the darkness and the light. He needs people to serve as watchmen and intercede for His children. He needs people to give warning and speak truth until Christ's return. The Lord commands you to be strong and to stand firm, to fix your eyes on Him, to live with courage and boldness through the power of His Spirit. *You are the one* the Lord calls to intercede for His people. Cry out to the Lord on behalf of you family, your community, and your nation. *Pray* for people to turn back to Him as their one true God. Speak truth into this generation today. Be the *one* to stand in the gap.

---

*I searched for a man among them who would repair the wall and stand in the gap before Me on behalf of the land so that I might not destroy it, but I found no one.* —Ezekiel 22:30

---

Further Scripture: Psalm 1:1; Isaiah 59:16; Ephesians 6:13

# September 29

*Week 39, Day 273: Ezekiel 24–26*

The Parable of the Boiling Pot

The Lord instructed His prophet Ezekiel to share a parable about a boiling pot to those remaining in Jerusalem, the rebellious house. Ultimately the people chose not to purify themselves or cleanse themselves before the Lord; therefore, God brought judgment and wrath. Ezekiel prophesied with confidence from the Lord and in obedience, without holding back. It was the hard truth God's people needed to hear.

Think of your life like a boiling pot. Are *you willing to allow God's "hot water" to cleanse* and purify your heart, your mind, your body? Are you willing to let God's love and grace clean you from the inside out? It means surrendering to Him *all* of whatever uncleanliness you have in your heart—pride, envy, outbursts of anger, selfish ambitions, or idolatry. Ask the Lord to have His way. He will forgive you. He will purify you. He will wipe you clean with His love. The first step is turning to Him, repenting of your sins, and walking away with His strength and power. You will step into His love and His great faithfulness.

---

*Because of the indecency of your uncleanness—*
*since I tried to purify you,*
*but you would not be purified from your uncleanness—*
*you will not be pure again*
*until I have satisfied My wrath on you.* —Ezekiel 24:13

---

Further Scripture: Psalm 51:10–13; 2 Corinthians 7:1; 1 John 1:9

## *Week 40, Day 274: Ezekiel 27–29*
### The Fall of Tyre's Ruler

Tyre's empire grew with the king's wisdom, understanding, wealth, and great trading skills. Although the king was wise, the Lord saw how his heart had become prideful. Therefore, the Lord brought judgment and destruction, and the kingdom of Tyre fell.

It's tempting to build your own kingdom. You may try to justify your actions by saying everyone else is building their own kingdoms, for example, living the "American Dream." Ask yourself: *Do I find greater comfort and peace in my business, my marriage, my wealth, my family, or even myself rather than in the Lord?* The Lord knows and will reveal the truth to you. *Sometimes* you have to go to the bottom to realize your pride at the top. The Lord doesn't want you to play god in your kingdom. He has specific roles and purposes for you in His kingdom. He says, "Seek first the kingdom of God and His righteousness, and all these things will be provided for you." The Lord wants you to ask Him, lean on Him, and trust His promises. Remember, He is able to do above and beyond what you can even imagine, and He will reveal your path in life. Put your life in His hands and seek Him first.

*Your heart became proud because of your beauty;*
*for the sake of your splendor*
*you corrupted your wisdom.*
*So I threw you down to the earth;*
*I made you a spectacle before kings.* —Ezekiel 28:17

Further Scripture: Psalm 25:4; Proverbs 11:2; Matthew 6:33

# October 1

## Week 40, Day 275: Ezekiel 30—32
### Personal Responsibility for Sin

The word of the Lord came to Ezekiel saying Egypt would continue to grow weaker. If one arm was already broken, then God would break the other. They would not be bandaged or given medicine, allowing zero opportunity for Egypt to fight back. The Egyptians faced punishment because they had refused God and were an idolatrous, pagan nation that stood against His chosen people. The Egyptians would lose their strength completely, and the Babylonians would prevail against them.

Are there things falling apart around you? Perhaps your car, your house, or your health? Have you ever stopped and asked the Lord: *Are You trying to communicate something to me?* It takes humility to stop, listen, and lean into the Lord. The Lord may be trying to refine you. Or it could be because, like the Egyptians, you have completely rejected the Lord in an area in your life. In either situation, stop and ask the Lord to reveal His plan, His purposes, and what He wants for you in this season. Ask Him what He wants to show you or teach you. As you journey with the Lord, remember every season carries a reason.

---

*Son of man, I have broken the arm of Pharaoh king of Egypt. Look, it has not been bandaged—no medicine has been applied and no splint put on to bandage it so that it can grow strong enough to handle a sword.*
—Ezekiel 30:21

---

Further Scripture: Ecclesiastes 3:11; John 15:2; 16:13

## *Week 40, Day 276: Ezekiel 33—34*
## The Lord Is Your Shepherd

The word of the Lord came through Ezekiel as he prophesied against the shepherds of Israel. He addressed how they were not fulfilling their role as shepherd to God's people. God instructed them to strengthen the weak, heal the sick, bandage the injured, bring back the strays, and seek the lost. Because they had not done this, the Lord promised to rescue the people, saying: "You are My flock, the human flock of My pasture, and I am your God." The Lord would soon send Jesus, in the lineage of David, as the ultimate shepherd to His people. Jesus would indeed strengthen, heal, bandage, bring back, and seek out the sheep— His chosen people.

You may need to hear *the Lord is your Shepherd*. You lack nothing in Christ. He makes you lie down in green pastures, and He restores your soul. Yes! Jesus is your good shepherd, and He cares for you, strengthens you, heals your hurt, brings you back when you have strayed away, and will seek after you if you are lost. Jesus loves you. Today, receive this truth for your life: *The Lord is your Shepherd, and you are seen by Him.*

---

*"Then they will know that I, Yahweh their God, am with them, and that they, the house of Israel, are My people." This is the declaration of the Lord* GOD. *"You are My flock, the human flock of My pasture, and I am your God." This is the declaration of the Lord* GOD. —Ezekiel 34:30–31

---

Further Scripture: Psalm 23:1–2; Ezekiel 34:15–16; John 10:14–15

## *Week 40, Day 277: Ezekiel 35—36*
Restoration of Israel's People

God's people had turned against Him and His commands. They had unclean ways and behavior. Therefore, the Lord poured out His wrath on them. He scattered the people among other countries and judged them according to their conduct and actions. However, the Lord, rich in mercy and grace, promised to bring them back to their own land and cleanse them. He promised to *give them a new heart and a new spirit*. He would remove their hearts of stone and replace them with hearts of flesh. The Lord would place His Spirit in them, causing them to follow His ways.

The Lord desires for you to receive His mercy and sufficient grace. If you feel numb and hardened to the Lord, He is able to remove your heart of stone and put a new heart within you. He is able through His Son, Jesus Christ. By faith, receive this grace for your life. Your hard heart filled with anger, lust, materialism, hurt, or selfishness will be set free. *The Holy Spirit will soften your heart as though God is giving you a spiritual heart transplant!* He will fill your heart with the joy of your salvation and the peace of Jesus your Savior. The presence of the Holy Spirit will be with you, and love will be the evidence of your new heart. Receive this heart transplant today!

---

*I will give you a new heart and put a new spirit within you; I will remove your heart of stone and give you a heart of flesh. I will place My Spirit within you and cause you to follow My statutes and carefully observe My ordinances. —Ezekiel 36:26–27*

---

Further Scripture: Galatians 2:20; Ephesians 2:3–5; Hebrews 8:10

# October 4

*Week 40, Day 278: Ezekiel 37–38*

The Valley of Dry Bones

The hand of the Lord rested on Ezekiel as His Spirit led Ezekiel to a valley of dry bones. The Lord commanded Ezekiel to prophesy to the bones: "Dry bones, hear the word of the LORD! . . . I will cause breath to enter you and you will live! . . . Then you will know that I am Yahweh." Ezekiel did as the Lord commanded, and *the dry bones came to life.*

As a believer, *Jesus brings you life.* He lives in you. He promises you full restoration. He promises to wake you up from a dead-like sleep and restore your soul. Ezekiel followed God's specific commands, spoke *life* over the bones, and those bones came alive. Today, as you think about people or situations around you needing to find *life*, choose to become the bearer of the life-giving power of Jesus. Begin to *speak words of hope and love* into your home, your spouse, your child, or your friend. May the Spirit of God raise them up, in Jesus' name, with life, with power, and with love. No longer may people live as though they are dead. Today, turn to Jesus in His Word, His presence, even with His people, and allow His Spirit to breathe life into you and those around you!

---

*Then He said to me, "Son of man, can these bones live?"*
*I replied, "Lord GOD, only You know."*
*He said to me, "Prophesy concerning these bones and say to them:*
*Dry bones, hear the word of the LORD! This is what the Lord GOD says to*
*these bones: I will cause breath to enter you, and you will live."*
*—Ezekiel 37:3–5*

---

Further Scripture: Proverbs 18:21; Ezekiel 37:10; John 6:63

## *Week 40, Day 279: Ezekiel 39*
Display God's Glory

Ezekiel prophetically declared the Lord would put an end to Gog and to his land, Magog. The Lord would stand against these forces on behalf of His beloved Israel, bringing destruction to Israel's enemies. Then the Lord would display His glory among all the nations as He restored and offered compassion to Israel. Israel would know Yahweh was their God, and He would not hide His face from them. He would pour out His Spirit on all of Israel.

You may feel as though you have enemies all around you and your world has fallen apart. People turn against you. The market fails. The health report lingers, and fear creeps in. Remember, chosen child of God, *the Lord is with you.* He stands in your midst. He sees the enemy. He sees the health report. *He knows the situation.* And He will defend you. He will fight for you. Today, He will be your refuge and your safe place. You can hide yourself in His great compassion for you. He will go before you, so you know He is your God. He will bring restoration to those He loves and to those who seek Him. He will pour out His loving Spirit upon you and display His glory to all.

---

*I will display My glory among the nations, and all the nations will see the judgment I have executed and the hand I have laid on them. From that day forward the house of Israel will know that I am Yahweh their God.*
—Ezekiel 39:21–22

---

Further Scripture: Psalm 5:11; 89:18; Ezekiel 39:28–29

### Week 40, Day 280: Ezekiel 40–41

## Details that Give Hope

God gave Ezekiel a vision of the new temple in the city of Jerusalem. The Lord appointed a man to walk Ezekiel around the city, viewing the temple, the altars, the courts, the gates, and all the exact details. The man instructed Ezekiel, "Look with your eyes, listen with your ears, and pay attention to everything I am going to show you." The Lord showed Ezekiel many details. If Ezekiel closed his eyes just for a minute, he'd miss them. God desired for Ezekiel to not miss any of the important details He had designed.

God speaks specifically to you. You may wonder . . . *was that the Holy Spirit's voice?* Or you may question . . . *what was that?* The enemy likes to discourage you, to put you in a place of discontentment and fear, and to steal your joy, time, and energy. However, the Lord will speak truth, hope, and specific convictions of the heart. He knows you, and He knows your situation. He knows when you sit up and when you lie down. Every single step has been established by the Lord because He delights in your way. Today, open your eyes, listen with your ears, and pay attention to the details. God wants to speak to you. *Don't be so busy that you miss Him.*

---

*He spoke to me: "Son of man, look with your eyes, listen with your ears, and pay attention to everything I am going to show you, for you have been brought here so that I might show it to you. Report everything you see to the house of Israel." —Ezekiel 40:4*

---

Further Scripture: Psalm 37:23; 95:7; Psalm 139:13–17

## *Week 41, Day 281: Ezekiel 42—44*
### Filled with God's Glory

Ezekiel saw the temple in his vision, the place where God's throne will rest and where the soles of God's feet will dwell among the Israelites forever. The house of Israel will no longer defile God's name but *rather worship His name above all other names for eternity. The temple will be filled with God's glory*, His voice will sound like the roar of mighty waters, and the earth will shine with His glory.

How often do you think about eternity? Remember your body is a temple for God's glory and His Spirit dwells in you. You can give praise and honor to the Lord and all He is preparing for you in eternity! As a believer of Jesus Christ, you will be in the *presence of God forever and ever*, and the whole earth will be filled with His glory. Praise the Lord for eternal salvation. Praise the Lord for this gift of eternal hope. Praise the Lord for the weight of His glory—His holiness manifested in beauty. Give thanks for the beauty God placed around you: the works of His hands through people, through His creation, and through circumstances pointing to His grace and mercy. Today, come into His presence with thanksgiving. Enter His courts with praise. Holy, holy, holy is the Lord God almighty! Worship His holy name, today!

---

*While the man was standing beside me, I heard someone speaking to me from the temple. He said to me: "Son of man, this is the place of My throne and the place for the soles of My feet, where I will dwell among the Israelites forever."* —Ezekiel 43:6–7

---

Further Scripture: Isaiah 6:3; Ezekiel 43:2–3; 1 Corinthians 3:16

## *Week 41, Day 282: Ezekiel 45—46*
### The Lord's Portion of the Land

Ezekiel received specific instructions that when the land is divided as an inheritance, a donation to the Lord must be set aside—a holy portion of the land given for the Lord's purposes. This donated land would be used by the priests who minister in the sanctuary and draw near to serve the Lord. It would provide a place for their houses, as well as a holy area for the sanctuary. But first the land had to be released and offered up as a donation to the Lord.

Have you ever asked the Lord if anything He entrusted to you is meant to be set aside as a "holy donation"? Perhaps He has plans and purposes for something He has given you to steward. It's something to pray through—donating part of your property, resources, time, or belongings to the Lord for His purposes. Take the time to ask the Lord. Then do it. Give it away freely, trusting Him and believing every good and perfect gift belongs to the Lord. Don't get tempted to judge others or simply follow what others are donating. Seek the Lord on your own and *ask Him how to specifically donate for His purposes.* He is a God of specifics. He is a God of honesty. He is a God who answers you when you ask. Ask Him today!

---

*When you divide the land by lot as an inheritance, you must set aside a donation to the LORD, a holy portion of the land, $8^1/_3$ miles long and $6^2/_3$ miles wide. This entire tract of land will be holy.* —Ezekiel 45:1

---

Further Scripture: Proverbs 3:9–10; Ezekiel 45:4; Mark 12:43–44

## *Week 41, Day 283: Ezekiel 47—48*

## Rivers of Living Water

Ezekiel remained in the vision with a man guiding him step by step. Eventually the man led Ezekiel through river water that originated as a trickle from the city of Jerusalem toward the Dead Sea. First, they stepped into ankle-deep water, then knee deep, then waist deep, and soon they swam in the water. In this prophetic vision the river brought life everywhere it flowed.

Wow! What a picture for today! Jesus is your living water. When you are planted in the river water of Jesus, He brings the dead to life and makes all things new. Jesus gives the gift of abundant life. Ask yourself: *Where am I in the river water?* Are you *ankle deep* as you walk and believe in Jesus? Are you *knee deep*, perhaps on your knees praying through concerns on your heart? Are you *waist deep* as you serve the Lord in a capacity you once only prayed about? Or perhaps you are swimming in the water, and your feet aren't even touching the bottom. You are experiencing the fullness of the Lord, living fully surrendered as you trust His living water to empower you through each moment of your day. Step into the river water with Jesus. As you remain in Him, He'll take you deeper and deeper!

---

*He said to me, "This water flows out to the eastern region and goes down to the Arabah. When it enters the sea, the sea of foul water, the water of the sea becomes fresh. Every kind of living creature that swarms will live wherever the river flows, and there will be a huge number of fish because this water goes there. Since the water will become fresh, there will be life everywhere the river goes."* —Ezekiel 47:8–9

---

Further Scripture: Ezekiel 47:3–5; John 7:38; Ephesians 3:19

### *Week 41, Day 284: Daniel 1–2*

Be a Daniel

King Nebuchadnezzar's court officials chose Daniel, one of several young Israelite men, to train for three years in preparation for service to the king's court in Babylon. The king assigned the men daily provisions from the royal table—food and wine that would compromise Daniel's faith. Boldly, Daniel asked permission to receive a different diet of vegetables and water. *God granted Daniel and three others favor from the chief official.* At the end of training, Daniel and his friends not only excelled physically above the others but the Lord also gave them wisdom and knowledge tenfold!

The Lord honors a heart that does not fear man but rather fears the Lord. Jesus says that if anyone wants to come with Him, they must deny themselves, take up their cross, and follow Him. Like Daniel, this may mean making a choice different from the crowd and trusting the Lord will make a way when there seems to be no way. You must believe the Lord will be with you when you honor Him and walk in integrity. Today, *make the right choice in God's eyes,* even if it seems foolish, risky, or lonely. He's asking you to follow Him, walk in His ways, and not compromise your faith. Be a Daniel in your world today!

---

*Daniel determined that he would not defile himself with the king's food or with the wine he drank. So he asked permission from the chief official not to defile himself. God had granted Daniel favor and compassion from the chief official.* —Daniel 1:8–9

---

Further Scripture: Daniel 1:17, 20; Matthew 16:24; Luke 16:10

## *Week 41, Day 285: Daniel 3—4*
### Nebuchadnezzar's Golden Statue

King Nebuchadnezzar commanded people to worship a gold statue. If anyone refused, they would be thrown into a blazing, fiery furnace. In spite of this decree, Shadrach, Meshach, and Abednego *took a stand for their God,* refusing to bow down and worship this idol. Consequently, they were thrown into the furnace. However, their hope remained in the Lord as they declared that even if the Lord did not save them, they would not serve Nebuchadnezzar's gods. After a night in the blazing furnace, these men walked out untouched and unharmed by the heat and fire! The Lord delivered them. When the king saw this miracle, he proclaimed the great deliverance of the one true God.

When you face a fiery trial, does your confidence rest in the Lord to deliver you? Is your hope *found in Him alone?* Today, whatever trial you face, *believe the Lord is mighty to save.* He's your deliverer. His presence is near. Trust the Lord will be your rock, your fortress, and your shield. Right now, call upon His name. Refuse to compromise your worship and your commitment to the Lord. Trust He will deliver you through this fire. And even if He does not, continue to worship the name of the Lord. He will be with you. Stand and praise His name right now in the middle of your "fire."

---

*Nebuchadnezzar exclaimed, "Praise to the God of Shadrach, Meshach, and Abednego! He sent His angel and rescued His servants who trusted in Him. They violated the King's command and risked their lives rather than serve or worship any god except their own God. . . . For there is no other god who is able to deliver like this."* —Daniel 3:28–29

---

Further Scripture: Psalm 18:2; Isaiah 43:2; Daniel 3:18

## *Week 41, Day 286: Daniel 5—7*

### Daniel Delivered from Lions

King Darius enforced an edict stating anyone who worshipped a god beside the king would be thrown into a lion's den. Upon hearing this Daniel opened a window facing Jerusalem, and three times a day, got down on his knees, prayed, and gave thanks to his God. He was found worshipping God and thrown into the lion's den. During the night the Lord sent His angel to shut the lion's mouths, protecting Daniel! The Lord delivered Daniel as he walked by faith, worshipping the one and only true God.

Although culture says to follow this way for safety, that way for assurance, and another way for an anxious-free life, God says: "If you love Me, then follow Me." God promises to help you, guide you, deliver you, comfort you, and be your rock and refuge. *Trust the Lord without compromising your faith.* It may seem risky to take the road less traveled, but don't compromise. Take the risk and follow Christ. He has plans and promises He wants to reveal to you. But first you need to take that step of faith and follow Him. Trust the Lord and worship Him above all else.

---

*When Daniel learned that the document had been signed, he went into his house. The windows in its upper room opened toward Jerusalem, and three times a day he got down on his knees, prayed, and gave thanks to his God, just as he had done before.* —Daniel 6:10

---

Further Scripture: Daniel 6:16, 21–23; Acts 5:29

## *Week 41, Day 287: Daniel 8—10*
### Daniel's Prayer and Vision

As Daniel continued to follow the Lord, God delivered him and saved his life from the most impossible situations. He entrusted Daniel with visions foretelling the end of time and the last days. The visions overwhelmed Daniel, even caused him to lay sick for days. And yet *Daniel sought the Lord in the midst of his distress with prayer and petition.* He cried out to the Lord to show favor, to hear, to forgive, to listen, and to act. The Lord saw Daniel and heard his prayer. An angel confirmed that God heard Daniel's prayers and that God treasured him. Because Daniel prayed, this angel helped Daniel understand the visions. He instructed Daniel to not be afraid but *to have peace and be strong.*

When you are in anguish over this world, remember to seek the Lord in prayer on behalf of yourself, your family, and your nation. Ask the Lord to show His favor, to hear, to forgive, to listen, and to act. *The Lord will hear your prayers.* You are a treasured child of God. He wants you to understand His peace abides in you. Be strong. Do not fear the end days. Rather stand firm. Trust the Lord. Seek the Lord in prayer, and He will hear you and answer you. Trust him today.

---

*Therefore, our God, hear the prayer and the petitions of Your servant. Show Your favor to Your desolate sanctuary for the Lord's sake. Listen, my God, and hear. Open Your eyes and see our desolations and the city called by Your name. For we are not presenting our petitions before You based on our righteous acts, but based on Your abundant compassion. Lord, hear! Lord, forgive! Lord, listen and act! My God, for Your own sake, do not delay, because Your city and Your people are called by Your name.*
—Daniel 9:17–19

---

Further Scripture: Deuteronomy 7:6; Daniel 10:12, 19

## *Week 42, Day 288: Daniel 11–12*
### Shine Until the End

Daniel continued to see a vision of the final days. At the end of time, the wise will shine like the bright expanse in the heavens, and those who lead many to righteousness will shine like stars. Many will be purified, cleansed, and refined until the end. However, the wicked will act wickedly and will not understand. Only the wise will understand. The vision Daniel saw from the Lord was to be sealed until the end of time. Daniel would rest and then rise to his destiny.

Like Daniel, you may ask, "How long until the end of time?" You read the visions, you imagine the end days, and what do you do until then? *Hold fast and draw near to Jesus.* As you do, He will draw near to you. Resist the devil and flee from wickedness. Walk in the righteousness of Christ as you receive His love. In faith, continue to purify your heart, cleanse your hands, and, as the Lord allows refinement in your life, lean even further into Him. In doing so, it will prepare you to be like one of the stars shining in the heavens. The Lord will honor your faithfulness as you seek Him. Do not be afraid of what tomorrow holds. Hold firmly to the Lord, and He will bring you peace and understanding.

---

*Many of those who sleep in the dust*
*of the earth will awake,*
*some to eternal life,*
*and some to shame and eternal contempt.*
*Those who are wise will shine*
*like the bright expanse of the heavens,*
*and those who lead many to righteousness,*
*like the stars forever and ever.* —Daniel 12:2–3

---

Further Scripture: Daniel 12:9–10; Philippians 2:14–16; James 4:7–8

***Week 42, Day 289: Hebrews 1***

## Jesus Is Greater than the Angels

God appointed Jesus heir of all things. Jesus, creator of the universe, lived on earth as the human flesh of God. He shines with God's glory and *holds all things together by His command*. Jesus died to cleanse and purify you of your sin. Then He rose from death and sat down at the right hand of God in heaven. Therefore, *Jesus is far better than the angels*.

Yes! Jesus holds all things together. He sustains all things by His powerful word. He knows every detail of your life, even the burdens you carry. Jesus reigns on the throne forever—a strong, mighty, superior God, and yet He desires for you to talk to Him, to sit with Him, to pour out your heart to Him. Today, give thanks for Jesus, the Son of God, your sustainer. As you rest in the Lord, close your eyes. Picture Jesus like a glue stick in your life—*holding all things together*. Believe He is in all things and above all things. You will not fall. *He holds you.* He will anoint you with joy. The Lord sustains the weak and the weary because He is the Lord God almighty! You are precious in His sight, child of God.

---

*The Son is the radiance of God's glory and the exact expression of His nature, sustaining all things by His powerful word. After making purification for sins, He sat down at the right hand of the Majesty on high.*
—Hebrews 1:3

---

Further Scripture: Psalm 54:4; Colossians 1:17; Hebrews 1:4

### *Week 42, Day 290: Hebrews 2*
### Tested and Suffered

Jesus became flesh and blood and dwelt among His brothers. Jesus shared in suffering and testing, and He shared in dying. However, Jesus' death and resurrection destroyed the one who held the power of death, the devil. Death was defeated because of Jesus. Yes, Jesus brought freedom to those enslaved to sin. But not only that, since Jesus was tested and suffered, now He is *able to help* you during times of testing. Jesus was fully human and full of compassion.

Testing and suffering are big parts of life everyone experiences. Yet you are never fully prepared for the heartache these times bring. The people mocked and spat on Jesus, and He died a physically painful death. Yes, Jesus understands the pain you face in the midst of testing and suffering. Emotional, physical, or spiritual—*the Lord sees your suffering and is able to help you.* Do you hear that promise? *Jesus is able to help you.* Yes, you need help during seasons of suffering. You were not created to do this alone. *Jesus is able to help.* Therefore, open your hands to receive His kindness, open your eyes to see His hope, and open your heart to feel His presence. Lay your pride to the side and receive His help in the midst of your pain. You are not alone.

---

*For since He Himself was tested and has suffered, He is able to help those who are tested.* —Hebrews 2:18

---

Further Scripture: Psalm 121:1–2; Hebrews 2:14–15; 1 Peter 5:10

*Week 42, Day 291: Hebrews 3*

## Through the Cross

The author of Hebrews affirmed to his audience several benefits of Jesus' death on the Cross. The deceiver in this world can cause even a believer to doubt, to become deceived, or to turn away from Jesus. Therefore, you must encourage one another and not be hardened by sin's deception. Remember, Jesus is better than even Moses. Jesus offers a better hope, a better covenant, a better promise, a better sacrifice, a better provision, and an eternal home. You must hold on to the courage and the confidence of hope found in Jesus.

God instructs believers to *encourage one another daily.* He commands you to love one another as He loves you. You may ask, "But how do I encourage someone?" Help them find courage to keep going. It may include listening over lunchtime, reminding them of God's promises, praying together, asking the Lord for an encouraging word to speak over them, or coming alongside them to help fold laundry, mow the grass, or provide a meal. The Lord uses these acts of love to spur one another on in faith and help navigate the deception and evil ways in the world. Today, whom can you encourage to press on with hope in Jesus?

---

*But encourage each other daily, while it is still called today, so that none of you is hardened by sin's deception.* —Hebrews 3:13

---

Further Scripture: 1 Thessalonians 5:11; Hebrews 3:6; 10:23–25

## *Week 42, Day 292: Hebrews 4*
### Enter His Rest

Rest in the Lord and receive your promised salvation in Him. As you receive your eternal promise of heaven, the Lord says to cease striving for good works and achievements on this earth. *Release yourself from being in charge.* Rest in the Him, in His truth, and in His promises. Know that He is God, and trust that victory belongs to Him. He says, "Come to Me, all of you who are weary and burdened, and I will give you rest." Jesus will give you rest in your present life as you embrace Him completely. As you rest in His Word, allow it to speak life into your spirit and soul.

Nothing is hidden from the Lord. He sees you, and He alone judges your heart. He knows whether or not you have authentically repented and turned to Him. Therefore, admit your weakness, admit your need for a Savior to bear your burdens, and admit you cannot do anything on your own. Picture yourself lying on your back in a field of wildflowers. *Rest in God's goodness every day*, and finally, at the end of life, trust you will rest with your Savior forever. Today, come to the Lord, lay your burdens before Him, and you will find rest.

---

*Therefore, a Sabbath rest remains for God's people. For the person who has entered His rest has rested from his own works, just as God did from His. Let us then make every effort to enter that rest, so that no one will fall into the same pattern of disobedience.* —Hebrews 4:9–11

---

Further Scripture: Psalm 46:10; Matthew 11:28–30; Hebrews 4:12–13

## Week 42, Day 293: Hebrews 5

## A High Priest

The Lord is a High Priest who can relate to you. When Jesus became flesh and dwelt among men, He prayed and cried out reverently to God. Jesus believed God the Father was able to save Him from death, and He asked God if that was possible. However, God allowed Jesus to suffer and die. Even God's Son *learned obedience through what He suffered.*

Jesus the High Priest *learned obedience through His suffering.* God promises you will suffer, but like Jesus, *it is during these times of suffering that you learn obedience.* Suffering produces endurance, proves character, and gives hope. A four-year-old who sits in time-out feels as though he or she is suffering. But it's through the pain of being in the time-out that the child learns to yield to his or her parents and grows in obedience. Likewise, during your suffering, when you lean into the Lord, you gain a revelation from Him and appreciate His role in your life. The Lord will take you to new depths with His love, and *you will learn to walk even more obediently to Him.* Today, lean into the Lord during your suffering. The Lord will guide you and grow you in obedience as you walk closely with Him.

---

*During His earthly life, He offered prayers and appeals with loud cries and tears to the One who was able to save Him from death, and He was heard because of His reverence. Though He was God's Son, He learned obedience through what He suffered. —Hebrews 5:7–8*

---

Further Scripture: Psalm 119:71; Romans 5:3–4; 1 John 2:17

### *Week 42, Day 294: Hebrews 6*

## This Hope as an Anchor

Jesus offers you eternal hope as an anchor for your life. His hope is safe and secure. No matter what goes on around you—the storms, the hard work, the sickness—one thing is true: *when you believe in Jesus, you will be saved and have eternal life.* Therefore, rest in hope even when you cannot see. You can hope in the darkness. You can hope during the storms in life. You can hope in the chaos.

The Lord promises strength. The Lord promises protection. The Lord promises His presence. The Lord promises His faithfulness. Therefore, you can hang on to Him. With hope in Jesus as your anchor, you won't be moved. Hang on. The enemy will deceive and tempt you to go this way or that way, but hold on because God is stronger. Today, tell the Lord that *He is your anchor.* Picture hope tied around your waist anchoring you in the Lord. In Christ, you will remain secure and steadfast. You can do today. You can face tomorrow. The Lord is your strength and your shield, and your hope is anchored in Him. You will not be moved.

---

*We have this hope as an anchor for our lives, safe and secure. It enters the inner sanctuary behind the curtain.* —Hebrews 6:19

---

Further Scripture: Philippians 3:12; 2 Thessalonians 3:3; 1 John 5:13

### *Week 43, Day 295: Hebrews 7*
### A Greater Priesthood

Jesus is the guarantee of a better covenant. A better hope. A better priesthood. Better than the law. He did not come to destroy the law, but rather *Jesus came to fulfill the law.* Jesus came as the eternal sacrifice for the sin of the world. When the veil in the temple was split in two, believers were allowed full access to Jesus as their eternal priest. Jesus will always save those who believe in Him as their Savior, and Jesus will always intercede for you. Always. Forever. Guaranteed. Yes indeed, Jesus is the better priest, and He died as a sacrifice for your sins.

How does this relate to you as you live your life today? You have *full access to Jesus*, the kind of high priest who is holy, innocent, unde-filed, separated from sin, and exalted high above the heavens. Jesus died so you could be set free from your sin. He is your hope—the better hope. So today, no matter what your day brings, draw near to God with expectant hope. Remember, *you have direct access to the most High Priest*, Jesus, and His presence. Draw near to Him, and He will draw near to you.

---

*So Jesus has also become the guarantee of a better covenant. Now many have become Levitical priests, since they are prevented by death from remaining in office. But because He remains forever, He holds His priesthood permanently. Therefore, He is always able to save those who come to God through Him, since He always lives to intercede for them.*
*—Hebrews 7:22–25*

---

Further Scripture: Matthew 5:17; Hebrews 7:18–19; James 4:8

## *Week 43, Day 296: Hebrews 8*
## The New Covenant Is Superior

The author of Hebrews emphasized the main point about this new covenant to his readers: *People now have access to this better, superior, guaranteed covenant because of Jesus.* Jesus now serves as the Great High Priest, and He sits right next to God in the heavens. He leads worship in a tabernacle not built by man but built by God Himself. People need to recognize the access available to them and draw near to this eternal high priest, Jesus.

Are you getting stuck in the Old Covenant, trying to obtain salvation through your own good works, trying to make up for your sin? Remember, Jesus paid the sacrifice for your sin. He promises: "I will be merciful to their wrongdoing, and I will never again remember their sins." *Jesus is your Great High Priest*, and *you have direct access to Him every moment of every day.* He loves you as you are. He desires a relationship with you as you to live to glorify Him every day. It's not about acting good enough or doing all the correct "Christian activities." In Christ, you are enough. Today, rest at His feet, talk to Him, and listen to Him. Not because you must but because you *want to* have fellowship with your Savior, your Eternal High Priest.

---

*Now the main point of what is being said is this: We have this kind of high priest, who sat down at the right hand of the throne of the Majesty in the heavens, a minister of the sanctuary and the true tabernacle that was set up by the Lord and not man.* —Hebrews 8:1–2

---

Further Scripture: Jeremiah 31:31; Hebrews 8:6, 12

### *Week 43, Day 297: Hebrews 9*
Comparing the Old and New Covenants

The author of Hebrews described how the New Covenant—the ministry of Jesus, is better than the Old Covenant—the Law. The New Covenant has a greater, more perfect tabernacle. It is not made with earthly materials but is actually heaven itself as you enter into the presence of God. *In the New Covenant, you obtain redemption,* not from the sacrificial blood of animals year after year *but from the sacrifice of Jesus.* He died for the sins of the world once and for all. His obedience in death guaranteed your eternal salvation and redemption, thus allowing you to serve and glorify Jesus as Lord of lords and Kings of kings.

Give thanks for the New Covenant in Jesus, remembering your relationship with Him does not rest on rituals or owing God anything. It is not about earning your salvation through good works. Going to church, reading the Word of God, and praying reflects your love for God. You walk out these disciplines because they draw you near to the heart of God and facilitate His presence in your life. Today, ask yourself: *Am I drawing close to the Lord because I feel like I have to or because I desire to worship Him and seek His presence?* The Lord desires you to live freely in His love.

---

*But the Messiah has appeared, high priest of the good things that have come. In the greater and more perfect tabernacle not made with hands (that is, not of this creation), He entered the most holy place once for all, not by the blood of goats and calves, but by His own blood, having obtained eternal redemption.* —Hebrews 9:11–12

---

Further Scripture: Romans 6:8–11; Galatians 5:1; Hebrews 9:13–15

### Week 43, Day 298: Hebrews 10

Let Us Draw Near

Jesus' death on the Cross tore the veil in the temple, allowing you access to His grace, His mercy, and His love. In the New Covenant, Jesus serves as a great high priest over the entire the house of God—all who believe. You can *draw near* to Him. Come to Jesus fully assured by faith you will be saved.

Jesus wants you to *draw near* and *hold on to Him*. Pray. Seek him. Don't set up other gods or turn to false idols for hope, life, or victory. Jesus Christ is all you need. *Hold fast to Jesus, His power, and His Word.* He fills you with wisdom. He alone satisfies your hunger and thirst. As you hold on to Jesus, He instructs you to encourage others to seek Him just as you seek Him. Meet together. *Be concerned about each other.* Promote love and good works. Spur each other on, even when it hurts. And don't give up. Press on, encouraging each other to draw near to God. Jesus doesn't want you to live for Him in isolation. Whom can you be concerned about today? Go and love someone in the power of Jesus your Savior!

---

*Therefore, brothers, since we have boldness to enter the sanctuary through the blood of Jesus, by a new and living way He has opened for us through the curtain (that is, His flesh), and since we have a great high priest over the house of God, let us draw near with a true heart in full assurance of faith, our hearts sprinkled clean from an evil conscience and our bodies washed in pure water.* —Hebrews 10:19–22

---

Further Scripture: 2 Corinthians 4:1; 1 Thessalonians 5:17; Hebrews 10:23–25

*Week 43, Day 299: Hebrews 11*

Living by Faith

After discussing the better new covenant ministry of Jesus, the author of Hebrews said: "But we are not those who draw back and are destroyed, *but those who have faith and obtain life.*" What is this faith? "Faith is the reality of what is hoped for, the proof of what is not seen." Faith does not just believe Jesus is the Son of God, *it responds obediently to His voice as you draw near to Him.* This may include walking out what God is asking you to do, worshipping God alone, standing up for your belief in Jesus, or waiting in faith, not getting ahead of God.

Is there something you need to live out by faith? As you draw near to God, you take a step in obedience by faith. Open your mouth. Send an email and ask. Make the change. Faith requires you to trust God, release control, and understand it may sound unusual. Can you imagine what Noah went through building the ark without a drop of rain in sight? But by faith, Noah built the ark, and then it began to rain. You don't know the story the Lord is writing. You just know the steps He's asking you to take. *Without faith, it is impossible to please God.* Today, surrender your will. Say *yes* to the unseen. God will be with you, and you will obtain life!

---

*Now faith is the reality of what is hoped for, the proof of what is not seen. For our ancestors won God's approval by it.* —Hebrews 11:1–2

---

Further Scripture: Proverbs 3:5–6; Hebrews 10:39; 11:6–7

### *Week 43, Day 300: Hebrews 12*

## Run the Race with Endurance

Walking by faith can feel like such a challenge. Much like training to run a marathon, you begin with gentle steps of faith and slowly *build up the endurance to take larger leaps of faith with Jesus.* As a child of God, the Lord loves to teach you endurance in walking by faith. And yet when your heavenly Father recognizes an area He wants to strengthen, He will discipline you. It may feel hard. The discipline may make you cry. You may want to give up. But press on with faith, *believing in what you cannot see and trusting God's work in your life.* Through discipline and training, you will yield the fruit of peace and righteousness.

Yes, discipline and training from God is worth it. God is healing what needs healing in you. As you endure this season of discipline and training, fix your eyes on Jesus. Lay aside the things entangling you: bitterness, immorality, burdens, or other sin. Pursue peace. Even through this discipline, your faith in God cannot be shaken. You are walking on a solid, unshakable rock. His grace is sufficient to carry you through the difficulties. God's love is a consuming fire. He will light up your life. Just press on running toward His love.

---

*Therefore, since we also have such a large cloud of witnesses surrounding us, let us lay aside every weight and the sin that so easily ensnares us. Let us run with endurance the race that lies before us, keeping our eyes on Jesus, the source and perfecter of our faith, who for the joy that lay before Him endured a cross and despised the shame and has sat down at the right hand of God's throne. —Hebrews 12:1–2*

---

Further Scripture: Hebrews 12:7; 12:28–29; James 1:2–3

## *Week 43, Day 301: Hebrews 13*
### Sacrifice of Praise

The author of Hebrews established the point: *Jesus is better than the Law.* Then he shared pointers on how to live life as New Covenant believers in Christ. Love each other, show hospitality, remember prisoners, respect marriage by remaining pure, and have satisfaction with Christ because He is enough. Your home will be in eternity, not here on earth. Therefore, you will no longer offer up sacrifices in the temple but *rather a sacrifice of praise should continually be on your lips.*

Praise is essential in your relationship with Jesus. Just as you would encourage and lift up your spouse, your child, or your friend in a relationship, *you need to praise the name of Jesus.* Praise is an offer of worship. Praise is an offer of sacrifice. Praise is your battle cry. Lift up and confess the name of the Lord your God with thanksgiving and praise! As a believer in Christ, start your day in a place of worship and praise to the Lord. Pour out your heart and give Him thanks. Draw near to the Lord in worship and the other areas in life will come into alignment as you release your heart to the Lord God Almighty! Praise the Lord, your helper, who never leaves you nor forsakes you. May He alone satisfy you today!

---

*Therefore, through Him let us continually offer up to God a sacrifice of praise, that is, the fruit of our lips that confess His name.*
—Hebrews 13:15

---

Further Scripture: Psalm 34:1; 113:3; Hebrews 13:5–6

## *Week 44, Day 302: James 1*
### Joy in the Midst of Trials

The Lord says *you will* face trials and suffering in life. These trials produce endurance in you. Cultivating endurance may not be on your mind when you get the call about an accident, the news about test results, the burden of a hurt relationship, or when you just feel down and unable to do the next thing. But James challenged believers to consider it *great joy even in the midst of trials.* Remember, God promises to be with you, to walk with you, and to lift you up. He is your rock. He will provide everything you need.

As you need wisdom and strength to navigate through difficult days, seek the Lord *with faith, and ask Him for wisdom.* You don't have to have it all together before you ask the Lord. Rather, by faith, believe God has the answers and wisdom you need for today. He promises to give wisdom generously, without questioning or criticizing you. He will anchor you through the storm so that the worries of the world don't toss you around. God loves you so much, and He sees your hard place. Ask God for wisdom, and He will answer you.

---

*Now if any of you lacks wisdom, he should ask God, who gives to all generously and without criticizing, and it will be given to him. But let him ask in faith without doubting. For the doubter is like the surging sea, driven and tossed by the wind.* —James 1:5–6

---

Further Scripture: Psalm 25:9; Hebrews 11:6; James 1:2–3

## *Week 44, Day 303: James 2*
### An Outward Expression of Your Inward Faith

Faith *causes* you to do good works. It's your faith *in action*. Good works are the *outward sign of an inward faith*. Yes, you are saved by your faith in Jesus alone. And because God created you as His workmanship, He designed works for you to walk out. Therefore, the Holy Spirit will prompt you to do good works for His kingdom to outwardly express your love of God and love for others. You don't do good works because you must but rather as an expression of your faith in Jesus.

If your neighbors lose electricity at their home, the Holy Spirit may prompt you to invite them over for a home-cooked meal as an expression of God's love. You can choose to quench the Spirit, not listen, and have a quiet night. Or you can walk obediently in the Lord and unselfishly give up your time, energy, and resources, putting your faith into action. You love your neighbors not because you have to do good works but because walking by faith in Jesus causes you to express it with acts of love. Today, ask the Lord to lead you in expressing His love to others.

---

*What good is it, my brothers, if someone says he has faith but does not have works? Can his faith save him?*
*If a brother or sister is without clothes and lacks daily food and one of you says to them, "Go in peace, keep warm, and eat well," but you don't give them what the body needs, what good is it?* —James 2:14–16

---

Further Scripture: Matthew 22:36–39; Romans 3:28; Ephesians 2:8–10

### *Week 44, Day 304: James 3*
### Controlling the Tongue

Ask yourself these questions: *Do the words leaving my mouth edify others? Am I producing healing words or demeaning words?* James describes the tongue as a small part of the body, and yet it boasts great things. The tongue has the power and ability for great impact, positive or negative, in just a moment, like a rudder affects a boat. Even the smallest words can make a positive impact or create havoc, like a small fire igniting an entire forest. Just as a small bit controls the course of a horse on a path, your tongue controls the path of your life.

It may seem like an overwhelming responsibility to control your tongue. Ask the Lord for help. He will empower you with grace and power as you abide in Him, rest in Him, and walk with Him. The more time you spend in His Word, soaking His truth into your heart, the more He will empower you with self-control over your tongue. You will walk in His Spirit and not in your flesh. When you abide in God, His Spirit will guide you to choose words wisely, to listen rather than speak, and to sprinkle love and kindness with your spoken words. Today, *ask the Lord to help you control your tongue.* With Jesus, all things are possible.

---

*So too, though the tongue is a small part of the body, it boasts great things. Consider how large a forest a small fire ignites. And the tongue is a fire.*
—James 3:5–6

---

Further Scripture: John 15:5; Ephesians 4:29; James 1:19

***Week 44, Day 305: James 4***

## Love vs. Judging

Who are you to judge others? You have never walked in their shoes. You don't know their stories. So how can you be the judge? Critical comments made under your breath do not benefit anyone. Therefore, don't judge the way others parent, purchase things, what they are wearing, or even why they have a bad attitude. *Everyone has a story.* You don't need to judge others before hearing their story.

Ask the Lord to help you turn judgmental thoughts or comments into prayers. God says to submit to Him, resist the devil, and he will flee from you. Draw near to God, and He will draw near to you. Therefore, *draw near to God and resist the temptation to be critical and judgmental of your neighbors.* The Lord says to love your neighbor as yourself. Ask yourself, *how do I want to be loved as a neighbor?* Express love the way you want to be shown love. And if you don't have anything good to say—then you probably don't need to say it! The person you are tempted to judge could most likely use prayer and kindness. Therefore, seek the Lord on how to show them love like Jesus.

---

*Don't criticize one another, brothers. He who criticizes a brother or judges his brother criticizes the law and judges the law. But if you judge the law, you are not a doer of the law but a judge. There is one lawgiver and judge who is able to save and to destroy. But who are you to judge your neighbor?*
—James 4:11–12

---

Further Scripture: Romans 2:1–3; James 2:8; 4:7–8a

## *Week 44, Day 306: James 5*
## Pray and Believe

Paul wrote in Romans: "If you confess with your mouth, 'Jesus is Lord,' and believe in your heart that God raised Him from the dead, you will be saved." Yes, when you believe in Jesus, He calls you righteous. You don't have to do any specific sacrifice or good works to earn righteousness. When James wrote, "The urgent request of a righteous person is very powerful in its effect," he was talking about you, child of God. Yes, the Lord longs for you to *come before Him and ask Him your request.* You, in your human nature like Elijah, *have the power to ask the Lord for anything.*

Pray to the Lord. He hears every prayer. He will answer with either a resounding *yes,* perhaps a *no,* or to *wait* just a bit. By faith and with certainty, believe the Lord hears your prayers when you cry out to Him. Bring everything to the Lord. Praise Him. Thank Him. Ask for healing, provision, or salvation for a loved one. Pray without ceasing. Like a child who constantly makes requests to his father, in the same way, talk to your heavenly Father. Your prayers are effective. *Your prayers offered up with faith can move mountains,* cause it to rain, heal the sick, and bring back the lost. Today, pray and believe the Lord hears you.

---

*The urgent request of a righteous person is very powerful in its effect. Elijah was a man with a nature like ours; yet he prayed earnestly that it would not rain, and for three years and six months it did not rain on the land. Then he prayed again, and the sky gave rain and the land produced its fruit.*
—James 5:16–18

---

Further Scripture: 1 Kings 18:41–42; Romans 10:9–10; 1 John 5:14

## *Week 44, Day 307: 1 Peter 1*
## Living Hope

Peter addressed suffering believers and encouraged them to stand firm for Jesus as they faced persecution for their faith. Even in the midst of despair, Peter encouraged them to praise the Lord. Peter focused on the benefits of Jesus Christ: *His great mercy, the gift of a new birth into a living hope, Jesus' sacrifice on the cross, and an inheritance in heaven.* He described the inheritance in heaven as imperishable, uncorrupted, and unfading. Nothing but your gift of salvation can be described this way.

As you or someone you know faces a difficult situation—*focus on Jesus.* Yes, even in the pain, *praise His name.* Close your eyes and reflect on God's gifts and blessings, despite your troubling circumstances. Jesus promised you would face trouble in this world—but do not despair because greater is He who is in you, than he who is in the world. Jesus is your living hope and is preparing a forever-place for you in heaven. Jesus will encourage you. He will strengthen you for every good work. Take it one day at time and praise Jesus, your living hope!

---

*Praise the God and Father of our Lord Jesus Christ. According to His great mercy, He has given us a new birth into a living hope through the resurrection of Jesus Christ from the dead and into an inheritance that is imperishable, uncorrupted, and unfading, kept in heaven for you.*
—1 Peter 1:3–4

---

Further Scripture: Romans 5:3–4; 1 Thessalonians 5:16–18; 2 Thessalonians 2:16–17

### *Week 44, Day 308: 1 Peter 2*
Jesus—The Living Stone

Peter reminded the believers facing persecution of the Living Stone, Jesus. Yes, Jesus is the cornerstone given to people to follow and to stand upon as the firm foundation. Therefore, build your life on Jesus, the Living Stone. He chose you to proclaim and praise His name alone!

Believe the truth about your identity. Work, kids, possessions, or even the pain you've endured do not define who you are. Today, you need to walk in this truth: *As a follower of Christ, you are a child of God. You are chosen. You are hand selected for the high calling of priestly work. You are holy in Christ Jesus. You are selected by God to be an instrument for Him to proclaim praises of the Lord.* Build your life on the Living Stone, Jesus. With your identity in Him, you will not be shaken. Proclaim God's goodness and mercy in your life and His calling you out of the darkness into His marvelous light. He chose you and created you for purpose. Shake off whatever lie you hear from the enemy. Today, whatever comes, walk as a chosen child of God.

---

*But you are a chosen race, a royal priesthood,*
*a holy nation, a people for His possession,*
*so that you may proclaim the praises*
*of the One who called you out of darkness*
*into His marvelous light.* —1 Peter 2:9

---

Further Scripture: 1 Corinthians 2:7–9; 2 Timothy 1:9; 1 Peter 2:4

### *Week 45, Day 309: 1 Peter 3*
### Drawn by Your Love Within

Peter encouraged believers to *stand firm* on the living hope of Jesus during difficult times. He wrote to them about submission *after* he confirmed *who they were in Christ.* In Christ, they were chosen, purpose-filled, and highly called as God's possession. With that as the backdrop, Peter asked believers to walk out their calling with *respectful behavior and godly character.* Peter desired for those in the world to be won over to Christ without being preached to but rather by observing pure and reverent behavior. Just like the hymn goes, "They will know we are Christians by our love."

As you walk with Christ and abide in Him, spiritual fruit will grow, and godly character will present itself naturally in your life. The condition and health of your heart is more important to the Lord than your clothing, hairstyle, or jewelry selection. The world certainly entices you to do more and more with your outward appearance. Yet, as you walk confidently in who you are in Christ, *people will be drawn to Christ's love within you.* Allow Christ to be your all and hide yourself in Him. Then His beautiful love and grace will radiate through you!

---

*Instead, it should consist of what is inside the heart with the imperishable quality of a gentle and quiet spirit, which is very valuable in God's eyes.*
—1 Peter 3:4

---

Further Scripture: Proverbs 4:23; John 1:12; 13:35

### *Week 45, Day 310: 1 Peter 4*

Get Serious and Pray

Peter got right to the point—*the end is near. Jesus, your Savior, is returning. It's time to get serious and get disciplined in prayer. Above all, maintain an intense love for one another. The kind of love that forgives repeatedly.* The bottom line—*pray and love others.* Why? There's no time to waste before Jesus returns.

*Knowing* you should pray is easy. But to actually pray with discipline and focus, now that's another story. The world has a lot of distractions, right? "Oh, I need to send this text. Oh, I need to quickly do the laundry. Oh, let me check this email. Oh, I just had a baby; I'll join a prayer group when she goes to kindergarten!" No more excuses, dear friends. *It's time to get serious.* Turn to the Lord and pray. While you pray, ask Jesus for strength to love others intensely. Intense love comes from a place of abiding in Christ. Yes, you first need to receive and rest in His love. Then you are able to love others, forgive others, and unselfishly serve others. And love is what this world needs. Pray and ask the Lord to help you live out this kind of love today because He is returning quickly. There's no time to mess around with unforgiveness and petty issues. Get serious and pray. Then *love.*

---

*Now the end of all things is near; therefore, be serious and disciplined for prayer. Above all, maintain an intense love for each other, since love covers a multitude of sins.* —1 Peter 4:7–8

---

Further Scripture: Ephesians 6:18; 1 Peter 4:11; Revelation 22:20

## *Week 45, Day 311: 1 Peter 5*
Humility and Trust

In the same way that God called Christ to humble Himself, taking on the role as the Chief Shepherd in your life, God calls you to clothe yourself with humility and to trust Him. *God resists people who walk in pride*—those who think of themselves more highly than others. However, *God gives grace as you walk with humility.* Peter encouraged believers to humble themselves. As you walk humbly, trust your cares to the Lord and rest in His loving care.

*Humility and trust.* Satan roams like a roaring lion, prowling around and seeking to destroy your trust and desire to walk in humility. He's tempting you to live pridefully and self-sufficiently, to worry more and live in fear. Therefore, you must be firm in your faith. Don't act out of your feelings. Stand firm in your faith and trust the Lord in the unseen. Believe God is with you and remains sovereign today, like He was yesterday and will be tomorrow. As you walk in humility, God will give you the grace and strength to withstand Satan's schemes. Stand firm. The Lord will lift you up—*don't try to do it yourself.* Remain humble and trust in the Lord.

---

*And all of you clothe yourselves with humility toward one another, because*
*God resists the proud*
*but gives grace to the humble.*
*Humble yourselves, therefore, under the mighty hand of God, so that He*
*may exalt you at the proper time, casting all your care on Him, because*
*He cares about you.* —1 Peter 5:5–7

---

Further Scripture: Proverbs 3:5–6; Luke 14:11; 1 Peter 5:8–9

### *Week 45, Day 312: 2 Peter 1*

Everything You Need

Peter continued to encourage believers regarding how to live in the New Covenant by faith versus the Law. He reminded them that God's divine power had given them *everything* required for life and godliness. *Everything!* God's promises allow believers to escape corruption by evil desires and instead share in His divine nature. Peter longed for believers to remain strong in their faith and gave instructions on how to supplement, or strengthen, their faith.

Perhaps, like other believers, you woke up this morning with faith in Jesus. Now what do you do? Pray and thank the Lord for His power in you, *giving you everything you need for life and godliness.* Receive and rest in God's abundant promises: eternity in heaven, His Holy Spirit to guide you, His love for you, His constant presence with you, and more! As you press on walking by faith and not by sight, ask the Lord to supplement your faith with these qualities: goodness, knowledge, self-control, endurance, godliness, brotherly affection, and love. God desires for you to grow in your faith. Therefore, press on in your faith today! God has given you *everything* you need!

---

*His divine power has given us everything required for life and godliness through the knowledge of Him who called us by His own glory and goodness. By these He has given us very great and precious promises, so that through them you may share in the divine nature, escaping the corruption that is in the world because of evil desires.* —2 Peter 1:3–4

---

Further Scripture: Philippians 3:10; Hebrews 11:6; 2 Peter 1:5–8

## *Week 45, Day 313: 2 Peter 2*

Be Aware

Peter warned believers that false prophets would rise up. The enemy has deceptive ways and will disguise himself, even as a false teacher. Remember, Jesus is the only way, the truth, and the life. He remains the right path, the narrow path, and the only path that leads to everlasting life.

False teachers delight in deceiving you. Their haughty eyes look for sin. They lure and seduce you with greedy hearts. However, Jesus said *the gate is wide that leads to destruction and there are many who go through it. The narrow gate leads to life and few find it.* Therefore, fix your eyes on Jesus and stand guard. But don't be afraid of false teachers—remember *you have victory in Jesus' power.* He gives you the Holy Spirit to guide you, teach you, and empower you with discernment. Don't fear—*just be aware.* Draw near to the Lord, and He will guide you on His path.

---

*But there were also false prophets among the people, just as there will be false teachers among you. They will secretly bring in destructive heresies, even denying the Master who bought them, and will bring swift destruction on themselves. Many will follow their unrestrained ways, and the way of truth will be blasphemed because of them.* —2 Peter 2:1–2

---

Further Scripture: Matthew 7:13–14; John 14:6; 2 Peter 2:13b–14

### *Week 45, Day 314: 2 Peter 3*

### Stand Firm

Peter ended his letter with a final warning to the brethren about false teachers but also added an encouragement about the day of the Lord's return. Many people will live out their own desires, but believers must be on guard against lawless people who would lead them to fall from their foundation in the Lord. *God's people need to be ready for Jesus' return and stand in the truth.* The Lord does not delay His promise to return. Rather He is being patient with you. He doesn't want anyone to perish but all to come into repentance.

*Indeed, the Lord is returning.* While you wait for His return, *stand firm in your faith.* Have eyes to see the false teachers around you. Live with confidence in Him! Press on to know Him more with pure motives and a clear conscience. Make every effort to be at peace with the Lord. If you feel led to say something in Jesus' name, do it in the power of His love. Be bold and courageous so you don't miss an opportunity. Don't be intimidated by the false teachers out there—*you know the truth.* Proclaim it and save others for all eternity. Today, live ready for Jesus' return as you stand in the firm foundation of His truth.

---

*Therefore, dear friends, since you know this in advance, be on your guard, so that you are not led away by the error of lawless people and fall from your own stability. But grow in the grace and knowledge of our Lord and Savior Jesus Christ. To Him be the glory both now and to the day of eternity. Amen.* —2 Peter 3:17–18

---

Further Scripture: Ephesians 5:15–16; 2 Peter 3:8–9, 13–14

# November 10

*Week 45, Day 315: 1 John 1*

Back to the Basics

John wrote to believers to encourage Christians to get back to the basics of their faith and walk in the truth of God's perfect love. He shared this truth—*God is light, and in Him there is absolutely no darkness.* None. If Christians believe they have fellowship with Jesus and yet walk in sin, they are lying. Anyone who says they are in fellowship with Jesus but walk in darkness is fooling themselves. The truth is not in them. But anyone who confesses their sin will find that Jesus is faithful to forgive and then cleanse them from *all* unrighteousness.

Perhaps you have tried to deceive God and others by saying: "Jesus is my Lord," and yet, you're lying in your heart and don't fully trust God. Are you making your own plans and selfish choices? Friend, you don't have to live in heavy darkness, ashamed of your sin. There's no point in lying. God sees all. He is the light of the world. *Allow the light of Christ's perfect love to break through your darkness.* Just receive His light! Confess your sin today! Jesus will forgive you and cleanse you! Come before the Lord in full surrender and honesty and walk into the *light!*

---

*Now this is the message we have heard from Him and declare to you: God is light, and there is absolutely no darkness in Him.* —1 John 1:5

---

Further Scripture: Psalm 27:1; John 8:12; 1 John 1:6–9

### *Week 46, Day 316: 1 John 2*

Bring Darkness into the Light

The Apostle John got back to the basics of abiding in Christ by saying: "This is how we are sure that we have come to know Him: by keeping His commands." Yes, that's the bottom line! If you say you know Christ, then keep His commands. Don't say, "I know Christ!" but go on hating your brother. John would call you a liar walking in darkness. You don't know where you are going because the darkness blinds you.

Can you honestly say, "I love my brothers and sisters"? Or do you have hatred, envy, or unforgiveness toward someone? *Answer honestly.* If these questions make your stomach hurt or put angst in your heart, it may be time to seek the Lord and pursue loving your brother or sister. Listen to His Spirit guide you, humble yourself to repent and forgive. If you want to live honestly, loving and walking with God, then be open about the dark, hidden, or tucked away areas in your life. *Let all the darkness come into the light* so the Lord can bring freedom and healing to your life. Then you will follow His commands and know the depth of God's forgiving love. Today, put on compassion, humility, and forgiveness as you walk in the light.

---

*The one who loves his brother remains in the light, and there is no cause for stumbling in him. But the one who hates his brother is in the darkness, walks in the darkness, and doesn't know where he's going, because the darkness has blinded his eyes.* —1 John 2:10–11

---

Further Scripture: Ephesians 4:31–32; Colossians 3:12–13; 1 John 2:3–6

## *Week 46, Day 317: 1 John 3*
## Love in Action

John reminded believers of God's command from the beginning—*love your brothers and sisters as you receive God's love in your life.* John clearly stated that it's the evidence of *love*, or lack thereof, that defines God's children and the devil's children. If you do not love your brother or sister, then you are not doing what is right.

*Check your heart.* Think about those brothers and sisters who have hurt you. Maybe you've chosen to just move past them in life, avoiding them and the hurt. But have you truly forgiven them? Can you say you love them? Love causes action. Forgiving your brother or sister is a choice. God calls you to forgive and love like Jesus. Today, *ask Jesus if there is anyone He wants you to forgive.* It's time to walk in freedom. Perhaps this includes no longer hating someone but choosing to love. You are called to lay down your life for your brothers and sisters as an act of God's generous love. That's hard when the hurt is deep. Jesus said love covers a multitude of sin. You receive this love from Jesus, but do you offer this love to others in your life? As you humbly love others like Jesus, forgiving them as the Lord leads you, you will begin to grasp His great love.

---

*This is how God's children—and the Devil's children—are made evident. Whoever does not do what is right is not of God, especially the one who does not love his brother. For this is the message you have heard from the beginning: We should love one another.* —1 John 3:10–11

---

Further Scripture: Luke 17:3–4; 1 Peter 4:8; 1 John 4:20–21

### *Week 46, Day 318: 1 John 4*
### Knowing God Through Love

John declared to believers that *Christ's perfect love drives out fear.* Christ demonstrated this love by dying for you while you were still a sinner. His love for you is perfect and drives out all fear in your life. Even in your fear, Jesus stands with you, He loves you, and His promises go with you. *Now you love because of His great love.*

If Christ died so you may be loved, and you love others because He first loved you, then you must die to yourself to love others like Christ. Did you get that? Die to *yourself.* If you are having a difficult time loving others, then die to your *selfish ambition*, die to your *pride*, and die to the *control you desire.* Let it go. Remain in Christ. Love from a place of giving up your life for someone else, just as Christ did. Dying to self means not living in fear of "what if" but living with hope in the truth. Love like Jesus. That's what you are called to, and that's what you are able to do when perfect love remains in you.

---

*In this, love is perfected with us so that we may have confidence in the day of judgment, for we are as He is in this world. There is no fear in love; instead, perfect love drives out fear, because fear involves punishment. So, the one who fears has not reached perfection in love. We love because He first loved us.* —1 John 4:17–19

---

Further Scripture: Roman 5:8; Galatians 2:19b–20; 1 John 4:16

## *Week 46, Day 319: 1 John 5*
### Victory in Christ!

John understood the surrounding darkness and how the devil seeks to steal, kill, and destroy. John empathized with the suffering and the hurting. He encouraged believers with the truth—because they were born of God and had received new life in Christ, *believers are conquerors of the world. Victory is in Christ!* Yes, the victory that conquers the world is faith. Believe that what is unseen will come forth. Because you believe in Jesus as Savior, you will be victorious.

Friends, when you believe in Jesus, you have victory. Victory over the world. Victory over darkness. *You have victory!* Close your eyes and picture yourself conquering the world. You stand firm and strong. You don't give into the worry, fear, depression, or lies from the enemy saying you can't, you aren't, you won't, you'll die, you'll fail, or you'll be alone. Walk by faith and *have victory over the lies.* Set your mind on the promises of God, believe in Him, and remain in Him. Today, declare out loud—"I have victory! With Christ, I can conquer the world!"

---

*For this is what love for God is: to keep His commands. Now His commands are not a burden, because whatever has been born of God conquers the world. This is the victory that has conquered the world: our faith. And who is the one who conquers the world but the one who believes that Jesus is the Son of God?* —1 John 5:3–5

---

Further Scripture: 1 Corinthians 15:57; 1 John 4:4; 5:14

### *Week 46, Day 320: 2 John 1*
### Walking in Love

John wrote to a believer, instructing her and her children to walk in the love and truth of Christ. He warned them to watch out for false teachings that denied the truth about Jesus. John instructed them to not even invite deceivers into their home but to *remain in Christ's teachings.*

You are called to *walk in truth and love* as you follow God's path for your life. When you say yes to Christ, you walk in victory. You keep walking in love, even when you are weary and heavy-burdened. When you walk in love, you imitate Christ, remaining in Christ's commands. As you remain in Him, you choose to forgive, you choose to give, you choose to rise above offense, and you choose to stand firm when false teachers come along your path. God will give you the wisdom to overcome and conquer. The path you walk in the truth and love of Christ is not promised to be easy or smooth. But friend, the Lord will bless you with goodness and mercy to follow you all the days of your life as you press on *walking in love.*

---

*And this is love: that we walk according to His commands. This is the command as you have heard it from the beginning: you must walk in love.*
*—2 John 1:6*

---

Further Scripture: Psalm 143:8; Ephesians 5:1–2; 2 John 1:4

*Week 46, Day 321: 3 John 1*

No Greater Joy

John found no greater joy than hearing that *his children*, converts, or believers who had been encouraged by his ministry, *were walking in the truth*. Testimonies of their hospitality and support to strangers who were in ministry encouraged John's heart. John instructed his children to imitate what was good, not what was evil.

You can't force the people you disciple to walk in faith with Jesus, just as you can't force your children to follow Jesus with all their hearts, souls, and minds. But *you* are someone's child. *You* are a child of God. How would others testify of your faithfulness? Are you imitating Christ? Or imitating what is evil? Are you showing hospitality? Are you walking in the grace of God or striving in your own strength to keep things together? Friend, receive Christ's perfect love for you today. He loves you as you are. As you receive His love, fix your eyes on Him and grow in knowing Him as your friend, your Savior, and your heavenly Father. *Imitate His love to others*. Ask yourself how Christ would love this person. Then walk out that faithfulness you know to be true, following the perfect example, Jesus.

---

*For I was very glad when some brothers came and testified to your faithfulness to the truth—how you are walking in the truth. I have no greater joy than this: to hear that my children are walking in the truth.*
—3 John 1:3–4

---

Further Scripture: Ephesians 5:2; 3 John 1:5–6, 11

### *Week 46, Day 322: Jude 1*

## Contending for the Faith

Jude, a half-brother of Jesus, wrote his letter to those called, loved, and kept by Jesus. Just let that soak in. *You are called, loved, and kept by your Savior.* Jude wanted to discuss the basics, like salvation. However, he found it necessary to encourage those called by God *to contend for the faith*—to remain strong, to fight, and keep the faith. He urged his brothers and sisters to build themselves up in the faith and pray in the Holy Spirit. Expect mercy from the Lord and show mercy to others. Hate what is evil and cling to what is good. Walk in the Spirit and not in the flesh.

Friends, evil exists in the world and temptations surround you. Truth seems to easily fade away. The forces in this world wage war around you, wanting to keep you from trusting and walking in Jesus. Therefore, gird yourself up, put your boxing gloves on, and *contend to keep the faith.* Remain in the Word of God and grow in Him. Receive His fresh mercies each morning. But also love others by offering mercy. You are a contender for your faith. Remain strong in the Lord and walk in humility. Victory is in the Lord!

---

*Dear friends, although I was eager to write you about the salvation we share, I found it necessary to write and exhort you to contend for the faith that was delivered to the saints once for all.* —Jude 1:3

---

Further Scripture: Philippians 2:5–8; Jude 1:1, 20–23

## *Week 47, Day 323: Hosea 1—4*
## Hosea's Marriage and Children

Hosea not only proclaimed prophetic messages for Israel but also lived them out in obedience to the Lord's instructions. Upon the Lord's command, Hosea married a promiscuous woman named Gomer. Although Gomer broke her marital promise to Hosea, he followed the Lord's command to love his adulteress wife in the same way God loved the Israelites who repeatedly turned to other gods.

Just as Hosea loved his wife again and again despite her unfaithfulness, the Lord demonstrated His love by sending His Son Jesus to die for you while you were still a sinner. When you believe in Jesus, you receive God's grace, unconditional love, and eternal life as a free gift. You didn't do anything to deserve Christ's love. He loves you as you are. *The love the Lord has for you never ends.* Even if you walk away from God, He will go again to you and show you love. God's love will never separate from you. In the same way, you are called to love others, even when they hurt you or walk away. You are called *to go again and show love*, just like Hosea loved Gomer. Today, go again and show Christ's love to those around you.

---

*Then the LORD said to me, "Go again; show love to a woman who is loved by another man and is an adulteress, just as the LORD loves the Israelites though they turn to other gods and love raisin cakes."* —Hosea 3:1

---

Further Scripture: Romans 5:8; 8:38–39; 1 John 4:19

### *Week 47, Day 324: Hosea 5—8*

## False Repentance

Just as God loved Israel, Hosea loved Gomer, despite her lack of loyalty in their marriage. As much as the Lord desired for Israel to repent, He called their bluff when they said: *Let us strive to know God. Let us return to the Lord, He will heal us.* The Lord desired surrendered hearts, not external religion in which the people strove to act like they followed God. Despite their ungodly actions, the Lord remained patient, and His love for Israel continued.

In many ways, this same lip-service religion is offered to the Lord today. *The Lord wants your heart.* He desires *your loyalty* to Him. He wants you to draw near to Him. He doesn't want empty religious activity. He wants you to *love Him wholeheartedly.* Don't try fake repentance without a broken heart. Honestly turn to the Lord with full humility and authentically ask for forgiveness, desiring His love. Acknowledge He is the *only* one who can fill your cup, He is the *only* one to satisfy your longing, and He is the only one to heal you. But you must be real with Him. Come before Him today. Cease striving in your own strength. Be real. Be honest. Lay it all down before Him at the Cross. Receive His love, and then walk in obedience.

---

*For I desire loyalty and not sacrifice,*
*the knowledge of God rather than burnt offerings.* —Hosea 6:6

---

Further Scripture: 1 Samuel 15:22; Psalm 51:16–17; Isaiah 57:15

## *Week 47, Day 325: Hosea 9—11*
## The Lord's Love for Israel

The Lord's compassion stirred despite Israel's rebellious spirit. God cared for His children. He yearned for them to come back to Him. His heart broke for them; therefore, He couldn't just give them up. He loved unconditionally, and nothing would separate that love. The Lord demonstrated mercy and grace to His children.

Hosea described God leading His children with "ropes of love" out of captivity in Egypt. Imagine a dad leading his son through a busy airport. For his son not to walk away and get lost, the son wears a backpack with a rope on it for the father to grasp. This is a picture of God's heart for you, His child. He loves you so much. He desires to lead you with ropes of love out of bondage by sending you Jesus, His only Son. God loves you unconditionally and will not let you go. No matter how long the ropes of love may go—*the Lord's love will never, ever let you go.* The Lord's compassion remains for you. When you think no one else cares, God cares, and He promises to be with you. His love is wide and high and deep. Today, will you receive His great love and allow the Lord to lead you?

*How can I give you up, Ephraim?*
*How can I surrender you, Israel?*
*How can I make you like Admah?*
*How can I treat you like Zeboiim?*
*I have had a change of heart;*
*My compassion is stirred!* —Hosea 11:8

Further Scripture: Hosea 11:1, 4; Romans 5:8; Ephesians 3:17–19

## *Week 47, Day 326: Hosea 12—14*

## Repentance and Restoration

Hosea continued to love Gomer despite how she rejected him and loved others. Even though Gomer broke her marriage vow to Hosea, he remained willing to receive her when she returned to him. He loved her unconditionally. The Lord God loves Israel unconditionally. Despite their covenant with God, Israel rejected Him and worshipped other gods. Even so, Israel can always return to Yahweh their God. The Lord will *receive their repentance and restore them to new life rooted in Him.*

Do you need this truth today? No matter how many times you have turned against God and sought other idols, the Lord's love remains. Do you hear His voice calling you back to Him? Do you have a tug in your heart to turn to Him in humility as your one source for love and satisfaction? Turn to the *one*, Jesus Christ, and His unconditional love. He will heal you. He will restore you. He will give you new life. Take root in Him, and He will bring you growth. You will blossom in new ways as you surrender completely to Him. Today, surrender and ask the Lord to be the king of your heart.

---

*Israel, return to Yahweh your God,*
*for you have stumbled in your sin.*
*Take words of repentance with you*
*and return to the Lord.*
*Say to Him: "Forgive all our sin*
*and accept what is good,*
*so that we may repay You*
*with praise from our lips."* —Hosea 14:1–2

---

Further Scripture: Hosea 14:4–7a, 9; Ephesians 2:8–9

# November 22

*Week 47, Day 327: Joel 1—3*

## Judgment of the Nations

Joel instructed God's people to gather and blow the trumpet—for the day of the Lord is coming! Locusts invaded the land of Israel causing destruction, but the Lord came to restore. A great army rose up against Israel because they did not seek the Lord. But even so, the Lord restored His people. The Lord provided plenty to eat, and they were satisfied. If His people will praise the name of Yahweh, they will never again be put to shame. The great I Am is present in Israel, and He is their God. There is *no other* god. The Lord will display wonders among His people. And everyone who calls upon the name of the Lord will be saved.

Are you ready for the day of the Lord? God may bring destruction, but He will bring you restoration. He will satisfy you when you turn to Him. All the nations will gather and know there are no other gods besides the one true God, the Great Redeemer. His Spirit will move miraculously—through dreams, visions, prophecies, and wonders in the heavens and on earth. Just as Christ came to love all, you are called to love like Christ. From the place of His love flowing through you, His Spirit will move so the whole world will proclaim that Jesus Christ is Lord. Today, *stand firm and ready yourself* for the day of the Lord.

---

*You will have plenty to eat and be satisfied.*
*You will praise the name of Yahweh your God,*
*who has dealt wondrously with you.*
*My people will never again be put to shame.*
*You will know that I am present in Israel*
*and that I am Yahweh your God,*
*and there is no other.*
*My people will never again be put to shame.* —Joel 2:26–27

---

Further Scripture: Psalm 22:26; Isaiah 44:6; Joel 2:28–30a

### *Week 47, Day 328: Amos 1—3*

Reason for Punishing Israel

The Lord called Amos, a sheep breeder from Tekoa, and gave him a prophetic message to proclaim to Israel. The message described punishment for Israel and its neighbors. Over and over, Amos said God would not relent in punishing, judging, and destroying these nations because they had turned against the Lord. Amos repeatedly declared God would "send fire . . . and it will consume."

Even today the Lord is a consuming fire in your life. The Lord sees when you worship other gods or when you seek satisfaction from the world instead of seeking Him first. God loves you unconditionally, but *He is a jealous God.* He longs for you to worship and love Him above all else. He longs for you to revere and stand in awe of who He is. He may take you through a trial *so His fire can bring refinement to create you into who He's called you to be for His purpose in His kingdom.* When you walk through fiery trials, know the Lord your God is with you. Seek Him in the fire. He is there. Praise His name even through the heat. Allow Him to burn off anything in your life not of Him. Praise the name of the Lord as your restorer and redeemer. You will not be shaken.

---

*I will not relent from punishing Judah*
*for three crimes, even four,*
*because they have rejected the instruction of the LORD*
*and have not kept His statutes.*
*The lies that their ancestors followed*
*have led them astray.*
*Therefore, I will send fire against Judah,*
*and it will consume the citadels of Jerusalem.* —Amos 2:4–5

---

Further Scripture: Deuteronomy 4:23–24; Isaiah 33:14; Hebrews 12:28–29

*Week 47, Day 329: Amos 4—6*

Seek Me and Live!

Amos continued to speak to Israel, pointing out times the people did not return to the Lord. Over and over again, the people did not return to the Lord. God boldly, clearly, and simply spoke to the House of Israel: *Seek me and live. Seek Yahweh and live.* And yet what did the people continue to do? Walk away from the Lord.

The Lord desires an intimate relationship with you—His chosen, beloved people to whom He sent His Son, Jesus, to redeem. God commanded you to love Him above all else—with all your heart, soul, and mind. The Word of God states over and over: *Seek and you will find God. Draw near to God and He will draw near to you. Ask God and you will receive. Knock and the doors will be open. Seek first God's kingdom, and all things in life will be added to you.* God longs for you to pursue a relationship with Him. Pray, read His Word, have fellowship with other believers, and look for the Lord working in your life. When you seek Him, when you love Him with everything, *He will be found, and you will live.* He promises that as you seek Him, you will live abundantly in the love He desires to lavish on you.

---

*For the* LORD *says to the house of Israel:*
*Seek Me and live!* —Amos 5:4

---

Further Scripture: Deuteronomy 4:29; Jeremiah 29:13; Amos 5:14

## *Week 48, Day 330: Amos 7—9*
### Amos's Visions

As Amos walked obediently with the Lord, proclaiming messages to Israel, he faced opposition from Amaziah. Amos's role as prophet for the Lord may not have made sense to others because he worked as a herdsman and didn't come from a family heritage of prophets. However, Amos stood confidently in his calling and continued receiving visions and proclaiming the messages from the Lord.

Has the Lord called you into something? Perhaps you work at a factory or are an elementary teacher. Maybe you are even retired. And yet the Lord has called you to teach and proclaim His Word to this next generation. You may question this calling because you don't come from a family of pastors or haven't been to seminary. Even so, remember, *when the Lord calls you into something, He will provide.* He will guide you. He will strengthen you. Beware of opposition from the world and lies from the enemy. Stand firm as a child of God and follower of Christ. He will be your confidence and keep your foot from slipping. He who calls you is faithful and will always be faithful.

---

*So Amos answered Amaziah, "I was not a prophet or the son of a prophet; rather, I was a herdsman, and I took care of sycamore figs. But the LORD took me from following the flock and said to me: 'Go, prophesy to My people Israel.'"* —Amos 7:14–15

---

Further Scripture: Proverbs 3:26; John 15:16; 1 Thessalonians 5:24

## *Week 48, Day 331: Obadiah 1*
### Love in the Midst of Wrath

The Lord called Obadiah to proclaim a prophetic message to the country of Edom—*You will be covered in shame and destroyed forever because of the violence done to Israel.* The Lord's message through Obadiah communicated that all nations who brought opposition to Israel would suffer the Lord's judgment. Why does this judgment against other nations take place? Because God's covenant with Israel will always prevail.

The Book of Obadiah warns of the wrath of God, but it also reminds you to *celebrate the love of God.* Yes! The Day of the Lord is coming. Christ will return and ascend Mount Zion to rule overall. As you anticipate His glorious return, open your eyes to see people around you. When you see others struggling in their faith or in a season of destruction, don't be like the Edomites and mock them, rejoicing in their misfortunes and gloating in their miseries. Rather, as God's chosen instrument, *be a vessel of His love,* showing mercy, kindness, and gentleness. In this way, when Christ returns, *people will be ready. You will be ready.* And, Lord willing, all people will know of His faithful love and mercy.

---

*For the Day of the LORD is near,*
*against all the nations.*
*As you have done, so it will be done to you;*
*what you deserve will return on your own head.* —Obadiah 1:15

---

Further Scripture: Psalm 145:8; Acts 9:15; Revelation 11:15

## *Week 48, Day 332: Jonah 1—4*

### Jonah's Story

The Lord called Jonah to proclaim His message to the people of Nineveh. But Jonah fled and ran away from his call. Consequently, the Lord allowed storms in Jonah's life, even putting him in the belly of a whale until Jonah submitted to the will of the Lord. As Jonah preached in Nineveh, the people turned from their evil ways and sought the Lord. Jonah was angered by the Lord's mercy for Nineveh, and he questioned God's will. In response, God rebuked Jonah.

You may relate with some or even all of Jonah's story: running away from God's will, facing storms in life, faithfully walking out God's call, experiencing God moving powerfully, seeing God shine through people around you, questioning God's will, or getting rebuked by God. No matter where you are, *God is with you, He is sovereign, and He is working*. He is strength in your weakness. Today, have faith to believe in Jesus and trust He is working through every season of your life. Seek Him, fix your eyes on Him, and trust Him, even when you can't see it. He is with you. Yes, He is with you.

---

*As my life was fading away*
*I remembered Yahweh.*
*My prayer came to You,*
*to Your holy temple.*
*Those who cling to worthless idols*
*forsake faithful love,*
*but as for me, I will sacrifice to You*
*with a voice of thanksgiving.*
*I will fulfill what I have vowed.*
*Salvation is from the LORD!* —Jonah 2:7–9

---

Further Scripture: Matthew 12:39–41; Luke 11:30; Romans 10:9–10

## *Week 48, Day 333: Micah 1–3*
## Gather and Lead God's Remnant

The Lord called upon the prophet Micah to declare truth to Israel. The Lord continued to appear to Israel even though *Israel remained in rebellion.* Micah stood apart from the false prophets because the Spirit of the Lord filled him with power, justice, and the courage to proclaim truth to Israel about their sin and rebellion. Yet even with the strong message of justice, warning, and destruction, Micah offered the hope and deliverance of God *as their great Shepherd who would gather and lead His remnant.* The Lord will know them by name, and they will know His voice.

Dear friends, the Holy Spirit equips you, empowers you, and guides you. He will fill you with joy and peace so that you overflow with hope. The Lord longs to guide you as your Shepherd. *He sees your rebellion and your wandering ways, He knows your heart, and He longs to have you safe in His arms.* The Lord will equip you with authority in His name to do His work. You don't have to walk out your calling, doing the will of your heavenly Father in your own strength. *You are not alone.* The Holy Spirit's power speaks through you, counseling you, leading you, and guiding you. Today, call upon the name of the Lord, and He will be your strength.

---

*As for me, however, I am filled with power*
*by the Spirit of the L*ORD,
*with justice and courage,*
*to proclaim to Jacob his rebellion*
*and to Israel his sin.* —Micah 3:8

---

Further Scripture: Micah 2:12; John 10:11; Romans 15:13

### *Week 48, Day 334: Micah 4—5*

From Defeated Ruler to Conquering King

After the Babylonian exile, God promised to restore His people to Jerusalem. *Micah prophetically proclaimed of the coming King* from the line of Judah who would be born to rule over Israel. Indeed Jesus, God's Son, would be born in Bethlehem and shepherd the people of Israel. And then, after a time, Jesus would return in the strength of Yahweh and in the majestic name of Yahweh His God. All people who call upon His name will live securely in His greatness extending to the ends of the earth. Yes, *Jesus will be peace to all people.* He will reign from antiquity to eternity.

Jesus is both the Great Shepherd and the King of kings. He was born to redeem an entire world, offering hope and restoration to His people. He is your peace, your strength, and your security. Are your eyes focused on the world—on false gods, other forms of security, prized earthly possessions, or rich food and drink? Like He did with the Israelites, the Lord promises to remove things from your life that distract your vision and ability to fix your eyes on Jesus alone. He is the *only* peace. He is the *only* security. Today, give thanks for the birth of the Son given to the world named Wonderful Counselor, Mighty God, Eternal Father, Prince of Peace.

---

*He will stand and shepherd them
in the strength of Yahweh,
in the majestic name of Yahweh His God.
They will live securely,
for then His greatness will extend
to the ends of the earth.
He will be their peace.* —Micah 5:4—5

---

Further Scripture: Isaiah 9:6; Micah 5:2; Matthew 2:4–6

## *Week 48, Day 335: Micah 6–7*
### Judgment and Restoration

The prophet Micah continued to declare the Lord's message, *patterned with both warning and hope to God's people*, the nation of Israel. He pointed out how they outwardly performed all the offerings and sacrifices, trying to please God. Yet God continued to desire their heart offerings. Micah explained what the Lord required of His people—*to act justly, to love faithfulness, and to walk humbly with Him*. However, God's people continued to turn against Him. Therefore, the Lord judged them and brought punishment. As the pattern went, Micah concluded with a message of hope for God's people, reminding them of His character and His promises.

Today, remember the Lord your God is able to remove your sin and forgive your rebellion. He does not hold on to His anger forever because He delights in faithful love. He will have compassion on you again and again. He promises to cast your sin into the depths of the sea. He promises to show you loyalty and be faithful to His covenant promise. As you seek the Lord daily, He asks you *to act justly, to love faithfulness, and to walk humbly with Him as your God.* He desires the sacrifice and devotion of your heart.

---

*Mankind, He has told you what is good*
*and what it is the LORD requires of you:*
*to act justly,*
*to love faithfulness,*
*and to walk humbly with your God.* —Micah 6:8

---

Further Scripture: Psalm 89:33–34; Micah 7:7, 18–20

# December 1

## *Week 48, Day 336: Nahum 1—3*
### The Burden Bearer

The prophet Nahum brought a message of comfort to the Israelites and prophesied about the Lord's judgment on Nineveh and Assyria. He proclaimed that *the Lord is good, a stronghold in the day of distress. The Lord cares for those who take refuge in Him.* But Nahum also confirmed God would completely destroy Assyria for their destructive ways. Israel would no longer be in bondage to Assyria because the Lord would break off the yoke and tear off the shackles. The Lord would set them free, and one day, *the feet of One bringing good news and proclaiming peace would come.*

No matter what destructiveness is in your life, the Lord is your refuge and stronghold in your day of distress. Look to Jesus to be your burden bearer. *Whatever* you face today. *Whatever* feels heavy on your list, remember to seek the Lord with it. He will lighten your burdens. He will set you free. He will bring you peace. You are no longer in chains. You have been set free and made perfect through Jesus Christ. The Lord will bring justice to the destruction. *Now go* and walk in freedom and share the peace with those around you.

---

*The LORD is good,*
*a stronghold in a day of distress;*
*He cares for those who take refuge in Him.*
*But He will completely destroy Nineveh*
*with an overwhelming flood,*
*and He will chase His enemies into darkness.* —Nahum 1:7–8

---

Further Scripture: Nahum 1:13, 15; Matthew 11:30

## Week 49, Day 337: Habakkuk 1—3
### Habakkuk's Prophecy

The prophet Habakkuk lamented to the Lord about the injustice and violence in the world. As He faced the dilemma of understanding God's ways, he asked:

> How long, LORD, must I call for help
> and You do not listen
> or cry out to You about violence
> and You do not save?
>
> . . . . . . . . . . . . . .
>
> Why do you tolerate wrongdoing?

After God answered, *Habakkuk displayed faith* in the midst of not understanding. He demonstrated trust in the midst of trials. He found hope in the Lord in the midst of despair. How? By faith, *Habakkuk believed in the God of his salvation.*

What do you do when God isn't showing up the way you asked Him to? What do you do when you don't understand the injustice around you? Yes, you have questions for God. But right now, today, pause for just a minute. By faith, choose to declare: "*Yet* I will triumph in Yahweh; I will rejoice in the God of my salvation! Yahweh my Lord is my strength; He makes my feet like those of a deer and enables me to walk on mountain heights!" Fix your eyes on Jesus, rather than on the problem. As you turn to the Lord, give Him thanks. Choose to trust, even in the midst of not understanding. Rejoice *always.*

*Yet I will triumph in Yahweh; I will rejoice in the God of my salvation! Yahweh my Lord is my strength; He makes my feet like those of a deer and enables me to walk on mountain heights! —Habakkuk 3:18–19*

Further Scripture: Habakkuk 1:2–3; Philippians 4:6–7; Hebrews 4:16

## *Week 49, Day 338: Zephaniah 1–3*
### The Day of the Lord

The prophet Zephaniah proclaimed that judgment would come for Jerusalem, for Judah, for all the nation, and even for the whole earth. Zephaniah proclaimed the Day of the Lord for his current time, but ultimately, for the end. And yet *Zephaniah also declared that God would gather a remnant* in His amazing grace, offsetting His jealous anger against those seeking evil. God is a warrior. He is mighty to save. The Lord will rejoice over His people with gladness and delight in them with shouts of joy. He is in their midst and will save.

Oh, friend, the Lord will bring you quietness in the midst of destruction and despair. Imagine the picture of a battle . . . *As you look out over the horizon, you see a warrior standing out among the others, victoriously riding toward you. As you watch this warrior, you know he is coming to rescue you. As he arrives to you, he celebrates with a cheer of joy. He cares for your safety and saves you.* This is a picture of the love of your heavenly Father. Look up from the battle. Look up and seek the Lord alone. *He is in your midst.* He fights for you and will rescue you. He delights over you with shouts of *joy.* He rejoices over you with gladness. Do not fear. The Lord is near.

---

*On that day it will be said to Jerusalem:*
*"Do not fear;*
*Zion, do not let your hands grow weak.*
*Yahweh your God is among you,*
*a warrior who saves.*
*He will rejoice over you with gladness.*
*He will bring you quietness with His love.*
*He will delight in you with shouts of joy."* —Zephaniah 3:16–17

---

Further Scripture: Deuteronomy 7:21; Psalm 9:10; Zephaniah 2:3

# December 4

## The Temple of the Lord

The prophet Haggai spoke to the people after the Babylonian captivity regarding their lifestyle. He commanded them to rebuild the temple after its destruction. The prophet confirmed the word of the Lord saying, *I am with you.* He longed for them to *consider carefully* how they lived. Their choice to live faithfully and obediently mattered to the Lord. They had misplaced their priorities upon returning to Jerusalem. God had a *greater temple* for them, but they had to turn to God and *carefully consider* their ways.

Just as Haggai spoke to the Israelites, the same is true for you. The Lord longs to bless you and restore you. Therefore, consider your actions. Consider your ways. In this volatile world full of temptations, with the enemy luring and deceiving you, you must *consider carefully* how you live. *Pray.* Seek the Lord. Ask for clarity and confirmation. Walk humbly. Do not fear, for God is with you. He wants to rebuild His love in you. Jesus will provide you peace because He *is* peace. Today, *carefully consider* your decisions, actions, and words, and walk with the Lord. It matters to God. And He has something even greater for you.

---

*Consider carefully from this day forward; from the twenty-fourth day of the ninth month, from the day the foundation of the LORD's temple was laid; consider it carefully.* —Haggai 2:18

---

Further Scripture: Haggai 2:9, 15–17; Ephesians 5:15–17

# December 5

***Week 49, Day 340: Zechariah 1—4***

## Zechariah's Visions

After Israel returned from exile, the word of the Lord came upon the prophet Zechariah through a series of dreams. He dreamt about Joshua, the high priest, standing before the people in filthy clothes, a symbol of Israel and their unclean sin. Then Joshua received clean clothes. *Zechariah declared this symbol of hope and restoration* for Israel if they walked in obedience to the Lord. He challenged the people to wholeheartedly seek the Lord as they rebuilt the temple.

Jesus was pierced for your iniquities, and His grace washes away your filthy sin and guilt. Whoever believes in Jesus as Savior and humbly repents will be forgiven. Then the Lord will freely give you robes of righteousness. Therefore, confidently come before the Lord with a humble heart and receive His grace and mercy. The clean robe is not just put on over your old, dirty robe. *Jesus completely removes the filthy robe of shame and guilt.* You are a child of the King, a royal heir, and you have access to God the Father. He calls you worthy. He loves you. Picture a white robe neatly wrapped around you and receive His gift today.

---

*Then I said, "Let them put a clean turban on his head." So a clean turban was placed on his head, and they clothed him in garments while the Angel of the LORD was standing nearby.*
*Then the Angel of the LORD charged Joshua: "This is what the LORD of Hosts says: If you walk in My ways and keep My instructions, you will both rule My house and take care of My courts; I will also grant you access among these who are standing here."* —Zechariah 3:5–7

---

Further Scripture: Zechariah 3:3–4; Galatians 2:20; Revelation 19:8

## *Week 49, Day 341: Zechariah 5—8*
### Fasting for the Lord

Zechariah spoke as a prophet to God's chosen people in Israel upon their return from exile. The Lord gave Zechariah prophetic messages of judgment but also of blessing and hope, through dreams and visions. When the people fasted in exile, the Lord saw their hearts were like rock and questioned, "Did you really fast for Me?" The Lord asked the remnant to walk in obedience and to fast with *pure hearts leaning into the Lord.* He promised joy, gladness, and cheerful festivals in return.

Fasting encourages you to purify your heart, mind, and soul before the Lord. It often forces you to face a challenging situation by removing the extras in your life and truly focusing on the Lord for your strength, your sustenance, and your hope. Today, pray about fasting. Then obediently begin your fast, remembering to keep your motives for fasting pure. Don't fast to lose weight, be more productive with your time, or to make someone else happy. *Fast with a pure and obedient heart.* Love truth and peace, trusting the Lord to powerfully move in your midst.

*The LORD of Hosts says this: The fast of the fourth month, the fast of the fifth, the fast of the seventh, and the fast of the tenth will become times of joy, gladness, and cheerful festivals for the house of Judah. Therefore, love truth and peace.* —Zechariah 8:19

Further Scripture: Exodus 34:28; Zechariah 7:4–6; Luke 4:2–4

### *Week 49, Day 342: Zechariah 9–12*

## Mourning for the Pierced One

Zechariah proclaimed that one day the Jewish people will realize they pierced the Messiah. They will mourn and weep. They will know He is the One. They will grieve their disobedience and rejection of the Cornerstone, the Shepherd. They will lament piercing the heart of God. Yes, one day, Jesus will return on the clouds, and all will know He is the One they waited for.

Ask yourself: *Have you acted like the Israelites, rejecting and walking in disobedience? Will you be surprised that Jesus is the Messiah?* The Lord longs for you to *wake up* to His love, truth, and peace and receive Him into your life. Don't wait like the Israelites. Don't walk in your own ways and miss the Messiah right in front of you. Wake up and receive the truth. It's here for you. Yes, Jesus will come back. He wants you to know the truth so you may be set free and walk in peace. The Lord will never leave you. He loves you. Allow Him to be the cornerstone of your life, allow him to be your Great Shepherd, leading and guiding you. Allow Him to be your Messiah. Receive Him today.

---

*Then, I will pour out a spirit of grace and prayer on the house of David and the residents of Jerusalem, and they will look at Me whom they pierced. They will mourn for Him as one mourns for an only child and weep bitterly for Him as one weeps for a firstborn.* —Zechariah 12:10

---

Further Scripture: Zechariah 10:4; Romans 11:25–27; Revelation 1:7

# December 8

*Week 49, Day 343: Zechariah 13—14*

## Finding the Messiah in Zechariah

As the prophet Zechariah concluded, he announced the Day of the Lord and the vision given to him—*Jesus will fight in battle,* and His feet will stand on the Mount of Olives facing Jerusalem to the east. The Mount of Olives will be split in half from east to west, forming a huge valley, so that half the mountain will move to the north and half will be south. When the Lord returns, there will no longer be impurity in His midst. Everyone will call upon the name of the Lord. Hallelujah! Jesus is returning. Wait for the Day of the Lord's return!

Behold, *the Lord reigns in your midst as a mighty warrior.* On the day of His return, He will fight for you because He loves you. He will be victorious. *Forever and ever, He will reign.* No longer will people be impure or hypocritical. No longer will there be idols or false worshippers. In the end, when Christ the Messiah returns, all will proclaim: "Our Lord and God—You are worthy to receive glory and honor and power because You have created all things, and because of Your will they exist and were created!" All the earth will see He is the Messiah. Prepare the way and go forth, proclaiming His name so all the world will know.

---

*Then the LORD will go out to fight against those nations as He fights on a day of battle.* —Zechariah 14:3

---

Further Scripture: Zechariah 14:11, 21; Revelation 4:11

## *Week 50, Day 344: Malachi 1—4*
### Sun of Righteousness

The Lord heard the people say, "Look, what a nuisance," as they scorned His table. The people asked: "Have we wearied the Lord? How can we return? What have we spoken against you?" God's people were ignorant about how their words, actions, and heart condition affected the Lord. However, on the Day of the Lord, everyone will witness the arrogant and those who commit wickedness become stubble. But, *for those who fear God's name,* the sun of righteousness will rise with healing in its wings, and they will go out and playfully jump like calves from the stall.

Like the Israelites, God hears you when you mock Him. Yes, He sees you in your rebellion. Yes, He knows your thoughts. And He will consume you with fire if you do not turn back to Him. However, *for those who seek the Lord and fear Him, be prepared to dance and sing and play! The Day of the Lord will be upon us.* Stop arrogantly questioning God. Stop trying to figure out how far you can push it with Him. He sees you, He hears you, He knows you, and He wants your heart to be surrendered to Him. *That's it.* Then you will have joy, peace, and salvation. Jesus will be enough, and this truth will set you free to playfully jump like a calf!

---

*"But for you who fear My name, the sun of righteousness will rise with healing in its wings, and you will go out and playfully jump like calves from the stall. You will trample the wicked, for they will be ashes under the soles of your feet on the day I am preparing," says the LORD of Hosts.*
—Malachi 4:2–3

---

Further Scripture: Psalm 16:11; 73:25–28; Malachi 1:13; 3:13–14

*Week 50, Day 345: Revelation 1*

John's Vision of the Risen Lord

God gave the Apostle John a revelation to testify about Jesus Christ. The Book of Revelation shares the vision the Lord entrusted to John. All who read, hear, and keep the words in the Book of Revelation will be blessed because the time is near.

You may think the Book of Revelation doesn't apply to you. Or you may assume it's over your head. You may even feel a sense of fear when you begin to think about the Book of Revelation. However, John encouraged his readers by saying those who heed Revelation's words will be blessed because the time is near. John followed this by powerfully describing Jesus. Today, as you read John's descriptions of Christ, ask the Lord to expand your heart to this revelation entrusted to John— *Jesus is the One who is, who was, and who is coming. Jesus Christ is the faithful witness, the firstborn from the dead and the rulers of the kings of the earth. Jesus loves you and set you free from sins. He made you a kingdom and a priest to His God and Father. Jesus is coming on the clouds. Jesus is the Alpha and the Omega, the Almighty. Jesus is the Living One, alive forever, and He holds the keys of death and Hades.* Praise the mighty name of Jesus! Fall before the Lord as you enter into His presence in worship.

---

*The one who reads this is blessed, and those who hear the words of this prophecy and keep what is written in it are blessed, because the time is near!*
—Revelation 1:3

---

Further Scripture: Matthew 5:6; Revelation 1:4–6, 17–18

## *Week 50, Day 346: Revelation 2*
### The First Four Church Letters

John followed God's instructions to write and deliver letters to seven churches. As the Lord addressed the churches of Ephesus, Smyrna, Pergamum, and Thyatira, He repeated Himself with the phrase, "I know your . . ." Yes, the Lord knew their strengths, their works, how they stood strong in the place of suffering or temptation, and how they gave in. *Each church received a different challenge from the Lord.* Some He asked to repent. Others were encouraged to hold strong and be faithful until death because they would be victorious and would be granted a crown of life. John reminded the churches: "Anyone who has an ear should listen to what the Spirit says."

If you have received a convicting message from the Lord, perhaps through a friend, a sermon, or a post you read online, don't be ignorant and turn the other way. *Listen to the Holy Spirit's prompting.* You may be like the churches of Ephesus, Pergamum, or Thyatira, needing to repent and turn back to your first love, Jesus. Remember, God knows you. God knows your works, love, faithfulness, and endurance. He knows your affliction and poverty. He knows the temptations you face, and He knows all you tolerate. If God wrote *you* a letter, what would He say to you? How would you respond?

---

*Anyone who has an ear should listen to what the Spirit says to the churches.*
—Revelation 2:29

---

Further Scripture: Psalm 26:2; Acts 3:19; Revelation 2:4

# December 12

*Week 50, Day 347: Revelation 3*

## Letters to Three More Churches

The letters continue to unfold as John proclaimed his vision from the Lord to the three remaining churches: Sardis, Philadelphia, and Laodicea. Each had a different challenge: to be alert and strengthen what remained; to endure all things by keeping God's command with faithful, courageous, and humble love; and to repent from a lukewarm way of life and be committed to Jesus.

Specifically, the Lord declared to the church of Laodicea, "Listen! I stand at the door and knock. If anyone hears My voice and opens the door, I will come in to him and have dinner with him, and he with Me." *This message is for you.* Do you know the voice of the Shepherd? Jesus said, "My sheep hear My voice, I know them, and they follow Me." Today, do you hear the voice of the Lord? Do you hear the Lord knocking? Take time to pause from the busyness and sit quietly. Ask the Lord: *Jesus, what do You want me to know about You? If we were having dinner, what would You say to me?* When you ask these questions, sit and listen like you would to a friend. Today, listen to the One who guides you, knows you, and loves you. Remain alert and ready.

---

*As many as I love, I rebuke and discipline. So be committed and repent. Listen! I stand at the door and knock. If anyone hears My voice and opens the door, I will come in to him and have dinner with him, and he with Me. —Revelation 3:19–20*

---

Further Scripture: John 10:3–4; Revelation 3:2–3, 15–16

### *Week 50, Day 348: Revelation 4*
### The Throne Room of Heaven

Imagine John all alone on an island when the Spirit of God entrusted him with visions of what was to come and instructions to send his visions to the seven churches of Asia. As John was in the Spirit, he saw the One seated on a throne encircled by 24 elders on 24 thrones. He described four living creatures continuously saying, "Holy, holy, holy, Lord God Almighty, who was, and is, and who is coming." The 24 elders cast their earned crowns before the throne of the One and proclaim, "Our Lord and God, You are worthy to receive glory and honor and power, because You have created all things."

You may not physically be gathered around the throne of heaven, but you can take time to worship the Lord. Posture yourself to worship Him. Give Him the "crowns" in your life. Whatever you feel you have gained, *surrender it all to the Lord*. Give thanks to the Lord. Recognize God as the author and creator of all things, who is deserving of all honor, power, and glory. Worship Him because He is truly worthy of it all. This life is not about you on earth, it is about the Lord and His kingdom that is to come in heaven. Day and night, let your praise rise to the one who is worthy of it all.

---

*The 24 elders fall down before the One seated on the throne, worship the One who lives forever and ever, cast their crowns before the throne, and say:*
*Our Lord and God,*
*You are worthy to receive*
*glory and honor and power,*
*because You have created all things,*
*and because of Your will*
*they exist and were created.* —Revelation 4:10–11

---

Further Scripture: Jeremiah 10:7; Colossians 1:16; Revelation 4:8

*Week 50, Day 349: Revelation 5*

Worship in Heaven

As John's vision continued, one of the elders declared who was worthy to open the scroll and break its seal: "The Lion from the tribe of Judah, the Root of David, has been victorious so that He may open the scroll and its seven seals." Jesus, the Lamb, is worthy to open the scroll. He was slaughtered, and His blood redeems people from every tribe and language and nation for God. Yes, indeed, Jesus alone is worthy. John witnessed an angelic choir worshipping: "The Lamb who was slaughtered is worthy to receive power and riches and wisdom and strength and honor and glory and blessing!"

You may face suffering, trials, persecution, and unmet expectations. For a moment, rest in the hope of heaven. *There will be a day when the whole earth will worship the One who is worthy, the Lamb of God.* Picture this moment of worship in heaven. Reflect on His redemption in your life. Jesus is worthy to receive power, riches, wisdom, strength, honor, glory, and blessing. Will you stand to worship, or will you fall down to worship Him? Give Jesus your whole heart as you worship Him today. He is worthy of it all.

---

*Then one of the elders said to me, "Stop crying. Look! The Lion from the tribe of Judah, the Root of David, has been victorious so that He may open the scroll and its seven seals."* —Revelation 5:5

---

Further Scripture: Genesis 49:9–10; John 1:29; Revelation 5:11–12

## *Week 50, Day 350: Revelation 6*
## In Christ's Name—Stand Up!

Just as it was determined, the Lamb opened the six seals of the scroll. Each seal revealed something to come: conquest and overturn of power, war, famine, scarcity, death, martyrdom, and wrath. Not one of the seals reveled something enjoyable or comfortable. Each one would bring fear and pain. *You may wonder who is able to stand under all the hardship.* Who is able to withstand the pain of what is to come?

*You are able to stand up and endure because of your faith in Jesus Christ.* Paul encouraged believers to stand strong in the Lord and in His strength during battle. The Lord equips your hands for battle. The Name of the Lord is a strong tower you can run to and hide in. He will protect you. The Lord is a stronghold in the day of distress because He cares for all who take refuge in Him. You are declared righteous by faith. Through your faith, you are justified and have peace with God through Jesus Christ. Rejoice in the hope of glory, no matter how bleak life may appear. Remember, God remains in control; you can stand in Him and in His promises. He is with you and will never leave you nor forsake you.

---

*And they said to the mountains and to the rocks, "Fall on us and hide us from the face of the One seated on the throne and from the wrath of the Lamb, because the great day of Their wrath has come! And who is able to stand?"* —Revelation 6:16–17

---

Further Scripture: Proverbs 18:10; Nahum 1:6–7; Ephesians 6:10

# December 16

*Week 51, Day 351: Revelation 7*

## A Multitude from the Great Tribulation

After the sixth seal was opened, John described an angel from the east sealing 144,000 servants of God from every tribe of Israel. Then he described *a vast multitude from every nation, tribe, people, and language standing before the throne* and before the Lamb in heaven. The Lamb refers to Jesus, the redemptive sacrifice for the whole earth. Robed in white, the innumerable crowd cried out in a loud voice, "Salvation belongs to our God, who is seated on the throne, and to the Lamb!"

How will a "vast multitude from every nation, tribe, people, and language" know about the Lamb? This image seems to fulfill Jesus' Great Commission to His disciples to *go* because all authority had been given to make disciples of all nations. Even today, Jesus commands believers to *go* and share God's love to the nations. Who in your life needs to hear about Jesus, the sacrificial Lamb of God, who died for the sins of every nation, tribe, people, and language, offering redemption and eternal life? As you *go* and share, you will receive power from the Holy Spirit to bear witness wherever the Lord leads you. Today, it's time to *go*.

---

*After this I looked, and there was a vast multitude from every nation, tribe,*
*people, and language, which no one could number, standing before the*
*throne and before the Lamb. They were robed in white with palm branches*
*in their hands. And they cried out in a loud voice:*
*Salvation belongs to our God,*
*who is seated on the throne,*
*and to the Lamb!" —Revelation 7:9–10*

---

Further Scripture: Matthew 28:19–20; Acts 1:8; Revelation 7:3–4

### *Week 51, Day 352: Revelation 8*
### The Trumpet Judgments Begin

The seventh seal brought half an hour of silence in the throne room of heaven, and an angel offered incense and the prayers of the saints in the presence of God. John's vision continued as the first four angels blew the first four trumpets. The trumpets brought forth havoc on earth—fires destroying a third of the earth, a third of the sea filling with blood, a third of all freshwater becoming bitter, followed by darkness covering a third of the sun, moon, and stars. Finally, an eagle cried out in warning: "Woe! Woe! Woe!" Things were about to get *even worse* with the three remaining trumpets.

Do you find it difficult to imagine living through the images in John's vision? Yes, the reality is you could possibly experience this turmoil, even as a follower of Christ. However, even in the face of *darkness*, even in the face of *turmoil*, even in the face of *destruction, the Lord promises His presence.* He is your protector, and He is your hope. No matter what you will face—darkness, bitter water, or fire—the Lord promises to never forsake you. He is in your midst. He will be your strength when you are weak. Today, share the Lord's promises so others can find security, even in the midst of turmoil. Go!

---

*I looked again and heard an eagle flying high overhead, crying out in a loud voice, "Woe! Woe! Woe to those who live on the earth, because of the remaining trumpet blasts that the three angels are about to sound!"*
—Revelation 8:13

---

Further Scripture: Deuteronomy 31:6; Proverbs 18:10; Revelation 8:1–2

## *Week 51, Day 353: Revelation 9*
## The Fifth and Sixth Trumpets

When the fifth trumpet sounded, smoke covered the earth, bringing darkness. Locusts with the power of scorpions were told not to harm the grass but *only harm people who did not have God's seal on their foreheads.* They were not permitted to kill but only torment for five months. The people wanted to die, but death would flee them. The sixth trumpet brought death to a third of the human race as a demonic invasion of 200 million mounted troops were sent out, bringing more fire, smoke, and sulfur.

Torment and death came upon people who did not repent of their disobedience to God. However, even in the final days, *people will have the opportunity to turn and repent.* Why wait? *Choose to turn to the Lord today!* Perhaps you know some who haven't given their lives to Jesus. Pray for them, fast for them, share and model God's love so they will want to know the Jesus in you. The woes will come, the pain will come, and it will be miserable. Today, share with someone the hope you have in Jesus, despite difficult circumstances. Jesus promises hope, peace, and eternal love to all those who believe and repent of their wicked ways.

---

*They were told not to harm the grass of the earth, or any green plant, or any tree, but only people who do not have God's seal on their foreheads. They were not permitted to kill them but were to torment them for five months; their torment is like the torment caused by a scorpion when it strikes a man. In those days people will seek death and will not find it; they will long to die, but death will flee from them.* —Revelation 9:4–6

---

Further Scripture: Luke 24:47; Acts 26:20; Revelation 9:20–21

## *Week 51, Day 354: Revelation 10*
## The Mighty Angel and the Small Scroll

Before the seventh trumpet was blown, John saw a mighty angel coming down from heaven surrounded by a cloud. When the angel cried out, seven thunders spoke, but a voice told John not to write it down. Then the angel announced there would no longer be an interval of time—no more delay, the wait is over. When the seventh angel blew the seventh trumpet, *then God's hidden plan, His mystery, will be completed.*

As you read these words and this vision of John, trust a time will come when the mystery of the Gospel and of Christ will be fully revealed. The time will come when the wait is over, and the plan is completed. Until then the Lord will provide you the strength and motivation to reveal truth. The Lord will provide grace to share about the mysteries of Christ and the fullness and the riches of His glory. The time to turn away from evil ways, to repent, and to seek the Lord *is now*. May any hesitation and pause in receiving Christ in your life cease, so when Christ does return, and His plan is completed—you are ready!

---

*There will no longer be an interval of time, but in the days of the sound of the seventh angel, when he will blow his trumpet, then God's hidden plan will be completed, as He announced to His servants the prophets.*
—Revelation 10:6–7

---

Further Scripture: 1 Corinthians 2:7; Ephesians 3:8–9; Revelation 10:10–11

## *Week 51, Day 355: Revelation 11*
### The Two Witnesses

During the tribulation brought by the first six trumpets, the Lord empowered two witnesses to prophesy for 1,260 days, or three and a half years. As the two witnesses finished their testimony, the beast from the abyss, a presence of Satan, killed them. However, after three and a half days, God's breath of life restored them, and *they were resurrected to heaven.* Then the seventh angel blew his trumpet and loud voices in heaven proclaimed victory: "The kingdom of the world has become the kingdom of our Lord and of His Messiah, and He will reign forever and ever!" People were terrified *but gave God glory.*

The two witnesses brought a *picture of revival during the tribulation.* They had the power of the Resurrected Savior *in them.* You have this same power of the Resurrected Savior in *you.* You are a treasured vessel to be used for His glory. God gave you authority over darkness, over demons, and over sickness because of His power alive in you. He promises to give you everything you need to be a witness so people will be saved from eternal judgment. Today, *go* and proclaim the good news in the power and authority of the Lord.

---

*The 24 elders, who were seated before God on their thrones, fell facedown
and worshiped God, saying:
We thank You, Lord God, the Almighty,
who is and who was,
because You have taken Your great power
and have begun to reign.* —Revelation 11:16–17

---

Further Scripture: Luke 9:1; Romans 8:11; Revelation 11:6

## *Week 51, Day 356: Revelation 12*

## The Great Dragon

Two signs appeared to John. First, a pregnant woman was crying out in labor before giving birth. Symbolically, this most likely represents the Messiah's birth in Israel. Second, a fiery red dragon, a symbol of Satan, was standing in front of the pregnant woman, ready to devour her child. The woman gave birth to a son, a male who would shepherd all nations. In the vision, the child was *not devoured by Satan* but rather caught up to God to His throne. In the end, *the dragon did not win the war against the woman*, and he did not gain her baby son. This vision likely illustrates Jesus remaining on the throne and Satan left to wage war against those who have kept God's commands and have the testimony about Jesus.

From the beginning, the enemy has attempted to defeat the plans of God. Even today, victory belongs to the Lord and to His people who keep His commands and hold fast to the testimony of Jesus. Satan seeks to steal, kill, and destroy. Be ready. Stand strong in the battle. You are equipped. *The enemy is defeated by the power of Jesus' name.* Jesus is the Good Shepherd to the nations. Therefore, follow His voice and hold fast to Jesus.

---

*And the dragon stood in front of the woman who was about to give birth, so that when she did give birth he might devour her child. But she gave birth to a Son—a male who is going to shepherd all nations with an iron scepter—and her child was caught up to God and to His throne.*
—Revelation 12:4–5

---

Further Scripture: Genesis 3:15; John 10:10–11; Revelation 12:17

# December 22

The Beasts from the Earth and Sea

As John's vision continued, two more beasts emerged—the antichrist from the sea and a false prophet from the earth. Satan will give the antichrist his power, his throne, and great authority. The false prophet will deceive all those who live on the earth through the signs he performs. The whole earth will be amazed. Many will follow the antichrist and worship him, except those whose names are written in the Book of Life, determined by Jesus the Lamb who was slain for their salvation. Yes, they will continue to worship the Lord. However, they may be destined for captivity and even killed by the sword. *The Lord will grant the saints perseverance and faith.*

In the tribulation, as a believer of Christ, you will possibly face captivity or even be killed by a sword. But as you think of all the possible torture and pain, remember the saints who have gone before you have already experienced persecution for their faith. Because of their pain, others can now live in Christ. In the last days, *the Lord will grant you faith and perseverance.* Remember, Jesus said those who are persecuted for righteousness are blessed and the kingdom of heaven is theirs. So you are to be glad and rejoice because our reward is great in heaven. Today, *rest in the hope from Jesus.* Walk by faith and not with fear. You will be blessed.

---

*All those who live on the earth will worship him, everyone whose name was not written from the foundation of the world in the book of life of the Lamb who was slaughtered.* —Revelation 13:8

---

Further Scripture: Matthew 5:10–12; Colossians 1:11–12; Revelation 13:9–10

### *Week 52, Day 358: Revelation 14*
## Reaping the Earth's Harvest

John's vision shifted from the antichrist to the Lamb, and he saw and heard a series of powerful messages from five angels. As the end of the tribulation drew near, messages regarding both salvation and wrath were boldly declared. One message, a voice from heaven, instructed John to write: "The dead who die in the Lord from now on are blessed." And the Spirit responded, "Yes . . . let them rest from their labors, for their works follow them!"

Hang in there, friend. Stay strong in the Lord. None of what you do will be wasted, and in the end, you will be blessed. *Yes,* suffering hurts and open wounds bring pain. *Yes,* the things of this world attempt to satisfy you with temporary pleasures and sweep you away from following Christ fully. *Yes,* trials come along and devastate your heart. And yet, remember, Jesus is victorious. *Jesus is enough.* The Lamb, the One, the Savior of the world came to rescue you from wrath, judgment, and eternal fire. So now, more than ever before, stay strong, and you will be *blessed* because of your perseverance in keeping God's commands and faith in Jesus.

---

*Then I heard a voice from heaven saying, "Write: The dead who die in the Lord from now on are blessed."*
*"Yes," says the Spirit, "let them rest from their labors, for their works follow them!"* —Revelation 14:13

---

Further Scripture: 1 Peter 4:12–14, 19; Revelation 14:6–7

***Week 52, Day 359: Revelation 15***
## Celebrate Victory with a Song

God's wrath is coming to completion—the saints will have endured seven seals and seven trumpets. Now seven angels would distribute the seven bowls of wrath to usher in God's glory. But first the saints celebrated the victory over the beast, his image, and the number of his name as they stood on the sea of glass with harps singing and praising the Lord God Almighty!

John witnessed a victory song after a period of suffering, testing, and tribulation. May this song serve as a reminder to *praise the Lord* and glorify His name throughout your day. You may think you can't carry a tune or keep the rhythm with your toes, but don't let that stop you from *worshipping the Lord* with your heart. Sing Him a new song of praise. Rejoice in the work of His hands. Thank Him for His ways. Recognize His faithful promises and provision in Your life. Whether it's experiencing God answer the impossible or resting in His peace during the mundane, praise Him for victory in His presence. Now go and sing a song to the Lamb of God, Jesus Christ! Who was, and is, and is still to come!

---

*I also saw something like a sea of glass mixed with fire, and those who had won the victory over the beast, his image, and the number of his name, were standing on the sea of glass with harps from God. They sang the song of God's servant Moses and the song of the Lamb:*
*Great and awe-inspiring are Your works,*
*Lord God, the Almighty;*
*righteous and true are Your ways,*
*King of the Nations. —Revelation 15:2–3*

---

Further Scripture: Exodus 15:1; Psalm 98:1; Revelation 15:1

***Week 52, Day 360: Revelation 16***

## The Seven Bowls

The time came for the seven angels to pour out the seven bowls of wrath on the earth, to people with the mark of the beast and those who worshipped his image. Indeed, these people had not repented, had not turned to the Lord, did not bring God glory, and blasphemed His name. Now they would receive God's promised wrath and judgment: painful sores, blood in the sea, blood in the fresh water, burning fire and heat, darkness, lightning, thunder, earthquakes, and 100-pound hail stones. Even still, in the midst of torture, they continued to blaspheme the Lord God Almighty and refused to repent.

Don't delay repenting and giving your life to Jesus. If you have something hidden, just stop. Let it go. Repent and say: "Lord, forgive me of my sins. I give You my life." There is no sin, no mess, and no ugly situation too far beyond God's love for you. Let your pride go. For once in your life, humble yourself, repent, and receive God's grace. *You will never fully understand His love for you until you let go of control and let His love come into your life.* Give it up and stop running from the Lord. His goodness and mercy will be with you all the days of your life.

---

*And people were burned by the intense heat. So they blasphemed the name of God, who had the power over these plagues, and they did not repent and give Him glory.* —Revelation 16:9

---

Further Scripture: Acts 3:19–20; 2 Corinthians 6:2; Revelation 16:1–2

*Week 52, Day 361: Revelation 17*
## The Lamb Will Conquer

As John's vision continues, preparation takes place for the battle that will occur when Christ's return begins. The kings of the earth, who had been given authority for one hour, give their power and authority to the beast. The kings join the beast and together wage war against the Lamb. But the Lamb of God, Jesus, *has victory* because He is the Lord of lords and the Kings of kings. His followers, the believers, fight with Him. He calls them chosen and faithful.

Jesus, the Savior of the earth, *reigns victorious* over all kingdoms—neither beast, nor king of the earth will gain victory over Him. He brings purpose, sovereignty, and works all things together for His good, for those He has *called chosen and who are faithful.* Do not fear when you face a battle, hardship, or unknown moments in life. As His called, faithful, and chosen, when you dwell in the shadow of the Almighty, you can say to the Lord: "My refuge and my fortress, my God, in whom I trust." Call to Him, and He will answer you. He will rescue you, satisfy you, and give you salvation. Today, do not fear, and do not be dismayed. The Lord promises hope in Him. He is your shelter. Take a deep breath and rest in the shadow of His mighty wings. He will be with you always.

---

*These will make war against the Lamb, but the Lamb will conquer them because He is Lord of lords and King of kings. Those with Him are called, chosen, and faithful.* —Revelation 17:14

---

Further Scripture: Psalm 91:1–2; John 15:16; James 2:5

### *Week 52, Day 362: Revelation 18*
### The Fall of Babylon the Great

John's vision continued as the great city of Babylon fell to destruction forever. The political leaders fell, the merchants fell, and all who did business by the sea fell. All were destroyed. God wiped away everything they had built up with their hands and had placed their hope in. It affected other kingdoms, and the people wept and lamented. Pride and seduction filled Babylon. Now, at last, *they received this final judgment.*

Whom and what do you put your hope in? If the stock market crashed, if your car was destroyed, if you were laid off from your executive position, or if you were unable to exercise daily, would it cause you to crumble and lament? Or would you remain strong in the Lord because your hope rests in Him? When life falls apart, your response will honestly reveal what or whom you have placed your hope in. Choose to rest in the Lord's promise to work all things together for good. He has a plan, and He has control over all the earth. He will carry your burdens. Choose to not only believe His truth but live out your belief that *God is bigger than the temporary pleasures this life offers.* May your life reflect His faithfulness as you put your hope in Him.

---

*He cried in a mighty voice:*
*It has fallen,*
*Babylon the Great has fallen!*
*She has become a dwelling for demons,*
*a haunt for every unclean spirit,*
*a haunt for every unclean bird,*
*and a haunt for every unclean and despicable beast.* —Revelation 18:2

---

Further Scripture: 2 Corinthians 4:16–18; Revelation 18:16–17a, 23b–24

## *Week 52, Day 363: Revelation 19*

## Victorious in Battle

After the complete destruction of Babylon, a vast multitude of voices sang hallelujah and praises to the Lord for His deliverance, judgment, and sovereignty. Then, in John's vision, *heaven opened and a rider called Faithful and True, the Word of God—yes, Jesus—came out riding on a white horse.* His army of believers followed Him, and He fought the battle against the beast and the false prophet. When captured, the beast and false prophet were thrown alive into the lake of fire that burns with sulfur. With a sword in His mouth, Jesus killed the beast's entire army.

Allow Jesus' victory over the beast, the false prophet, and their army serve as an encouragement to you today as you *fight your own battles,* not against flesh and blood, but against the rulers, authorities, world powers of darkness, and spiritual forces of evil in the heavens. *You have victory in the Great I Am*—Jesus Christ—who is coming back to defeat the enemy. But until then, hold up the sword of the spirit and shield of faith. Walk with the breastplate of righteousness and the helmet of salvation. Steadily go with the feet of peace and with truth like a belt around your waist. Stand firm. Be alert. Pray at all times. *The enemy will flee when you boldly say the name of Jesus!* Hallelujah! Say it again. Hallelujah! Salvation, glory, and power belong to our God!

---

*But the beast was taken prisoner, and along with him the false prophet, who had performed the signs in his presence. He deceived those who accepted the mark of the beast and those who worshiped his image with these signs. Both of them were thrown alive into the lake of fire that burns with sulfur.*
—Revelation 19:20

---

Further Scripture: 1 Corinthians 15:57; Ephesians 6:14–18; Revelation 19:1, 11–13

## *Week 52, Day 364: Revelation 20*
### The Millennia Reign of Christ

After the devil was defeated and thrown into the lake of fire and sulfur to be tormented day and night, forever and ever, John saw the One, *Jesus, seated on the great white throne with the books opened.* The final judgment came, separating those who believe in Jesus and those who never repented and received Jesus as Savior. It was judgment time. *Anyone whose name was not written in the Book of Life was thrown into the lake of fire* to be tormented day and night, forever and ever, along with Satan, the antichrist, and the false prophet.

As you witness the victory Jesus has over Satan, you also witness the hard reality for the unsaved. As the Word of God states, those who have not confessed Jesus as Lord and Savior, whose names are not written in the Book of Life, will be thrown into the lake of fire. May John's vision of what is to come in the end prepare you to be ready. Today, seek the Lord as your Savior and eternal hope for salvation. May it stir compassion within you to share Christ's love with others. May it motivate you to pray and beseech the Lord to save people you know and love while there is still time. You wouldn't want someone you love to ask at the end, "*Why didn't anyone ever share this Jesus with me?*" Go now and share the Gospel. *What are you waiting for?*

---

*And anyone not found written in the book of life was thrown into the lake of fire.* —Revelation 20:15

---

Further Scripture: Psalm 33:4–5; Philippians 4:3; Revelation 20:10

# December 30

*Week 53, Day 365: Revelation 21*

The New Jerusalem

The marriage previously announced between the Bride and the Lamb finally occurs. John witnesses the holy New Jerusalem radiantly coming down out of heaven, ready for God like a bride meeting her husband. John sees the new heaven and new earth, where God will dwell with humanity. Death, grief, pain, and crying will no longer exist. The One seated on the throne instructs John to write these words because they are beautiful and true: "It is done! I am the Alpha and the Omega, the Beginning and the End. I will give water as a gift to the thirsty from the spring of life. The *victor will inherit these things,* and I will be his God, and he will be My son."

Who is the victor to inherit these things? If you simply have faith to believe Jesus is the Son of God, then you can reign victorious in heaven forever with the Alpha and the Omega and drink from the spring of life forever. You will experience no more tears and no more pain, you will walk on golden streets in the light of God's glory, and your name will be written in the Lamb's Book of Life. *Jesus gave you the power and authority to share this good, life-changing message. Why stay quiet?* Today, go and share the beauty and hope inherited by the victors who have faith in Jesus.

---

*"Write, because these words are faithful and true." And He said to me, "It is done! I am the Alpha and the Omega, the Beginning and the End. I will give water as a gift to the thirsty from the spring of life. The victor will inherit these things, and I will be his God, and he will be My son."*
—Revelation 21:5b–7

---

Further Scripture: 1 John 5:4–5; Revelation 21:3–4, 9b–11

### *Week 53, Day 366: Revelation 22*
### The Source of Life

As John's vision concluded, the angel of the Lord affirmed the words spoken as faithful and true in order to show believers what must quickly take place before Christ returns. The one who keeps these prophetic words will be blessed. John began to worship the angel, but the angel insisted he stop and commanded John to only worship God. Believers will be made holy as they seek the Lord. By drinking the living water Jesus offers, no one will ever be thirsty again. Jesus promised He would come quickly. Jesus, the Great I Am, the Alpha and Omega, the Lord God Almighty, the Root, the Offspring of David, the Bright Morning Star is *coming quickly*. Until then, John prayed for Jesus' gift of grace to be with the saints.

You are living the final days before Christ's return. *Will you be ready?* Receive Christ's love for you. Live ready by keeping His Word. Love the Lord with all your heart, soul, mind, and strength. Then love others, as you love yourself. Worship God alone. Nothing else will ever satisfy you besides the love of Jesus. Christ is enough. Come, Lord Jesus, come. He is coming quickly. Be ready!

---

*He who testifies about these things says, "Yes, I am coming quickly."*
*Amen! Come, Lord Jesus!*
*The grace of the Lord Jesus be with all the saints. Amen.*
—Revelation 22:20–21

---

Further Scripture: Matthew 22:37–39; Ephesians 2:8–9; Revelation 22:7–9

# Names of the Messiah Through the Bible

*revive*DAILY devotionals intentionally correspond with Time to Revive's reviveSCHOOL—a two-year program of biblical teaching. This study focuses on seeing the complete portrait of the Messiah as depicted in all 66 books of the Bible. Throughout the study, reviveSCHOOL identified *a theme word* for the Messiah in each book of the Bible. I have included this resource to encourage and guide you as you read through the Bible. As you read through this list, ask yourself, *Who is the Messiah in my life today?*

| Book of the Bible | Key Word for Messiah | Key Verse |
|---|---|---|
| *Pentateuch* | | |
| Genesis | Seed | Gen 3:15; Gal 3:16, 19 |
| Exodus | Deliverer | Jude 1:5 |
| Leviticus | Atonement | Hebrews 10:19–22 |
| Numbers | Rock | Num 20:11; 1 Cor 10:4 |
| Deuteronomy | Prophet | Deut 18:15; John 6:14 |
| | | |
| *The Gospels* | | |
| Matthew | King | Matthew 21:15 |
| Mark | Servant | Mark 10:43b–45 |
| Luke | Son of Man | Luke 19:20 |
| John | Son of God | John 20:30–31 |
| | | |
| *Historical Books* | | |
| Joshua | Commander | Joshua 5:13–15 |
| Judges | Judge | Colossians 1:13–14 |
| Ruth | Kinsman Redeemer | 1 Peter 1:18–19 |
| 1 Samuel | Anointed One | 1 Samuel 2:10 |
| 2 Samuel | Eternal Throne | Luke 1:30–33 |
| 1 Kings | Something Greater | Matthew 12:42 |

| 2 Kings | Surviving Seed | Psalm 89:3–4 |
|---|---|---|
| 1 Chronicles | Son of David | 1 Chronicles 17:11, 14 |
| 2 Chronicles | Royal Throne | 2 Chronicles 7:18 |
| Ezra | Promise Keeper | 2 Corinthians 1:19–20 |
| Nehemiah | Builder | Matthew 16:18 |
| Esther | Despised One | Isaiah 53:3 |

| *Acts* | Authority | Acts 2:33 |
|---|---|---|

| *Wisdom Books* | | |
|---|---|---|
| Job | Promised Redeemer | Job 19:25 |
| Psalms | King of Glory | Psalm 24:7–10 |
| Proverbs | Wisdom | 1 Corinthians 1:30 |
| Ecclesiastes | Eternal | Ecclesiastes 3:11 |
| Song of Songs | Bridegroom | Revelation 19:7 |

| *Paul's Letters* | | |
|---|---|---|
| Romans | Justifier | Romans 3:24 |
| 1 Corinthians | The Last Adam | 1 Corinthians 15:45 |
| 2 Corinthians | Treasure | 2 Corinthians 4:7 |
| Galatians | Liberator | Galatians 5:1 |
| Ephesians | The Head | Ephesians 1:22; 5:23 |
| Philippians | Exalted One | Philippians 2:9 |
| Colossians | Firstborn | Colossians 1:15, 18 |
| 1 Thessalonians | Coming Lord | 1 Thess 4:15–16; 5:23 |
| 2 Thessalonians | Faithful Lord | 2 Thess 3:3 |
| 1 Timothy | Mediator | 1 Timothy 2:5–6 |
| 2 Timothy | Righteous Judge | 2 Timothy 4:8 |
| Titus | Savior | Titus 2:13; 3:4–7 |
| Philemon | Master | Matthew 23:10 |

| *Major Prophets* | | |
|---|---|---|
| Isaiah | Immanuel | Isa 7:14; Matt 1:21–23 |
| Jeremiah | New Covenant | Jer 31:31–33; Heb 8:13 |

| Lamentations | My Portion | Lam 3:22 |
|---|---|---|
| Ezekiel | New David | Ezek 34:22–24 |
| Daniel | Stone | Dan 2:35, 45 |

| *Other Letters* | | |
|---|---|---|
| Hebrews | High Priest | Heb 4:14; 5:10; 10:19–22 |
| James | Perfect Law | James 1:25 |
| 1 Peter | Living Hope | 1 Peter 1:3 |
| 2 Peter | Master of Truth | 2 Peter 2:1–2 |
| 1 John | Perfect Love | 1 John 4:18–19 |
| 2 John | Truth | 2 John 1:1–2, 4 |
| 3 John | Perfect Example | 3 John 1:11 |
| Jude | Merciful Lord | Jude 1:21 |

| *Minor Prophets* | | |
|---|---|---|
| Hosea | Unconditional Love | Hosea 3:1; Rom 5:8 |
| Joel | Avenger | Joel 3:19–21 |
| Amos | Restorer | Amos 9:11–15 |
| Obadiah | Established King | Obadiah 1:21 |
| Jonah | Resurrection | Jonah 1:17; Matt 12:40; John 11:25 |
| Micah | The Shepherd | Micah 5:4; Matt 2:6 |
| Nahum | Burden Bearer | Nahum 1:7, 13; 2 Cor 5:21; Matt 11:30 |
| Habakkuk | Coming Salvation | Hab 2:3; 3:18; Heb 10:37 |
| Zephaniah | Mighty Warrior | Zeph 3:17 |
| Haggai | Greater Temple | Hag 2:9; Rev 21:22 |
| Zechariah | Pierced One | Zech 12:10; John 19:37 |
| Malachi | Sun of Righteousness | Mal 4:2 |

| *Revelation* | I Am | Rev 1:8, 17–18; Exod 3:14; John 8:58 |
|---|---|---|

# About Laura Kim Martin and Time to Revive

From the time Laura Kim Martin was a little girl growing up in Minnesota, she has sensed the Lord's calling to ministry. Her desire has always been to serve the Lord and tell the lost about Jesus Christ. A communication studies graduate of Taylor University (Indiana), Laura married Kyle Lance Martin, and together, they founded the Dallas-based ministry Time to Revive in 2010. As a couple, they surrendered their lives for the sake of the Gospel, reaching the lost, and encouraging the Church. With her heart for prayer and full dependence on the Lord, Laura began writing a weekly prayer and encouragement devotional, *Along the Journey*.

Through years of living out surrendered faith and trust in the Lord, Laura has tasted and seen that God is good. She has walked through trials and unknowns and personally witnessed God's faithfulness in the miracle moments of her own life, believing God through the impossible. She's received the love of Christ and freedom found in resting in His presence, while walking in His grace and truth. Laura joyfully walks with Jesus through the power of His Holy Spirit and listens to His voice. Now, she shares the lessons the Lord has written on her own heart, encouraging others to press on in their personal faith journeys with Jesus.

When not writing or opening up her home with her heart for hospitality in Richardson, Texas, Laura relishes time with Kyle and their four kids: Maya, Nadia, Selah, and Jude. Whether spending time outside or getting involved in activities that bring her kids joy, she loves seeing her family laugh and play well. Laura also enjoys exploring new coffee shops with friends, shopping for meaningful gifts for others, and sitting in her comfy chair at home where she can spend intimate time with the Lord.

Follow Laura Kim Martin:
www.laurakimmartin.com
(f) Facebook: Laura Kim Martin and reviveDAILYdevo
(⊙) Instagram: @laurakimmartin and @revivedailydevo

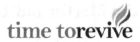

# time torevive

Time to Revive (TTR) equips the believers to get ready for the return of Christ. TTR partners with the church in communities, bringing believers together across denominational lines and inspiring them to obey the Great Commission to go in the power of the Holy Spirit and make disciples. Through hands-on training, the TTR team empowers the saints to leave familiar church walls and walk by faith to share the Gospel in authentic and life-changing ways.

www.timetorevive.com
info@timetorevive.com
https://www.facebook.com/timetorevive

If you have enjoyed this devotional and would like to dig even deeper into studying the Word of God, we invite you to register online to reviveSCHOOL.org. reviveSCHOOL is a two-year interactive Bible study that teaches through the Bible daily from Genesis to Revelation. Teaching and study are focused on seeing the Complete Portrait of the Messiah in all 66 books of the Bible. Additional resources include a 29-minute video teaching for each lesson, daily teaching notes, study guide questions, and a painting that summarizes each book of the Bible.

www.reviveSCHOOL.org
info@reviveSCHOOL.org

# Reading Plans for *revive*DAILY

I don't know about you, but I love to check boxes off after I complete something. Therefore, I have included these reading plans for *Year One* and *Year Two* of *revive*DAILY. You can look ahead at what is coming as well as check off the boxes as you read daily through the Bible. Keep in mind, however, that reading and studying through the Bible is not a sprint race. It's more like a marathon. And the purpose isn't just to check off boxes and get through another chapter in the Bible. Give yourself grace on this journey as you daily spend time with Jesus and in the Word of God.

Remember, you can find additional study resources, including a daily video teaching for each daily reading, at www.reviveschool.org.

Enjoy the journey!

# YEAR 1

**WEEK 1**
- 1 Genesis 1-3
- 2 Genesis 4-6
- 3 Genesis 7-9
- 4 Genesis 10-12
- 5 Genesis 13-15
- 6 Genesis 16-17
- 7 Genesis 18

JAN 1

**WEEK 2**
- 8 Genesis 19
- 9 Genesis 20-21
- 10 Genesis 22
- 11 Genesis 23-24
- 12 Genesis 25-26
- 13 Genesis 27-28
- 14 Genesis 29

JAN 8

**WEEK 3**
- 15 Genesis 30
- 16 Genesis 31
- 17 Genesis 32-33
- 18 Genesis 34-35
- 19 Genesis 36-37
- 20 Genesis 38
- 21 Genesis 39-40

JAN 15

**WEEK 4**
- 22 Genesis 41-42
- 23 Genesis 43-44
- 24 Genesis 45-46
- 25 Genesis 47-48
- 26 Genesis 49-50
- 27 Exodus 1
- 28 Exodus 2-3

JAN 22

**WEEK 5**
- 29 Exodus 4-5
- 30 Exodus 6
- 31 Exodus 7-8
- 32 Exodus 9-10
- 33 Exodus 11
- 34 Exodus 12-13
- 35 Exodus 14-15

JAN 29

**WEEK 6**
- 36 Exodus 16-18
- 37 Exodus 19-20
- 38 Exodus 21
- 39 Exodus 22
- 40 Exodus 23-24
- 41 Exodus 25
- 42 Exodus 26

FEB 5

**WEEK 7**
- 43 Exodus 27-28
- 44 Exodus 29
- 45 Exodus 30-31
- 46 Exodus 32-33
- 47 Exodus 34-35
- 48 Exodus 36
- 49 Exodus 37-38

FEB 12

**WEEK 8**
- 50 Exodus 39
- 51 Exodus 40
- 52 Leviticus 1-3
- 53 Leviticus 4-5
- 54 Leviticus 6
- 55 Leviticus 7
- 56 Leviticus 8-9

FEB 19

**WEEK 9**
- 57 Leviticus 10
- 58 Leviticus 11-12
- 59 Leviticus 13
- 60 Leviticus 14
- 61 Leviticus 15
- 62 Leviticus 16
- 63 Leviticus 17

FEB 26

**WEEK 10**
- 64 Leviticus 18
- 65 Leviticus 19
- 66 Leviticus 20
- 67 Leviticus 21
- 68 Leviticus 22
- 69 Leviticus 23-24
- 70 Leviticus 25

MAR 5

**WEEK 11**
- 71 Leviticus 26
- 72 Leviticus 27
- 73 Numbers 1-2
- 74 Numbers 3
- 75 Numbers 4
- 76 Numbers 5-6
- 77 Numbers 7

MAR 12

**WEEK 12**
- 78 Numbers 8-9
- 79 Numbers 10-11
- 80 Numbers 12-13
- 81 Numbers 14
- 82 Numbers 15-16
- 83 Numbers 17-18
- 84 Numbers 19-20

MAR 19

**WEEK 13**
- 85 Numbers 21-22
- 86 Numbers 23-24
- 87 Numbers 25-26
- 88 Numbers 27-28
- 89 Numbers 29-30
- 90 Numbers 31
- 91 Numbers 32

MAR 26

**WEEK 14**
- 92 Numbers 33
- 93 Numbers 34
- 94 Numbers 35-36
- 95 Deuteronomy 1-3
- 96 Deuteronomy 4-6
- 97 Deuteronomy 7-9
- 98 Deuteronomy 10-12

APR 2

**WEEK 15**
- 99 Deuteronomy 13-14
- 100 Deuteronomy 15-16
- 101 Deuteronomy 17-18
- 102 Deuteronomy 19-20
- 103 Deuteronomy 21-22
- 104 Deuteronomy 23-24
- 105 Deuteronomy 25-26

APR 9

**WEEK 16**
- 106 Deuteronomy 27
- 107 Deuteronomy 28
- 108 Deuteronomy 29-30
- 109 Deuteronomy 31
- 110 Deuteronomy 32-24
- 1 Matthew 1
- 2 Matthew 2

APR 16

**WEEK 17**
- 3 Matthew 3
- 4 Matthew 4
- 5 Matthew 5
- 6 Matthew 6
- 7 Matthew 7
- 8 Matthew 8
- 9 Matthew 9

APR 23

**WEEK 18**
- 10 Matthew 10
- 11 Matthew 11
- 12 Matthew 12
- 13 Matthew 13
- 14 Matthew 14
- 15 Matthew 15
- 16 Matthew 16

APR 30

| WEEK 19 | | WEEK 20 | | WEEK 21 | |
|---|---|---|---|---|---|
| 17 | Matthew 17 | 24 | Matthew 24 | 31 | Mark 3 |
| 18 | Matthew 18 | 25 | Matthew 25 | 32 | Mark 4 |
| 19 | Matthew 19 | 26 | Matthew 26 | 33 | Mark 5 |
| 20 | Matthew 20 | 27 | Matthew 27 | 34 | Mark 6 |
| 21 | Matthew 21 | 28 | Matthew 28 | 35 | Mark 7 |
| 22 | Matthew 22 | 29 | Mark 1 | 36 | Mark 8 |
| 23 | Matthew 23 | 30 | Mark 2 | 37 | Mark 9 |
| | MAY 7 | | MAY 14 | | MAY 21 |

| WEEK 22 | | WEEK 23 | | WEEK 24 | |
|---|---|---|---|---|---|
| 38 | Mark 10 | 45 | Luke 1 | 52 | Luke 8 |
| 39 | Mark 11 | 46 | Luke 2 | 53 | Luke 9 |
| 40 | Mark 12 | 47 | Luke 3 | 54 | Luke 10 |
| 41 | Mark 13 | 48 | Luke 4 | 55 | Luke 11 |
| 42 | Mark 14 | 49 | Luke 5 | 56 | Luke 12 |
| 43 | Mark 15 | 50 | Luke 6 | 57 | Luke 13 |
| 44 | Mark 16 | 51 | Luke 7 | 58 | Luke 14 |
| | MAY 28 | | JUN 4 | | JUN 11 |

| WEEK 25 | | WEEK 26 | | WEEK 27 | |
|---|---|---|---|---|---|
| 59 | Luke 15 | 66 | Luke 22 | 73 | John 5 |
| 60 | Luke 16 | 67 | Luke 23 | 74 | John 6 |
| 61 | Luke 17 | 68 | Luke 24 | 75 | John 7 |
| 62 | Luke 18 | 69 | John 1 | 76 | John 8 |
| 63 | Luke 19 | 70 | John 2 | 77 | John 9 |
| 64 | Luke 20 | 71 | John 3 | 78 | John 10 |
| 65 | Luke 21 | 72 | John 4 | 79 | John 11 |
| | JUN 18 | | JUN 25 | | JUL 2 |

| WEEK 28 | | WEEK 29 | | WEEK 30 | |
|---|---|---|---|---|---|
| 80 | John 12 | 87 | John 19 | 5 | Joshua 9-10 |
| 81 | John 13 | 88 | John 20 | 6 | Joshua 11-12 |
| 82 | John 14 | 89 | John 21 | 7 | Joshua 13-14 |
| 83 | John 15 | 1 | Joshua 1-2 | 8 | Joshua 15-16 |
| 84 | John 16 | 2 | Joshua 3-4 | 9 | Joshua 17-18 |
| 85 | John 17 | 3 | Joshua 5-6 | 10 | Joshua 19-20 |
| 86 | John 18 | 4 | Joshua 7-8 | 11 | Joshua 21-22 |
| | JUL 9 | | JUL 16 | | JUL 23 |

| WEEK 31 | | WEEK 32 | | WEEK 33 | |
|---|---|---|---|---|---|
| 12 | Joshua 23-24 | 19 | Judges 13-14 | 26 | 1 Samuel 1-2 |
| 13 | Judges 1-2 | 20 | Judges 15-16 | 27 | 1 Samuel 3-4 |
| 14 | Judges 3-4 | 21 | Judges 17-18 | 28 | 1 Samuel 5-6 |
| 15 | Judges 5-6 | 22 | Judges 19-20 | 29 | 1 Samuel 7-8 |
| 16 | Judges 7-8 | 23 | Judges 21 | 30 | 1 Samuel 9-10 |
| 17 | Judges 9-10 | 24 | Ruth 1-2 | 31 | 1 Samuel 11-12 |
| 18 | Judges 11-12 | 25 | Ruth 3-4 | 32 | 1 Samuel 13 |
| | JUL 30 | | AUG 6 | | AUG 13 |

| WEEK 34 | | WEEK 35 | | WEEK 36 | |
|---|---|---|---|---|---|
| 33 | 1 Samuel 14 | 40 | 1 Samuel 25 | 47 | 2 Samuel 7-8 |
| 34 | 1 Samuel 15-16 | 41 | 1 Samuel 26-27 | 48 | 2 Samuel 9-10 |
| 35 | 1 Samuel 17 | 42 | 1 Samuel 28-29 | 49 | 2 Samuel 11-12 |
| 36 | 1 Samuel 18 | 43 | 1 Samuel 30-31 | 50 | 2 Samuel 13-14 |
| 37 | 1 Samuel 19-20 | 44 | 2 Samuel 1-2 | 51 | 2 Samuel 15-16 |
| 38 | 1 Samuel 21-22 | 45 | 2 Samuel 3-4 | 52 | 2 Samuel 17-18 |
| 39 | 1 Samuel 23-24 | 46 | 2 Samuel 5-6 | 53 | 2 Samuel 19-20 |
| | AUG 20 | | AUG 6 | | SEP 3 |

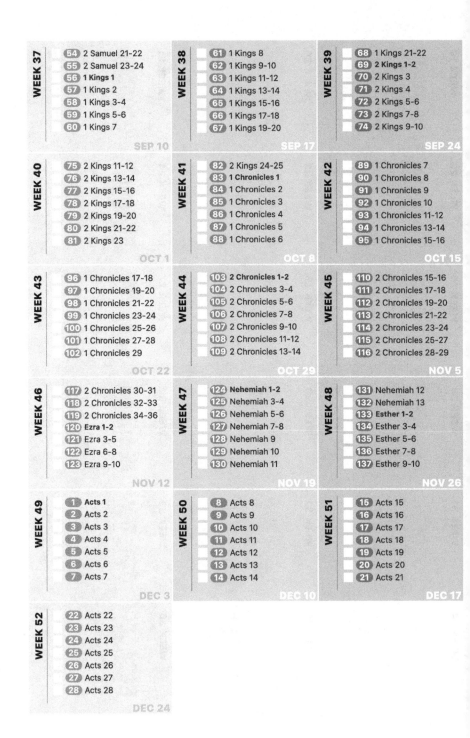

**WEEK 37**
- 54 2 Samuel 21-22
- 55 2 Samuel 23-24
- 56 **1 Kings 1**
- 57 1 Kings 2
- 58 1 Kings 3-4
- 59 1 Kings 5-6
- 60 1 Kings 7

SEP 10

**WEEK 38**
- 61 1 Kings 8
- 62 1 Kings 9-10
- 63 1 Kings 11-12
- 64 1 Kings 13-14
- 65 1 Kings 15-16
- 66 1 Kings 17-18
- 67 1 Kings 19-20

SEP 17

**WEEK 39**
- 68 1 Kings 21-22
- 69 **2 Kings 1-2**
- 70 2 Kings 3
- 71 2 Kings 4
- 72 2 Kings 5-6
- 73 2 Kings 7-8
- 74 2 Kings 9-10

SEP 24

**WEEK 40**
- 75 2 Kings 11-12
- 76 2 Kings 13-14
- 77 2 Kings 15-16
- 78 2 Kings 17-18
- 79 2 Kings 19-20
- 80 2 Kings 21-22
- 81 2 Kings 23

OCT 1

**WEEK 41**
- 82 2 Kings 24-25
- 83 **1 Chronicles 1**
- 84 1 Chronicles 2
- 85 1 Chronicles 3
- 86 1 Chronicles 4
- 87 1 Chronicles 5
- 88 1 Chronicles 6

OCT 8

**WEEK 42**
- 89 1 Chronicles 7
- 90 1 Chronicles 8
- 91 1 Chronicles 9
- 92 1 Chronicles 10
- 93 1 Chronicles 11-12
- 94 1 Chronicles 13-14
- 95 1 Chronicles 15-16

OCT 15

**WEEK 43**
- 96 1 Chronicles 17-18
- 97 1 Chronicles 19-20
- 98 1 Chronicles 21-22
- 99 1 Chronicles 23-24
- 100 1 Chronicles 25-26
- 101 1 Chronicles 27-28
- 102 1 Chronicles 29

OCT 22

**WEEK 44**
- 103 **2 Chronicles 1-2**
- 104 2 Chronicles 3-4
- 105 2 Chronicles 5-6
- 106 2 Chronicles 7-8
- 107 2 Chronicles 9-10
- 108 2 Chronicles 11-12
- 109 2 Chronicles 13-14

OCT 29

**WEEK 45**
- 110 2 Chronicles 15-16
- 111 2 Chronicles 17-18
- 112 2 Chronicles 19-20
- 113 2 Chronicles 21-22
- 114 2 Chronicles 23-24
- 115 2 Chronicles 25-27
- 116 2 Chronicles 28-29

NOV 5

**WEEK 46**
- 117 2 Chronicles 30-31
- 118 2 Chronicles 32-33
- 119 2 Chronicles 34-36
- 120 **Ezra 1-2**
- 121 Ezra 3-5
- 122 Ezra 6-8
- 123 Ezra 9-10

NOV 12

**WEEK 47**
- 124 **Nehemiah 1-2**
- 125 Nehemiah 3-4
- 126 Nehemiah 5-6
- 127 Nehemiah 7-8
- 128 Nehemiah 9
- 129 Nehemiah 10
- 130 Nehemiah 11

NOV 19

**WEEK 48**
- 131 Nehemiah 12
- 132 Nehemiah 13
- 133 **Esther 1-2**
- 134 Esther 3-4
- 135 Esther 5-6
- 136 Esther 7-8
- 137 Esther 9-10

NOV 26

**WEEK 49**
- 1 **Acts 1**
- 2 Acts 2
- 3 Acts 3
- 4 Acts 4
- 5 Acts 5
- 6 Acts 6
- 7 Acts 7

DEC 3

**WEEK 50**
- 8 Acts 8
- 9 Acts 9
- 10 Acts 10
- 11 Acts 11
- 12 Acts 12
- 13 Acts 13
- 14 Acts 14

DEC 10

**WEEK 51**
- 15 Acts 15
- 16 Acts 16
- 17 Acts 17
- 18 Acts 18
- 19 Acts 19
- 20 Acts 20
- 21 Acts 21

DEC 17

**WEEK 52**
- 22 Acts 22
- 23 Acts 23
- 24 Acts 24
- 25 Acts 25
- 26 Acts 26
- 27 Acts 27
- 28 Acts 28

DEC 24

# Year 2

**WEEK 1**
- 1 Job 1
- 2 Job 2-3
- 3 Job 4
- 4 Job 5-6
- 5 Job 7-8
- 6 Job 9-10
- 7 Job 11-12

JAN 1

**WEEK 2**
- 8 Job 13
- 9 Job 14
- 10 Job 15
- 11 Job 16
- 12 Job 17-18
- 13 Job 19
- 14 Job 20

JAN 8

**WEEK 3**
- 15 Job 21
- 16 Job 22-23
- 17 Job 24
- 18 Job 25-26
- 19 Job 27
- 20 Job 28-29
- 21 Job 30

JAN 15

**WEEK 4**
- 22 Job 31
- 23 Job 32-33
- 24 Job 34-35
- 25 Job 36
- 26 Job 37
- 27 Job 38
- 28 Job 39-40

JAN 22

**WEEK 5**
- 29 Job 41-42
- 30 **Psalms 1-3**
- 31 Psalms 4-6
- 32 Psalms 7-9
- 33 Psalms 10-12
- 34 Psalms 13-15
- 35 Psalms 16-17

JAN 29

**WEEK 6**
- 36 Psalms 18
- 37 Psalms 19-20
- 38 Psalms 21-22
- 39 Psalms 23-25
- 40 Psalms 26-28
- 41 Psalms 29-30
- 42 Psalms 31-32

FEB 5

**WEEK 7**
- 43 Psalms 33-34
- 44 Psalms 35-36
- 45 Psalms 37
- 46 Psalms 38-39
- 47 Psalms 40-42
- 48 Psalms 43-45
- 49 Psalms 46-48

FEB 12

**WEEK 8**
- 50 Psalms 49-50
- 51 Psalms 51-53
- 52 Psalms 54-56
- 53 Psalms 57-59
- 54 Psalms 60-62
- 55 Psalms 63-65
- 56 Psalms 66-67

FEB 19

**WEEK 9**
- 57 Psalms 68
- 58 Psalms 69
- 59 Psalms 70-71
- 60 Psalms 72-73
- 61 Psalms 74
- 62 Psalms 75-76
- 63 Psalms 77-78
- 64 Psalms 79-80

FEB 26

**WEEK 10**
- 65 Psalms 81-82
- 66 Psalms 83
- 67 Psalms 84
- 68 Psalms 85
- 69 Psalms 86-87
- 70 Psalms 88
- 71 Psalms 89

MAR 5

**WEEK 11**
- 72 Psalms 90
- 73 Psalms 91
- 74 Psalms 92-93
- 75 Psalms 94-95
- 76 Psalms 96-97
- 77 Psalms 98-99
- 78 Psalms 100-102

MAR 12

**WEEK 12**
- 79 Psalms 103-104
- 80 Psalms 105-106
- 81 Psalms 107-109
- 82 Psalms 110-112
- 83 Psalms 113-115
- 84 Psalms 116-118
- 85 Psalms 119

MAR 19

**WEEK 13**
- 86 Psalms 120-121
- 87 Psalms 122-123
- 88 Psalms 124-125
- 89 Psalms 126-127
- 90 Psalms 128-129
- 91 Psalms 130-131
- 92 Psalms 132-133

MAR 26

**WEEK 14**
- 93 Psalms 134-136
- 94 Psalms 137-139
- 95 Psalms 140-142
- 96 Psalms 143-145
- 97 Psalms 146-147
- 98 Psalms 148-150
- 99 **Proverbs 1-2**

APR 2

**WEEK 15**
- 100 Proverbs 3-4
- 101 Proverbs 5
- 102 Proverbs 6-7
- 103 Proverbs 8-9
- 104 Proverbs 10-11
- 105 Proverbs 12-13
- 106 Proverbs 14-15

APR 9

**WEEK 16**
- 107 Proverbs 16-17
- 108 Proverbs 18-19
- 109 Proverbs 20-21
- 110 Proverbs 22-23
- 111 Proverbs 24
- 112 Proverbs 25-26
- 113 Proverbs 27-29

APR 16

**WEEK 17**
- 114 Proverbs 30-31
- 115 **Ecclesiastes 1-2**
- 116 Ecclesiastes 3-4
- 117 Ecclesiastes 5-6
- 118 Ecclesiastes 7-9
- 119 Ecclesiastes 10-12
- 120 **Song of Songs 1-3**

APR 23

**WEEK 18**
- 121 Song of Songs 4-5
- 122 Song of Songs 6-8
- 1 **Romans 1**
- 2 Romans 2
- 3 Romans 3
- 4 Romans 4
- 5 Romans 5

APR 30

**WEEK 19**
- 6 Romans 6
- 7 Romans 7
- 8 Romans 8
- 9 Romans 9
- 10 Romans 10
- 11 Romans 11
- 12 Romans 12

MAY 7

**WEEK 20**
- 13 Romans 13
- 14 Romans 14
- 15 Romans 15
- 16 Romans 16
- 17 **1 Corinthians 1**
- 18 1 Corinthians 2
- 19 1 Corinthians 3

MAY 14

**WEEK 21**
- 20 1 Corinthians 4
- 21 1 Corinthians 5
- 22 1 Corinthians 6
- 23 1 Corinthians 7
- 24 1 Corinthians 8
- 25 1 Corinthians 9
- 26 1 Corinthians 10

MAY 21

**WEEK 22**
- 27 1 Corinthians 11
- 28 1 Corinthians 12
- 29 1 Corinthians 13
- 30 1 Corinthians 14
- 31 1 Corinthians 15
- 32 1 Corinthians 16
- 33 **2 Corinthians 1**

MAY 28

**WEEK 23**
- 34 2 Corinthians 2
- 35 2 Corinthians 3
- 36 2 Corinthians 4
- 37 2 Corinthians 5
- 38 2 Corinthians 6
- 39 2 Corinthians 7
- 40 2 Corinthians 8

JUN 4

**WEEK 24**
- 41 2 Corinthians 9
- 42 2 Corinthians 10
- 43 2 Corinthians 11
- 44 2 Corinthians 12
- 45 2 Corinthians 13
- 46 **Galations 1**
- 47 Galations 2

JUN 11

**WEEK 25**
- 48 Galations 3
- 49 Galations 4
- 50 Galations 5
- 51 Galations 6
- 52 **Ephesians 1**
- 53 Ephesians 2
- 54 Ephesians 3

JUN 18

**WEEK 26**
- 55 Ephesians 4
- 56 Ephesians 5
- 57 Ephesians 6
- 58 **Philippians 1**
- 59 Philippians 2
- 60 Philippians 3
- 61 Philippians 4

JUN 26

**WEEK 27**
- 62 **Colossians 1**
- 63 Colossians 2
- 64 Colossians 3
- 65 Colossians 4
- 66 **1 Thessalonians 1**
- 67 1 Thessalonians 2
- 68 1 Thessalonians 3

JUL 2

**WEEK 28**
- 69 1 Thessalonians 4
- 70 1 Thessalonians 5
- 71 **2 Thessalonians 1**
- 72 2 Thessalonians 2
- 73 2 Thessalonians 3
- 74 **1 Timothy 1**
- 75 1 Timothy 2

JUL 9

**WEEK 29**
- 76 1 Timothy 3
- 77 1 Timothy 4
- 78 1 Timothy 5
- 79 1 Timothy 6
- 80 **2 Timothy 1**
- 81 2 Timothy 2
- 82 2 Timothy 3

JUL 16

**WEEK 30**
- 83 2 Timothy 4
- 84 **Titus 1**
- 85 Titus 2
- 86 Titus 3
- 87 **Philemon 1**
- 1 **Isaiah 1-2**
- 2 Isaiah 3-4

JUL 23

**WEEK 31**
- 3 Isaiah 5-6
- 4 Isaiah 7-8
- 5 Isaiah 9-10
- 6 Isaiah 11-13
- 7 Isaiah 14-16
- 8 Isaiah 17-18
- 9 Isaiah 19-20

JUL 30

**WEEK 32**
- 10 Isaiah 21-22
- 11 Isaiah 23-25
- 12 Isaiah 26-27
- 13 Isaiah 28-29
- 14 Isaiah 30-31
- 15 Isaiah 32-33
- 16 Isaiah 34-36

AUG 6

**WEEK 33**
- 17 Isaiah 37-38
- 18 Isaiah 39-40
- 19 Isaiah 41-42
- 20 Isaiah 43-44
- 21 Isaiah 45-46
- 22 Isaiah 47-49
- 23 Isaiah 50-52

AUG 13

**WEEK 34**
- 24 Isaiah 53-55
- 25 Isaiah 56-58
- 26 Isaiah 59-61
- 27 Isaiah 62-64
- 28 Isaiah 65-66
- 29 **Jeremiah 1-2**
- 30 Jeremiah 3-5

AUG 20

**WEEK 35**
- 31 Jeremiah 6-8
- 32 Jeremiah 9-11
- 33 Jeremiah 12-14
- 34 Jeremiah 15-17
- 35 Jeremiah 18-19
- 36 Jeremiah 20-21
- 37 Jeremiah 22-23

AUG 27

**WEEK 36**
- 38 Jeremiah 24-26
- 39 Jeremiah 27-29
- 40 Jeremiah 30-31
- 41 Jeremiah 32-33
- 42 Jeremiah 34-36
- 43 Jeremiah 37-39
- 44 Jeremiah 40-42

SEP 3

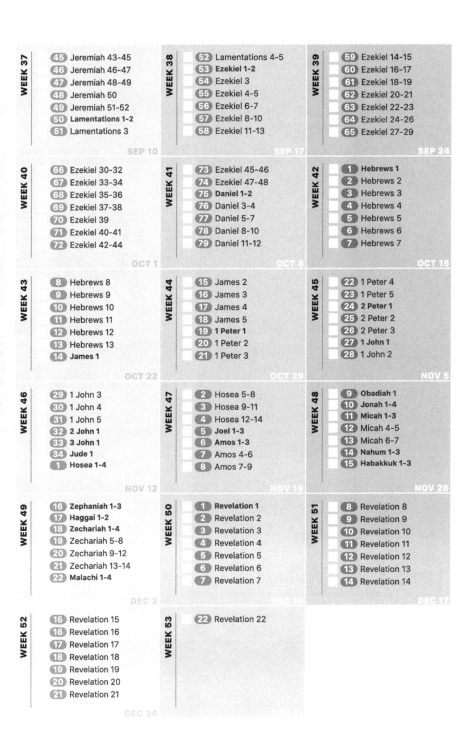

**WEEK 37**
- 45 Jeremiah 43-45
- 46 Jeremiah 46-47
- 47 Jeremiah 48-49
- 48 Jeremiah 50
- 49 Jeremiah 51-52
- 50 **Lamentations 1-2**
- 51 Lamentations 3

SEP 10

**WEEK 38**
- 52 Lamentations 4-5
- 53 **Ezekiel 1-2**
- 54 Ezekiel 3
- 55 Ezekiel 4-5
- 56 Ezekiel 6-7
- 57 Ezekiel 8-10
- 58 Ezekiel 11-13

SEP 17

**WEEK 39**
- 59 Ezekiel 14-15
- 60 Ezekiel 16-17
- 61 Ezekiel 18-19
- 62 Ezekiel 20-21
- 63 Ezekiel 22-23
- 64 Ezekiel 24-26
- 65 Ezekiel 27-29

SEP 24

**WEEK 40**
- 66 Ezekiel 30-32
- 67 Ezekiel 33-34
- 68 Ezekiel 35-36
- 69 Ezekiel 37-38
- 70 Ezekiel 39
- 71 Ezekiel 40-41
- 72 Ezekiel 42-44

OCT 1

**WEEK 41**
- 73 Ezekiel 45-46
- 74 Ezekiel 47-48
- 75 **Daniel 1-2**
- 76 Daniel 3-4
- 77 Daniel 5-7
- 78 Daniel 8-10
- 79 Daniel 11-12

OCT 8

**WEEK 42**
- 1 **Hebrews 1**
- 2 Hebrews 2
- 3 Hebrews 3
- 4 Hebrews 4
- 5 Hebrews 5
- 6 Hebrews 6
- 7 Hebrews 7

OCT 15

**WEEK 43**
- 8 Hebrews 8
- 9 Hebrews 9
- 10 Hebrews 10
- 11 Hebrews 11
- 12 Hebrews 12
- 13 Hebrews 13
- 14 **James 1**

OCT 22

**WEEK 44**
- 15 James 2
- 16 James 3
- 17 James 4
- 18 James 5
- 19 **1 Peter 1**
- 20 1 Peter 2
- 21 1 Peter 3

OCT 29

**WEEK 45**
- 22 1 Peter 4
- 23 1 Peter 5
- 24 **2 Peter 1**
- 25 2 Peter 2
- 26 2 Peter 3
- 27 **1 John 1**
- 28 1 John 2

NOV 5

**WEEK 46**
- 29 1 John 3
- 30 1 John 4
- 31 1 John 5
- 32 2 John 1
- 33 3 John 1
- 34 Jude 1
- 1 Hosea 1-4

NOV 12

**WEEK 47**
- 2 Hosea 5-8
- 3 Hosea 9-11
- 4 Hosea 12-14
- 5 Joel 1-3
- 6 **Amos 1-3**
- 7 Amos 4-6
- 8 Amos 7-9

NOV 19

**WEEK 48**
- 9 **Obadiah 1**
- 10 Jonah 1-4
- 11 **Micah 1-3**
- 12 Micah 4-5
- 13 Micah 6-7
- 14 **Nahum 1-3**
- 15 Habakkuk 1-3

NOV 26

**WEEK 49**
- 16 **Zephaniah 1-3**
- 17 **Haggai 1-2**
- 18 **Zechariah 1-4**
- 19 Zechariah 5-8
- 20 Zechariah 9-12
- 21 Zechariah 13-14
- 22 **Malachi 1-4**

DEC 3

**WEEK 50**
- 1 **Revelation 1**
- 2 Revelation 2
- 3 Revelation 3
- 4 Revelation 4
- 5 Revelation 5
- 6 Revelation 6
- 7 Revelation 7

DEC 10

**WEEK 51**
- 8 Revelation 8
- 9 Revelation 9
- 10 Revelation 10
- 11 Revelation 11
- 12 Revelation 12
- 13 Revelation 13
- 14 Revelation 14

DEC 17

**WEEK 52**
- 15 Revelation 15
- 16 Revelation 16
- 17 Revelation 17
- 18 Revelation 18
- 19 Revelation 19
- 20 Revelation 20
- 21 Revelation 21

DEC 24

**WEEK 53**
- 22 Revelation 22